PLÁCIDO

DOMINGO

Music advisor to Northeastern University Press

GUNTHER SCHULLER

PLÁCIDO
DOMINGO

by Cornelius Schnauber

TRANSLATED BY
Susan H. Ray

NORTHEASTERN UNIVERSITY PRESS • BOSTON

Northeastern University Press

German edition copyright 1994 by ECON Verlag GmbH, Düsseldorf.
English translation copyright 1997 by Susan H. Ray.

Library of Congress Cataloging-in-Publication Data

Schnauber, Cornelius.
Plácido Domingo / by Cornelius Schnauber ; translated
by Susan H. Ray.
p. cm.
Includes discography, bibliographical references, and index.
ISBN 1-55553-315-9 (cloth : alk. paper)
1. Domingo, Plácido, 1941– . 2. Tenors (Singers)—
Biography. I. Title.
ML420.D63S36 1997
782.1′092—dc21
[B]   97-9669

Designed by Virginia Evans

Composed in Bembo by Coghill Composition Co., Richmond, Virginia.
Printed and bound by Quebecor/Fairfield, Fairfield, Pennsylvania. The paper is
Quebecor Liberty, an acid-free stock.

MANUFACTURED IN THE UNITED STATES OF AMERICA
01 00 99 98 97   5 4 3 2 1

CONTENTS

{ v }

ILLUSTRATIONS

THIS BOOK IS NOT MEANT TO BE A BIOGRAPHY OF Plácido Domingo. Its purpose is rather to depict the artist and the man as a living and breathing individual active in today's cultural scene. The portrait naturally includes pertinent biographical information and important stages in Domingo's career, but readers expecting an encomium for the great singer and artist will be disappointed, I fear, for they will be confronted with critical observations as well. It is important to note, though, that even where they might seem sharpest, these critical remarks are not meant to detract from the unquestionable fact that Plácido Domingo possesses one of the great voices of our century. Occasionally there will arise in this book questions concerning the highest level of vocal and artistic competence and problems resulting from too much rather than from too little excellence and perfectionism, as paradoxical as that may sound at the moment.

Critical observations, even when they concern an artistic and vocal talent of the caliber of a Domingo, are of course highly subjective. What might strike one listener as imperfect can be just what another finds fascinating. What's more, one's mood at the time inevitably colors one's judgment of a performance, and this holds equally true for a live performance and a recording. And listening to the same recording a second time can change one's opinion about certain details established during the first exposure, with the result that one's appreciation is subjected to continual critical revision the more the particular piece is played. When I express a particular critical stance, whether of admiration or reservation, the reader should not consider it my final word on the subject. I hope that what I say in the following pages will serve as incentive for readers to return to the recording or performance in question to make their own evaluation.

This book focuses on Domingo's current work as well as on his accomplishments over the past ten years. It does not go back much farther than that, for the artist himself has discussed the period before 1983 in detail in his autobiography, *My First Forty Years* (1983); additionally, Daniel Snowman's book *The World of Plácido Domingo* (1985) adds authoritative documentation. My contribution focuses on the work and the person of the contemporary Domingo, with whom I had the opportunity to become acquainted during occasional engagements with the Los Angeles Music Center Opera. This organization is one of the three major opera houses in which Domingo currently performs on a regular basis. My employment there enabled me to gather the many facts and insights that inform this book. Plácido Domingo's professional commitment in Los Angeles is not limited to his role as singer and conductor; he also serves as artistic consultant and has recently been appointed a member of the board of directors of the Los Angeles Music Center Opera.

An essential aspect of this book focuses on the way Plácido Domingo is seen and described by other artists, his co-workers, and critics.

I want to thank the following individuals for interviews or otherwise informative conversations concerning Domingo the artist as well as Domingo the man. Foremost on the list is Plácido Domingo himself, followed by his wife, Marta Domingo. I also owe a debt of gratitude to Peter Hemmings, General Director of the Los Angeles Music Center Opera; Robin Thompson, Artistic Administrator of the Los Angeles Music Center Opera; Topper Smith, Music Administrator of the Los Angeles Music Center Opera; the stage director Christopher Harlan; Don Erik Franzen, Domingo's attorney and a member of the board of directors of the Los Angeles Music Center Opera; the singer Sheryn Abramian; and David Shostac, a recital flutist and member of the Los Angeles Chamber Orchestra.

In addition, I am grateful to the following persons for the help and information they provided: Nancy Seltzer, Domingo's public relations manager in Los Angeles; Domingo's secretaries Paul Garner and Nicholas Zoltan Marko; and Peter Hofstötter, the director of Domingo's base in Vienna.

May 1994

In September 1993 the Los Angeles Music Center Opera, in cooperation with London's Royal Opera House, Covent Garden, presented their production of Verdi's *Un ballo in maschera*. Plácido Domingo sang the role of King Gustav. During the premiere performance, he withdrew his royal handkerchief a number of times to wipe his noble nose; occasionally he lowered his head, the more easily to hide his nose between folded hands and to clear his throat in a manner befitting the dignity of his station. Contrary to what one might think, this was not a clever insertion on the part of the director, Stephen Lawless; what the audience perceived as part of the performance was the singer's skillful masquerading of a slight cough and stubborn cold.

Domingo learned how to deal with the unexpected onstage while still in his early twenties. His autobiography, *My First Forty Years,* starts off by recounting an unforeseen and potentially embarrassing situation toward the end of the second act of *La traviata* in a 1961 performance in Monterrey, Mexico. According to the original script, a messenger is supposed to appear at this moment and give Alfredo Violetta's farewell letter. Domingo sang the part as set down by the score and the text: "Someone is in the garden.—Who is there?" Since neither the messenger nor any other response followed, however, he quickly altered the text and answered his own question with "No one." Luckily for him, he found a small piece of paper on the stage and interpolated the news: "From Violetta."★ Domingo's presence of mind managed to

★Plácido Domingo, *My First Forty Years* (New York, 1983), 3–4. All subsequent quotes from Domingo's autobiography are indicated in the text as AB followed by the page number.

alter the scene in such a way as to give the impression that Violetta herself had left the note behind. Having successfully negotiated this hurdle, he continued with the music and the text as written.

Such episodes leave no doubt as to the consummate professionalism not only of the singer Plácido Domingo but of the actor as well. In the end, what constitutes theatrical professionalism is not least the skilled manipulation of unforeseen situations or accidents onstage so as to make the interference, whatever it may be, come across as an integral component of the overall portrayal of character and scene.

But what about the vocal quality of Domingo's singing during that Los Angeles performance, plagued as it was by a nasty cold?

Here, too, despite diminished dynamics and even weaknesses in certain pitches, the tenor succeeded in carrying everything off in such a way that even Martin Bernheimer, the Pulitzer Prize–winning critic of the *Los Angeles Times,* wrote of the premiere performance, "And it hardly mattered at all"—unusual praise from a critic generally inclined to be negative. In fact, Domingo's congestion was so successfully hidden behind skillful phrasings and subtle compensations that only the most sensitive ear was aware of it. Naturally, his voice sounded somewhat weaker and more muffled, especially to those sitting in the first rows of the orchestra. The result was that the dynamically expressive although occasionally forced singing of Leona Mitchell, in the role of Amelia, tended to dominate the performance. And yet, if you happened to be sitting in the last row of the highest balcony in the Dorothy Chandler Pavilion, Domingo's voice was once again the stronger of the two. His indisposition had absolutely no effect on his ability to project his high notes into the farthest recesses of the thirty-two-hundred-seat auditorium. This anticipates a general phenomenon we will deal with later on, and which we will see can also be a problem in the vocal quality of Domingo's singing.

During the week he was thus indisposed, Domingo also conducted Puccini's *La bohème* at the Los Angeles Music Center Opera without betraying any sign of fatigue and without forgetting any of the finer technical points of conducting he had acquired over the years. In fact, over the course of the next ten days he sang *Un ballo in maschera* three times and conducted *La bohème* four times.

Neither a strenuous week nor the cold he was suffering at the time managed to interfere with any of Domingo's professional duties or human qualities. Those who knew how miserable he felt were concerned he might cancel either his operatic performance or his conducting engagement, and many were sure he would renege upon the scheduled fundraising dinner for the opera. But it is precisely in situations like these that Plácido Domingo maintains his professionalism and demonstrates his dedication as a singer, a conductor, and a traveling salesman in the service of music.

Professionalism and artistic as well as personal reliability rank high among the characteristics distinguishing this extraordinary, predominately self-taught tenor. He has demonstrated these traits not only when confronted with unforeseen situations but also when his innate vocal qualities prove to be less strong in some areas than in others; here I'm referring to his high notes, beginning with a^1 (high A). By combining a skillful and elegant power of expression with musical bridgings and melodic phrasings that border on the vocally miraculous, Domingo accomplishes more than the perfect formation of these high notes. With the rare exception of the high c^2 (high C), he makes them radiate with a sound critics frequently describe as burnished, bronze, or velvety smooth.

It is always difficult to describe adequately the quality and expressive power of a voice, especially if that voice happens to be a great one. This is particularly true in Domingo's case, for many of the traditional concepts of the art apply only incompletely to his particular singing talent. Furthermore, voice teachers, singers, and critics are constantly introducing contradictions in the way they use these concepts. A case in point is the term *falsetto,* which for some is a general term for head voice, while others use it to designate a certain position of the vocal cords and therefore a particular sound within the head voice, while still others understand *falsetto* as meaning those highest tones outside the normal head voice region which already border on the acrobatic and thus lie beyond the range of the actual art of singing. I use the traditional concepts in the pages that follow but take care to explain them in context, which is to say, within the parameters of my appreciation of Domingo's art. I have also appended a brief glossary at the end of the book. Unfortunately, perhaps, such metaphorical or associative concepts as "burnished," "velvety," or "golden" are unavoidable when trying to describe the quality of a voice. Here, too, I have had to find my own words to a large extent. I leave it up to the reader to translate these associations into his or her own vernacular.

Much that follows in this book about Domingo's singing technique—such as legato, portamento, portato, head and chest register, falsetto, vocal colors—could be scientifically verified and expanded by electronic measurements. But the book is intended to be not so much a scientific treatise as a subjective representation open to the layman's verification. Instruments are precise and exact, whereas subjective impressions are alive and contradictory, giving rise to important and discriminating discussion.

THE
SINGER

Beginnings and Apprenticeship: From Madrid to Mexico City

Despite all the endearing qualities we will come to know about Plácido Domingo, one thing is certain: as a youngster he was already self-willed and self-directed. He knew where he wanted to go.

PLÁCIDO DOMINGO WAS BORN IN MADRID ON JANUARY 21, 1941, and the house he was born in already sports a commemorative plaque recording the event. Stubborn rumors to the effect that he is actually several years older (the Italian musicologist Rodolfo Celletti, for example, claims Domingo was born as early as 1934) lack all foundation. Were these rumors true, it would also mean that all the dates in *My First Forty Years* concerning his family, his parents' careers, and his own younger years would have been deliberately and consistently falsified. At the time of his alleged birth, his mother would have been not twenty-three, but rather sixteen years old, and he would have been not eight, but fifteen when he emigrated to Mexico. This in turn would not coincide with his descriptions of his childhood years in Spain and Mexico. Furthermore, he would have been an illegitimate child for the first six years of his life (his parents married on April 1, 1940), which is highly unlikely given his religious parents and Catholic Spain. It would also mean that the childhood photos in his autobiography were falsely dated as well, for the picture of him (in 1947) as a six-year-old alongside his sister, Mari

{ 3 }

Pepa, who is one year younger, could not possibly be that of a teenager. This is obvious to anyone. Had this photo been taken in 1940, however, so that the age but not the date on the picture would be correct, his younger-looking sister would have to have been seven years older at the time. And that, in turn, would mean that both siblings had publicly falsified their age, which is more than unlikely.

Plácido Domingo's mother was a native of the Basque country, his father half Catalan and half Aragonese, and both were singers. Domingo senior, who was also a professional violinist, was actually supposed to go to Germany to train as a Wagnerian heroic tenor, but personal reasons prevented him from leaving his native Spain at that time. His voice was predominantly baritone, and those were the roles he sang, especially in the zarzuelas. This genre, as will be discussed in greater detail later, had a most definitive musical influence on Domingo's early years. Suffice it to say here that the older Domingo, whose timbre was very similar to that of his son, combined the vocal colors and positions of baritone and tenor in his professional singing career. Many of the baritone roles in the zarzuelas are relatively high anyway, and they thus corresponded well to the father's vocal range.

A neglected cold later ruined his father's voice, for he forced himself to continue singing despite an infection of the vocal chords. Failure to seek any subsequent therapeutic treatment only made matters worse. Despite this setback, Domingo senior continued to perform in the zarzuelas, mainly because those roles demand more of a theatrical than a vocal talent.

Domingo's mother, Pepita Embil, was a famous zarzuela singer; in fact, her son feels she would have become an important opera singer as well, had she only pursued this career.

Her father had been a church musician who spent his leisure time playing operatic scores on the piano, and her uncle was known to be a theatrically inclined priest. Plácido Domingo's musical as well as theatrical talents thus seem to derive from both sides of the family.

His parents introduced their son to zarzuela performances at a very early age. Back then, zarzuela singers in Spain performed onstage once or twice a day, which naturally meant that their children spent a lot of time in the theater. The year 1946 was a decisive one for Plácido and his sister, for their parents had just finished a successful tour of Central America with a newly established troupe under the direction of the composer Frederico Moreno Torroba. They decided to remain in Mexico City and establish their own zarzuela troupe there. Two years later, in December 1948, both children left Spain as well, and on January 18, 1949, they first set foot on Mexican soil.

Shortly after his arrival in Mexico, young Plácido began to take piano lessons, helped behind the scenes (as he had also done in Spain) during zarzuela performances, and soon even played small parts in them as well. He could be heard, for instance, as one of the six boys in the first act of Manuel Penella Moreno's *El gato montés,* one of the most famous of all zarzuelas (premiere performance in 1916 in Valencia, Spain). Deutsche Grammophon has recently recorded the work, featuring Plácido Domingo and Veronica Villarroel in the main roles. It also proved successful for the Los Angeles Music Center Opera under the direction of Emilio Sagi (1994), both at the Opera Pacific in Costa Mesa and in the Dorothy Chandler Pavilion in Los Angeles, in a production based on Sagi's staging of the piece in Madrid two years earlier.

This is as good a place as any to examine the zarzuela in

general and *El gato montés* in particular, for without an appreciation of the genre we cannot understand Domingo's artistic development at the time, nor can we appreciate many of his current musical and artistic interests.

Zarzuela is a type of Spanish operetta that goes back to the seventeenth century and combines solo and ensemble singing with dancing and spoken dialogue. Originally conceived for courtly festivals and named after the Zarzuela Palace in the Pardo (a wooded area outside Madrid), this genre later increasingly became Spain's most popular form of music and theater. In fact, none less than Calderón de la Barca wrote what is believed to be the first zarzuela text, *El jardín de Falerina*.

Zarzuelas are cast in one, two, or three acts, and according to Domingo's description their prevailing mood is "either serious, semiserious, or comic." The great majority of them have a happy ending. Several zarzuelas, such as *El gato montés,* do indeed end tragically, but they still contain many comic elements. In the early years, that is, during the age of court performances, their themes were tailored to courtly taste, but later, especially during the age of Italian verismo as well as during our own century, they came to revolve around the daily lives, problems, and passions of the Spanish people. The music has always absorbed many European trends, with the result that some zarzuelas clearly betray the influence of Viennese walzes and operettas, especially those by Johann Strauss. *El gato montés,* for example, is strongly reminiscent of Giacomo Puccini (especially of *La bohème*), Pietro Mascagni (*Cavalleria rusticana*), and in one passage, even of Richard Wagner's *Siegfried Idyll*.

Still, the Spanish element, with its rhythms harking back to folk music and its characteristic melodic intervals and harmonies, is so dominant in most zarzuelas that even in a work like *El gato montés* (which also betrays the influence of Manuel de Falla) one cannot speak of plagiarism per se, but rather of a certain eclectic originality. Even so, Domingo himself admits that many zarzuelas do have considerable weaknesses, including the ones that played a decisive role in his own musical and theatrical formation and whose melody and ambiance he has never ceased to love. He tells us, for instance, that the composers of some of the shorter zarzuelas "were lazy; they would write precious little music and leave most of the piece as spoken dialogue" (AB, 5). Even in the three-act *El gato montés,* the first act, which is musically as well as dramatically almost perfect, and the thrilling first scene of the second act are unequaled in the rest of the piece, even though some impressive musical parts can still be found here and there. In an interview published in the *Los Angeles Times* on January 14, 1994, Domingo clearly expresses a critical distance to what he is otherwise very fond of: "I would have developed the last act a different way," he explains. "I would have made it a little more important, a little longer. But in many zarzuelas, the first act is strong and then perhaps it grows weaker. Maybe maestro Penella didn't have enough for the ending and just cut it short. But I think there is enough there for the public to really understand the work and to appreciate the color of Spain and Andalusia in it."

In a bilingual conversation with the audience during a pause in the dress rehearsal at the Opera Pacific, Domingo referred to the significance the zarzuela as well as Spanish music and culture as a whole have had in Southern California. His message was that California's Spanish-speaking population has good reason to be proud of its cultural heritage. In fact, this is one of the themes he addresses in the final chapter of his autobiography: the United States today, with its more than twenty million Spanish-speaking inhabitants, should become more familiar with the zarzuela and its Spanish musical heritage as well as with the rich Latin American tradition as fostered by such singers as Jorge Negrete, Carlos Gardell, and Pedro Infante. For Domingo, the Latin American heritage consists of much more than the Latin American soap operas viewed in the U.S., and much more than the harsh and agitating Caribbean rhythms so incessantly presented in the United States as being typical of Latin American music. Because all of this strikes Domingo as a clear distortion of the heritage, his video *The Songs of Mexico* shows the artist singing popular Mexican songs as well as talking with living singers and composers such as Roberto Cantoral in an effort to introduce their music to the United States.

Manuel Barajas was Domingo's first piano teacher in the New World. The young Plácido thought very highly of him and was strongly attracted by his human qualities as well as his professional expertise. Following the death of his mentor, Domingo, who was fourteen years old at the time, attended classes at the Mexican National Conservatory. His piano lessons there were less interesting than they had been under Barajas, but he learned other things in exchange: sight-singing, harmonic theory, composition. Domingo audited classes given by the famous Russian conductor Igor Markevitch, and they awakened his interest in symphonic works as well as in orchestral conducting itself. And it was here that the non-matriculated student Plácido Domingo sat in on classes given by singers of the Mexican National Opera, who introduced him to the world of opera.

These years also witnessed his first attempts at singing, and his accompanist, a fellow student in his piano classes two years his senior, soon became his first wife. Young Plácido left home at sixteen and secretly married his girlfriend. They lived together at the house of her older brother. Despite all the endearing qualities we will come to know about Plácido Domingo, one thing is certain: as a youngster he was already self-willed and self-directed. He knew where he wanted to go.

His parents were in Europe during this period, and their first intention upon returning to Mexico was to separate the young couple, but their attempts accomplished nothing. It was Plácido himself, suddenly a father at seventeen, who broke off the marriage with his first wife soon after the birth of his son José.

Domingo later came to understand that his first and pre-mature marriage had been irrational and irresponsible, but it represented a turning point in his life nonetheless. He was forced to leave the conservatory before finishing his studies in order to support his wife, his child, and himself. Had he remained at the conservatory, he believes, he undoubtedly would have learned a lot of theory but would never have developed into a real singer. His autobiography portrays one singing coach as an example of what he meant by this. This particular teacher knew everything there was to know about the physiology of the voice, but she bogged down in the theoretical and was unable to provide any practical assistance for his own growing interest in the art of singing. Thus his first real, if still informal, instruction in singing came from his parents, even before he started to study at the conservatory.

One of his teachers there did give him important vocal encouragement, however: Carlo Morelli, the brother of the famous Chilean tenor Renato Zanelli. Morelli was an out-spoken opponent of too much theory. For him, singing was bound up with mysticism, spirituality, and religion—a direction that Domingo didn't share in equal measure but that nevertheless did transmit more practical experiences and stimuli than did the pedantic and arid theory he got from his official coach. It was also under Morelli that Domingo, then still a baritone, managed to hit the high B (b¹) for the first time. He was so excited about his accomplishment that, while performing the tenor role in the quartet from *La bohème* during the Mexican president's visit to the conservatory, he more shrieked than sang it. (We will have more to say about Domingo's difficulties with certain high notes and specifically about how he has managed to master these notes so skillfully that today they are considered a marvel of musical phrasing and vocal structure.) Even then, Morelli must have recognized what talent lay in the young Plácido Domingo, for when he died, he left him his precious sapphire ring as a token of his esteem.

Particularly important for Domingo, however, were the musical evenings he attended in the house of his friend Pepe Esteva. These were almost exclusively devoted to Schubert's music. Up to twenty musicians got together every Monday evening, and although Domingo usually played the piano at these gatherings, they also gave him the chance to perfect his singing. Among the members of this group were also singers of the National Opera, and thus he became acquainted not only with the operatic repertoire but with some practical hints as well, such as how to comport oneself as a singer and how to follow other singers. He also learned a great deal about musical style and the different types of voice and timbre that could be employed to portray operatic characters.

After Domingo left the conservatory, he concentrated his energies on his professional career while keeping up his participation in the Schubertiads at Pepe Esteva's house. He accompanied his mother on the piano and sang the rather high baritone roles in zarzuelas. Once he even sang the main tenor role in a single performance, even though at the time he had a great deal of trouble with that tessitura. On the whole, he made himself generally useful to his parents' theater group: he sang in the chorus, played the piano when the orchestra needed beefing up, and declaimed the spoken dialogues. The practical experiences Domingo was able to garner during his teenage years unquestionably contributed to his extraordinary versatility in all practical matters of stage performance and helped him guard against becoming what might be called a pedantic tenor. No one can call him "Professor Otello" or "Professor Hoffmann" the way Dietrich Fischer-Dieskau, for instance, has been (unjustifiably) described as "Professor Rigoletto" or "Dr. Falstaff." And yet, Domingo has recently been appointed an adjunct professor at the University of California at Los Angeles (UCLA), and this in addition to the six honorary degrees he has already been awarded from leading universities in Europe, Mexico, and the United States. Even so, when lecturing to his students, he talks more about his practical experiences than about the theoretical underpinnings that inform the art of singing and acting.

It was not long before Domingo was singing in Mexico City in theaters other than that of his parents. He appeared, for example, in 185 performances as one of Alfred P. Doolittle's drunken friends in Lerner and Loewe's musical *My Fair Lady;* he accompanied singers in a nightclub; and he sang in a total of 170 performances of Lehár's *The Merry Widow,* playing Danilo forty times and Camille in the remaining 130. With the exception of a single substitution for the main tenor in the zarzuela *Luisa Fernanda,* these were the first substantial tenor roles he was to sing on a regular basis. Otherwise, he continued to sing leading baritone roles in his parents' zarzuela productions. The artist who sang the title role in *The Merry Widow* at the time, Evangelina Elizondo, was a famous Mexican soubrette, while Domingo himself was hardly eighteen years old. (This fact led even then to rumors that Domingo was actually older than he said he was.)

In 1959 Domingo sang in the National Opera, even though he had scarcely any regular singing instruction behind him and never studied singing in the conventional sense afterward. Although he sang baritone parts at first, it soon became evident that, as Morelli had previously indicated, he was really a tenor, and he was soon offered a contract to sing in that capacity. He now sang supporting roles during the so-called international season (every year the opera sponsored a "national season" featuring local talents in the main roles and an "international season" with the local talents singing secondary roles). These included Borsa in *Rigoletto*, Remendado in *Carmen*, Spoletta in *Tosca*, the Abbé in *Andrea Chénier*, Gaston in *La traviata*, the Emperor in *Turandot* (a very young father for Turandot!), and Cassio in *Otello*.

Singing minor roles in the international season rather than main roles in the national season between 1959 and 1961 was of great advantage to Domingo. It gave him a chance to appear onstage with the greatest singers of the time and to use this opportunity to study their singing technique as well as their acting style. He was especially impressed and influenced by Giuseppe Di Stefano, and this influence is still apparent today, as he recently admitted in a public conversation at New York's Metropolitan Opera. In his autobiography he writes: "Among all the tenors I have heard in person, he was the one who most impressed me. The beauty, warmth, and passion of his voice, the excellence of his phrasing, and, above all, his masterly delivery of every word were a great inspiration to me. Di Stefano made me realize that the sort of wonders I had heard in the recordings of Caruso, Gigli, Fleta, Bjoerling, and other giants of the past could be achieved by living human beings" (AB, 24).

Domingo continued his piano playing in those days and even accompanied the ballet troupe Concierto de Mexico on tour, replacing the orchestra. Today he looks back with amusement at the discipline he needed to resist the diversions presented by forty or fifty ballerina legs (and this holds true for after as well as during the performance), especially since he was the only male participant with an interest in women.

Domingo was also involved in television programs that claimed between twelve and fifteen weeks out of the year. In one series he appeared as the pianist, whose other duties regularly included arranging his own program featuring zarzuela, operetta, opera, and musical comedy selections, as well as choosing the singers (usually from the National Opera) and accompanying them on air. In another series he appeared as an actor and played small roles in works by Pirandello, Benavente, Lorca, Cassona, and Chekhov. At that time he learned to study each role according to the Stanislavsky method, a naturalistic, psychological approach that put great emphasis on the study of the familial and social background as well as the correspondingly appropriate manners and behavior patterns of the respective characters. To this day, Domingo's performances as singer and actor continue to betray the stamp of the Stanislavsky school, a modified version of which still dominates the American theater scene. Neither television series had much rehearsal time; everything had to be arranged, decided, and produced on the fly.

Another important element in Domingo's developmental
years in Mexico was his temporary employment as chorus
leader in a difficult zarzuela production. He has often pointed
out that zarzuela chorus members usually sing wide open and
make no attempt to dampen their voices, much less blend
with the other singers. Even so, he was satisfied with the
result and used this experience to reflect on and learn a great
deal about both vocal quality and conducting.

It was also during this time that Domingo cut his first recordings. They grew out of his activities as an arranger of
Hollywood hit tunes for well-known Mexican pop singers,
and he occasionally sang as well. In fact, as he reports humorously in his autobiography, he and a friend once happened to
land a gig in a bordello, where their performance received an
appropriate "honorarium." He then adds the rather veiled
words: "Afterward, we sometimes went to some of the city's
forbidden houses. One day we visited one where we knew
the madam quite well, and we both sang and had a sort of
social evening there" (AB, 27).

Domingo sang his first leading role as an operatic tenor on
May 19, 1961, in Monterrey, Mexico. It was the role of Alfredo in Verdi's *La traviata*. Although wages were very low at
that time, this engagement still marked the beginning of his
own great career. He had already appeared as Gaston alongside Di Stefano on the Monterrey stage, but this performance
marked Domingo's ascension as Di Stefano's successor. His
second leading role in the traditional operatic repertoire came
on September 30 in Mexico City, as Cavaradossi in Puccini's
Tosca.

Much of what Domingo learned and practiced during the
four or five years following the Mexican National Conservatory has remained with him to the present day: a versatility

in singing and piano accompaniment ranging from serious opera to pop music; positions ranging from chorus director to method actor; and not least, the quick appropriation and learning of new roles and unfamiliar music. The very beginning of his career was thus already marked by that versatility and multifaceted interest that many critics fault him for today. They feel he is dissipating his energies and thus depriving himself of the chance to wring the ultimate out of a role—that which most closely corresponds to his unique vocal material and his enormous artistic abilities.

Mexico was the site of his apprenticeship years, which ended in 1962 with several important roles in the operatic repertoire and included his first excursion to the United States. November 1961 found Domingo in Dallas, Texas, where he sang Arturo in *Lucia di Lammermoor* with Joan Sutherland as Lucia and Ettore Bastianini as Enrico; exactly one year later he sang Pinkerton in Puccini's *Madama Butterfly* in Tampa, Florida, and shortly thereafter Edgardo in *Lucia di Lammermoor* with the legendary Lily Pons in Fort Worth, Texas. These performances are significant because the encounters with Pons, Bastianini, and Sutherland gave Domingo the opportunity to observe and study the techniques and stylistic idiosyncrasies of some of the greatest singers of the century.

His primary activities during 1961–62, however, remained concentrated in Mexico. He was now singing with the National Opera during its national season, and his roles included, among others, that of Rodolfo in Puccini's *La bohème,* Cavaradossi in Puccini's *Tosca,* Maurizio in Francesco Cilea's *Adriana Lecouvreur,* and Fernando in Mozart's *Così fan tutte.* He established his own chamber opera group with the help of Marta Ornelas and Franco Iglesias, and they traveled together as a group throughout Mexico, performing works by Ermano Wolf-Ferrari and Carlo Menotti as well as excerpts from Viennese operettas. Domingo sang or accompanied the others on the piano. In television productions he sang not only zarzuela roles but also the leading roles in Franz Lehár's *The Count of Luxembourg* and *The Merry Widow*. Thus his first active involvement with the Viennese operetta—a musical genre that continues to follow him wherever he goes—also emerged during his apprenticeship years. It began with the 170 performances of *The Merry Widow* mentioned above with Evangelina Elizondo as Hanna Glawari.

Journeyman's Years in Tel Aviv

In this context, breath control and athletic build do not refer to body size, even though Domingo does have to contend with a weight problem from time to time and has been known to drink vegetable juice instead of alcoholic beverages. . . . A passionate amateur soccer player as well, Plácido Domingo is actually a physical phenomenon, and ever since his Tel Aviv days he has possessed and continues to maintain an exceptional stamina and reserve.

Domingo's journeyman years began after an adventurous trip through the United States and eventually brought him to Tel Aviv in December 1962. It was during these Tel Aviv years that the singer developed into what he has since come to be, a formation inconceivable without the direct and immediate influence of his second wife, Marta Ornelas, whom Domingo married on August 1, 1962. Domingo first met Marta Ornelas, a native of Veracruz, at the National Conservatory in Mexico City, but neither had much interest in the other at first. Marta Ornelas, a serious student of singing, looked on Domingo and his artistic escapades, which happened to include a great interest in women, as a rather hopeless case. Marta was considerably more goal-oriented than was her future husband; her interpretation of Susanna in Mozart's *Marriage of Figaro,* which she sang with Cesare Siepi and Teresa Stich-Randall, won her critical acclaim as early as

1962 and resulted in her being named Mexico's Singer of the Year. She and Plácido had gotten to know each other better only a short time before, toward the middle of 1961, and from then on there developed an artistic partnership between the two that has yet to be matched in the annals of singing. There is no doubt that Marta Ornelas's influence on Domingo was and continues to be stronger than the public knows. It was because of him that she gave up her own singing career a few years after they met; in fact, only recently has she resumed her public appearances, this time in the role of a highly sought-after opera director who has been known to refuse an offer if it should coincide or interfere with one of her husband's debuts.

It was Marta Ornelas who first introduced Domingo to Mozart. At the time he was still concentrating his efforts on Italian and Spanish roles. In retrospect, he now feels that Mozart was not a good choice for him back then. Ernst Römer, Marta Ornelas's Austrian teacher in Mexico, had introduced her to the musical world of Mozart, Schubert, Schumann, Wolf, Brahms, and Strauss early in her singing career. To this day Mozart remains the composer whom Domingo most conspicuously neglects in his repertoire, for his music presents a continual challenge for the singer. In fact, as far as technique is concerned, Domingo considers Mozart the most difficult composer to sing, the second most difficult being Verdi. The artist spoke about this to Helena Matheopoulos in 1986, when she was collecting the series of interviews with famous singers that eventually made up her book *Divo: Great Tenors, Baritones and Basses Discuss Their Roles:*

It's not true that Mozart cannot harm a young voice. On the contrary: singers singing Mozart without a good technique would soon strangle themselves. But if they *do* have a good technique, then Mozart and Verdi are healthier for the voice than many other composers, especially those of the *verismo* school. Puccini, for example, could be harmful on occasion, because his heavy orchestrations make it necessary for singers to push their voice to the limit. So, although one could get by singing Puccini without a good technique at the beginning, *continuing* to do so would be extremely dangerous." (*Divo,* 63)

Domingo repeated these views in a seminar held on January 27, 1994, with a group of music students at the University of California at Los Angeles. From time to time I shall have occasion to quote from this UCLA seminar which, until now, remains the only one of its kind.

The seminar must have left a lasting impression on every student fortunate enough to participate. In a medium-sized rehearsal hall the world-famous Plácido Domingo was standing there speaking to them in a warm and friendly tone. His audience was a group of approximately one hundred students, and he treated them with sincerity and humor. At hour's end he patiently posed for photographs with some of them and expressed his gratitude for being able to rehearse the next opera he was to conduct at the Vienna State Opera, Bellini's *I puritani,* with the UCLA student orchestra.

Domingo has given a great deal of thought to the nature of Mozart's music: "Mozart is definitely not good for a young singer. If a young tenor has dramatic talent, he will strangle himself with Mozart. If you don't have a clearly developed technique, you cannot and should not sing Verdi or Mozart. In this instance, Puccini is easier. And yet, even with Puccini, if you have no technique you can damage your voice if you sing him too often. In 1965 I still was not ready to sing Mozart." The latter remark was surely meant only as a warning, for as it turned out, Domingo had already sung the role of Ferrando in Mexico and that of Don Ottavio several dozen times in Tel Aviv without doing any damage to his voice. He once told me that singing Mozart

is not exactly difficult. It's the simplicity that's so difficult to attain. . . . To sing Mozart, I think, you have to have a certain kind of voice. . . . It's not a matter of being difficult or easy. It's simply that there are singers and there are Mozart singers. For [some] singers Mozart can be poison, the worst of the worse. Mozart is very difficult to sing if you don't have the appropriate sound. Yet I basically think that the simple things are the most difficult. There are arias in *The Abduction from the Seraglio, Don Giovanni,* and *The Magic Flute* that are impossible to sing. [Mozart] makes it really hard for you, and I admire every singer who has mastered these arias, who can do them justice. Two years ago I sang a Mozart album and felt very good about it. Nevertheless, I try not to sing too much Mozart because it's not all that good for my voice. I think it will go well with *Idomeneo;* and although no one has yet asked me to do it, I would gladly sing Don Ottavio in a production. The fact is, I have never recorded Don Ottavio, and I would love to.

In Domingo's view, Mozart's music is not only technically but also stylistically more difficult to sing than that of most other composers. I can only agree with him here and extend the statement to include instrumentalists as well. If an amateur orchestra plays Mozart (or Beethoven), one immediately notices, especially with the strings, if the overall sound doesn't quite strike the proper tone—and this has nothing to do with hitting a wrong note. This peculiarity isn't as immediately detectable with composers like Bruckner and Mahler, for example.

Domingo never really accepted the Mozart challenge, even though he did sing Ferrando in *Così fan tutte* in Mexico City and Don Ottavio in *Don Giovanni* in Tel Aviv. But he has never sung the roles of Belmonte in *Die Entführung aus dem Serail* or Tamino in *Die Zauberflöte*. This lacuna is difficult to fill now, for the critical Marta Ornelas was not the only one in Mexico to point out that, back then, Domingo's voice was particularly well suited to Mozart's music. Years later, no less a luminary than Josef Krips himself expressed the wish that, if he could, he would reserve Domingo's voice for Mozart alone. Perhaps it is the German language that makes Domingo keep his distance from Belmonte and Tamino, for he had no such qualms about singing the role of Idomeneo at the Met in the 1994 fall season. The Italian *Idomeneo,* moreover, has no spoken dialogue.

In many respects, the Tel Aviv period, from the end of 1962 to the middle of 1965, can be described as Domingo's true journeyman's years, and not only because he and Marta had to sing for relatively low wages in the beginning and had to share primitive dressing rooms (which were too cold in winter and too hot in summer), but also because they were compelled to make good on the opportunity to expand their repertoire by adding important operas such as Mozart's *Don Giovanni,* Gounod's *Faust,* Bizet's *Carmen* and *The Pearl Fishers,* Tchaikovsky's *Eugen Onegin,* and Mascagni's *Cavalleria rusticana.* Even more decisive, however, was the necessity of singing more than three times a week, often with little rehearsal time. Within the span of three days, for example, Domingo had to learn the role of Don José in French because the scheduled singer reneged on his obligation. Domingo describes these days in his autobiography:

> I made my Tel Aviv debut as Rodolfo in *La Bohème*, and Marta made hers as Micaela in *Carmen*. Our work was carried out under the very worst conditions. I sang most of my roles for the first time in my life without even a single orchestra rehearsal! Only new productions were rehearsed with orchestra. But Mme de Philippe made us work very hard, and we learned our craft in the best way—without a prompter and with no proper facilities to speak of. . . . Having grown up observing my parents, who had the stamina to run a rehearsal after doing three performances on a Sunday, and having then learned to anticipate any eventuality at the Tel Aviv opera, I could hardly have failed to become a professional man of the theatre. I developed the resources of energy that one must have in my field. (AB, 42–43)

His ability to learn and adapt quickly was not restricted to the appropriation of new roles. In addition to French, the Domingos had to learn English and Hebrew: *Eugen Onegin*, for example, was sung in Hebrew (Domingo sang the role of Lensky). It was predominantly through watching films in Tel Aviv that Domingo acquired the fundamentals of the English, French, and Italian languages. The couple spent a great deal of time in movie houses watching films with soundtracks in the original English, French, or Italian and subtitles in Hebrew and another European language.

The most decisive event, however, was that, with the help of Marta Domingo and Franco Iglesias, a friend and colleague from Mexico City who also happened to be engaged in Tel Aviv at the time, Domingo's voice finally established itself in the tenor range.

Domingo's autobiography reports how both the high B (b^1) and the high C (c^2) cracked during his first performance of *Faust* in Tel Aviv. That is when Marta and Franco, but mainly Marta, started working with him on his high notes. During the morning hours, on the empty opera stage, Domingo worked on both the sound and the volume of his high notes. The first important task facing him was perfecting his breath control. Since he lacked specific training in this regard, Domingo supported his singing with a purely instinctual breathing process. His autobiography contains some rather vague and anatomically not quite correct observations on this topic: "I had always thought that one must pull back the diaphragm in order to sing, and I had not been giving it enough space. Now I was learning how to breathe properly, how to fill the diaphragm [sic], and how to maintain correct breath support" (AB, 47). Even Helena Matheopoulos has a rather indefinite explanation of the process: "He realized that the reason was his failure to support the voice properly, from the diaphragm. So with the help of his wife and a baritone friend, Franco Iglesias, he set about learning the secrets of correct breath control, positioning himself against a piano in the process and pushing the thorax out during high notes. His voice gradually grew in size and security and began to project through the orchestra more effectively" (*Divo*, 64).

Both statements contain equal measures of truth and error. It is true that for good respiratory support one must first exhale completely, the starting point of every breathing exercise. The next obvious step is to inhale properly, which means that the diaphragm has to be pushed to its lowest point to give the lungs sufficient space to expand. The process follows some basic rules: the elastic lobes of the alveoli, which have a negative, or low, pressure following every exhalation, fill up upon inhalation by means of air pressure that pours into them from outside. To expand in this way, the lungs need a corresponding amount of space in the body, and this space is acquired primarily by means of the downward movement of the diaphragm and the expansion of the chest cavity (but not by raising the shoulders!). This, in turn, involves the use of certain stomach and chest muscles. The diaphragm itself cannot fill with air. Breath support per se is simply controlled exhalation while singing, and thus, to press the air out of the lungs, the diaphragm has to be raised and the chest cavity reduced. Once again, the muscles controlling the movement of the diaphragm as well as the corresponding stomach and chest muscles are called into play and kept under strict regulation. Instead of letting the muscles that control exhalation release too quickly, the singer has to hold them back while simultaneously working against them with the muscles that control inhalation. Although the site of this process is the stomach and the chest region, the most tangible changes occur in the latter. The oppositional tension in the chest area is a conscious sensation that actually strengthens its muscles and expands its capacity. Leaning against the piano, as Matheopoulos describes, could only be a temporary solution, a means of focusing one's awareness on the chest muscles and their movement.

Just how well Domingo has since learned to regulate his respiratory support was impressively demonstrated during the 1966 production of *La traviata* at the New York City Opera. During this particular production, Alfredo is required in the final act to hold his partner in his arms for the entire length of the duet he sings with Violetta (Patricia Brooks). Such a feat is possible only for someone with consummate breath support who is also physically fit. In this context, breath control and athletic build do not refer to body size, even though Domingo does have to contend with a weight problem from time to time and has been known to drink vegetable juice instead of alcoholic beverages. While offering his guests beer or wine, he himself will drink only his special green vegetable juice cocktail, the same concoction I have also enjoyed frequently at the Farmers' Market in Los Angeles. A passionate amateur soccer player as well, Plácido Domingo is actually a physical phenomenon, and ever since his Tel Aviv days he has possessed and continues to maintain an exceptional stamina and reserve.

Proper respiratory support was one of the techniques Domingo perfected during his years in Tel Aviv. The other was his vocal formation of high notes. These two aspects of the art of singing are mutually dependent. Domingo is the first to admit that he lacks the talent that distinguished Alfredo Kraus and enabled him to work up to or attack a high C (c^2) with no outward show of effort. Nor is he able, as Nicolai Gedda was, to add a tender, lyrical touch to the conclusion of his high C. Unlike Pavarotti or Alfredo Kraus, Domingo couldn't toss off nine high Cs in a row with little space between, as Tonio does in his aria from Donizetti's *La fille du régiment,* and he has never sung, nor will he ever sing, the role of Arturo in Vincenzo Bellini's *I puritani* with high notes above the c^2 (including f^2, even if he were to reduce it, as Alfredo Kraus did, to a d^{b2}). Nor will he ever sing the c^2 in the second act of *Turandot* simply because the audience expects him to, which is what Pavarotti does, even though Puccini never required it. In his autobiography Domingo deplores the fact that many performances of Verdi's *Il trovatore* have foundered simply because they could not find a tenor capable of producing the high C at the end of the aria "Di quella pira," even though Verdi himself only wrote a g^1. Yet, since several high-C tenors have introduced the tradition, the audience has come to expect this high C (like the high B in *Rigoletto*'s "La donna è mobile," which doesn't appear in Verdi's score either), even though every tenor, even a matador of the high C, "sweats blood and bullets" at this point. Domingo is said to have told Daniel Snowman: "I always transpose the arias in *La bohème, Il trovatore,* and *Faust.*" But why should he have to transpose *Il trovatore,* for example, when the highest note Verdi wrote for the entire Manrico role is only an a^1? It may be that a transposed b^1 at the end of the stretta is more thrilling than the original g^1, but since Domingo already respects the written notes in the duet of the second act of Puccini's *Turandot* (in other words, he does not sing the interpolated high C), why should he not do the same in *Il trovatore* as well? Incidentally, there exists a 1969 recording of a live performance where Domingo not only sings the high C at the end of the stretta but actually brings it off with great élan. He sings a high C at the end of the stretta on other, later recordings, as well.

All in all, an isolated high C or the notes above it are not Domingo's forte. Rather, his strengths lie in the unique vocal and musical technique with which he phrases the passaggio (the transition region between the chest and the head registers), even if there are some critics who fault him on precisely this point. Part of this technique also has to do with the way he builds the notes above the passaggio so that a somewhat less radiant and energetic c^2 or b^1 no longer sounds weak and dull in its context. Marta Domingo told me about the "columns" on which she and her husband worked so diligently in Tel Aviv, even though they were a natural component of his voice and only needed strengthening through improved breathing techniques. She explained:

> Plácido has by nature a beautiful voice: like a column, equal from bottom to top. So what he really needed was to discover the art of breathing. His high notes are neither metallic nor abrasive. Unlike so many other tenors, Plácido's high notes don't resemble a pyramid, heavy below and tapered on top; with him they are rounded, both above and below, full of vibrato and rich in harmonics. They're explosions of light and gold, like fireworks. Yes, the true secret lies in his harmonics. Proper harmonics are a gift of God. One can perfect one's technique, and one can learn how to make the voice more beautiful; but harmonics are an inherent quality of the voice itself.

The obvious question here is, Just what are "harmonics"? Strictly speaking, the word refers to the overtones, or partials, which occur in the relation of 1:2, 1:3, 1:4, and so on, above a fundamental tone and which contribute to the complex sound of that tone. With regard to the human voice, however, the word refers to both the complete overtone spectrum and the specific groups of partials produced, during both singing and speaking, by the vocal cords and the vocal tract via a multiple of pulsations of the fundamental tones. Every individual's vocal mechanism is also characterized by so-called resonant formants, which emphasize the overtones in certain pitch ranges and thereby determine the volume of a person's voice as well as his or her individual vocal color. It is generally held that a good singing voice depends on the quality of the formant span in the neighborhood of 3,000 Hz, the range that is also known as the singing formant. The beauty and the volume of a voice depend upon its structure and energy. My ongoing studies of this particular topic suggest, however, that the formants lying above and below this range also influence the beauty and volume of a voice—a point of no mean significance when it comes to the shaping of the text of vocal scores as well.

In addition to his natural columns, though, one can also distinguish broad sonorous arcs or vocal bridges in Domingo's higher ranges, which give the impression some critics have described as the velvet or burnished, bronzed quality of his voice.

This "bronze" quality of Domingo's voice, which is often compared to the sound of the French horn or the cello, is due to the baritone-like components of his voice, which are carried over into the higher ranges by means of a smooth transition of harmonics from the chest to the head register.

Daniel Snowman describes it this way:

> The tone is darker, richer, more covered than the honeyed sound of Pavarotti, more nasal perhaps, but less *stretto* or constricted than his famous Italian rival. Where Pavarotti would ride over the assembled forces of a big orchestra with his tight, bright, pinpointed tone rather as a flute or an oboe can do, Domingo's will blend and balance more like a horn—unless the score requires the independence of a trumpet, in which case Domingo has the resources to oblige. If there is a single musical instrument that Domingo's voice most resembles it is probably the rich, vibrant, generously bowed cello. (Snowman, 102)

Snowman also describes Domingo's support technique and phrasing:

> Like all good singers, Domingo integrates the high notes into the texture of the music that surrounds them. He

will not hold on to a high note longer than the natural flow of the music permits nor interfere with the musical pulse in order to help his run-up. Indeed, he will often not even pause for breath before a high note but rather take it as part of a single sweep of a phrase. Such feats could only be attempted by a man blessed with large and pliant lungs, tremendous diaphragm support—and, above all, great musical sensitivity. (Snowman, 104)

Christopher Harlan, a director and assistant stage director for the Los Angeles Music Center Opera whose acquaintance with Domingo goes back to collaborations that predate his activities in Los Angeles, has his own words to describe Domingo's unique passaggio and his formation of the high notes: "It's something quite special: the ease with which he moves through the passaggio into the head voice is wonderful; the way he runs up to a note, completes a phrase, or brings it back again in a diminuendo. The *way* a person produces a high note is important, not so much the note itself. The bridges, the arcs make all the difference."

Technique aside, there is no doubt that it was in Tel Aviv that Domingo developed into a full-fledged tenor, for it was there that he overcame his final difficulties in forming the high tones. This, in turn, gave him the freedom to make the best melodic use of the baritone-like qualities of his voice precisely where he was best able to employ them—for example, in the role of Otello. It was in Tel Aviv, too, that he finally felt free enough to resume his flirtation with the idea of baritone roles, which he would pursue seriously a few years later.

The Domingos left Tel Aviv in June 1965. Marta Domingo was pregnant and ended her public singing career. Plácido Domingo had summer contracts for Camille Saint-Saëns's

Samson et Dalila in Chattauqua, New York, and Bizet's *Carmen* in Washington, D.C.

Marta and Plácido Domingo planned the birth of their first child carefully. A number of instances in his later life clearly demonstrate how vitally important family ties are for Domingo. In fact, his autobiography tells about the birth of his son. In it, Domingo writes that the very day he and Marta decided to leave Tel Aviv was also the day they decided to start a family. Given the relatively modest circumstances they were living under in Tel Aviv, the idea of bringing children into the world had not seemed advisable. Marta had wanted and had needed to contribute to the family finances through her earnings as a singer. They moved from one apartment to another in Tel Aviv a total of seven times, and occasionally had to share their living quarters with Franco Iglesias and his wife. While Domingo was busy at rehearsals or was out singing, Marta was home cooking, and when she was professionally engaged, he prepared the meals. On the days they were both singing, they ate in unpretentious local restaurants. The upcoming engagements in the New World meant the end of this way of life.

Yet all their plans very nearly came to naught. While swimming in the ocean one day, the current carried both Domingos out to sea. Giuseppe Bertinazzo, another tenor, heard their cries for help, and although he managed to bring Marta back to safety, he was unable to do the same for Plácido. Fortunately a nearby lifeguard rescued the already semiconscious and half-drowned Domingo in the very nick of time. Years later Domingo can still recall the taste of the salt water and his feeling of helplessness against the ocean's fury.

Baritone or Tenor

The 1992 complete recording of Il barbiere *on the Deutsche Grammophon label was conceived partially in jest but presented in all seriousness; it features Domingo singing the baritone role of Figaro.*

THE GREAT RAMÓN VINAY, SO ADMIRED BY DOMINGO and one of the most moving (for many operagoers *the* most moving) Otello interpreters of our century, began and ended his career as a baritone. In a 1962 production in Texas, for instance, he sang Iago to Mario del Monaco's Otello. For Domingo, the occasional baritone role signifies neither the beginning nor the end of a career, as such roles did for Vinay; his excursions into this vocal range have been taken "on the side."

Domingo's autobiography reveals that he was planning to sing the role of Don Giovanni in Salzburg in 1986. He had mentioned his desire to sing this role as early as 1980 at the Met, and not long after that Herbert von Karajan sent him a telegram announcing his decision to produce *Don Giovanni* in Salzburg three years down the road with Domingo in the title role. Domingo thought that was too soon, for the role of Don Giovanni lies not in the range between a high baritone and a tenor but rather in that between a high bass and a baritone. Such a challenge would have been difficult for any "baritonal" tenor to master, regardless of how tempting the geniality of the score and the vitality of the role may have been when compared to the conventionality of Don Ottavio, which Domingo had already sung. At the time of this writing, he has yet to sing the role of Don Giovanni, and Marta Domingo, who keeps critical guard over her husband's voice as well as his roles, once told me:

> You know, somebody was interviewing Plácido some time ago, and in the course of the conversation he mentioned that he loves the Spanish characters. Don Giovanni is Spanish and so is Figaro. And he said, "Perhaps some day, I don't know." Karajan read about it and got in touch with Plácido. "Plácido, if you're ready to do Don Giovanni, do it right away." But Plácido replied, "Maestro, thank you very much, but you know, when I said that, I meant in a few years." Don Giovanni is one of those things people say when they're thinking out loud.

Fair enough, but a number of existing and still available recordings do feature Domingo in baritone roles. One, for instance, is the 1992 Deutsche Grammophon videotape release *Hommage à Sevilla,* with stage sets designed by Jean-Pierre Ponelle. This tape shows Domingo not only singing Don Giovanni's champagne aria, "Finch' han dal vino," but also portraying both Count Almaviva and Figaro in the duet "All' idea de quel metallo" from the first act of Gioacchino Rossini's *Barber of Seville*. The former aria is characterized by a rather consistent baritone coloration because of its relatively deep register, while the latter is charmingly playful. Despite all the baritone-like strength in his voice, Domingo sings Almaviva with an especially bright timbre, thus clearly distinguishing that role from the baritone of his Figaro. Yet, all its darker coloration as Figaro notwithstanding, the tenor qualities of his voice cannot be completely disguised. Thus he sings and plays the role of the Count with a particularly friendly, blasé, ironic air while portraying Figaro as somewhat coarse and rebellious. This video, unabashedly produced with the help of modern trick technology, is a spectacular jest, a joy to watch as well as to hear.

The 1992 complete recording of _Il barbiere_ on the Deutsche Grammophon label was conceived partially in jest but presented in all seriousness; it features Domingo singing the baritone role of Figaro.

In listening to this Figaro, one notices how Domingo's mastery of tonal coloration comes to his aid. He once told the music students at UCLA: "I don't believe in a single color for a singer or for all the different roles he sings. Different colors are important." He demonstrated how he sings "Una furtiva lacrima" from Donizetti's _L'elisir d'amore_ with a coloration different from the one he employs in singing Otello. As Figaro he frequently tries to place special emphasis on the baritone-like colors; one example of this is his successful rendition of the deeper notes in the famous aria "Largo al factotum." Even so, the tenor qualities predominate, especially in the higher notes, which is quite clearly the case in just about all the recitatives as well as in those passages where he sings _mezza voce_ ("with half voice"). Although Figaro is a baritone role, in Domingo's interpretations only in the deeper notes of the arias, duets, trios, and so on does he actually sound like a baritone. In the upper ranges the sound of the tenor breaks through; the listener is very aware that the "baritone" Domingo, even when he tries to suppress these tenor qualities, is really a tenor.

This recording is interesting for other reasons as well.

When Domingo sings duets or trios with Frank Lopardo in his role as Count Almaviva, many passages give the impression that these are two tenor roles. At times, Lopardo's voice has an even darker quality than do Domingo's radiant phrases. When Domingo records a baritone role, it might be advisable for him to take on the tenor roles as well; as the *Hommage à Sevilla* video shows, he knows how to make a clear distinction between the coloration of the tenor roles and that of his own baritone. Of course, Lopardo's voice contrasts with Domingo's, but on the CD Domingo fails to sing with as pure a baritone as he does on the video, and Lopardo fails to sing his Almaviva on the CD as brightly (almost metallically) as Domingo does in the video version.

Although Domingo is not seriously considering performing as a baritone with any frequency, his fascination with certain roles in this range remains as strong as ever. His decision is motivated only in part by the vocal challenge these roles present; by far the greatest temptation lies in their musical-theatrical representation. He finds the (baritone) role of Gérard in Umberto Giordano's veristic opera *Andrea Chénier,* for example, considerably more interesting than the tenor role of the titular hero of the work, simply because Gérard, unlike Andrea, actually grows, or as Domingo puts it, takes on "gigantic" human qualities. And the role of Don Giovanni is tempting, too, again not only because of its musical complexity. In this case, Domingo feels that Don Giovanni has been repeatedly the victim of misguided interpretations. He talks about this in his autobiography:

> Don Giovanni is usually portrayed as either a very aggressive, macho character or as a cold, calculating seducer. Both of these views seem shallow to me. This is

a man who must be capable of showing great tenderness to women. Perhaps after so many adventures he no longer feels that tenderness, but he must demonstrate it convincingly—otherwise he could not be so successful. There must be something of the sweetness and correctness of the *hidalgo,* the Spanish gentleman, in his behavior. At times he exaggerates and becomes theatrical, when he feels that that is necessary in order to reach his goal, but those moments must be temporary departures from his normal appearance. (AB, 195)

Early Mastery: New York and Hamburg

*Despite all the frenzy he never lost his calm or compo-
sure. This particular trait continues to lure him into
additional obligations as singer and conductor, whereas
the mere thought of taking on such extra duties would
conjure up a nightmare of anxiety and stress for other
artists. And in spite of an appointment calendar just
about filled to capacity through 1997, Domingo is also
scheduled to take on the role of artistic director of the
Washington Opera, starting in 1996.*

OFFERS TO SING IN *SAMSON ET DALILA* IN CHAUTAUQUA,
New York, during the summer of 1965 and in *Carmen* in
Washington later that same year were the operative forces
behind the decision to leave Tel Aviv. In looking back, both
Plácido and Marta Domingo still consider the years they
spent in Israel as pivotal for many of the reasons cited above,
though they were always aware that Domingo's career had
to be established in other parts of the world as well. Since
Mme Edis de Philippe, the director of the opera in Tel Aviv,
was not amenable to the idea of Domingo's appearing for
half a season in Israel and the other half somewhere else, the
only choice left them was to leave Tel Aviv altogether.

The fall of 1965 witnessed several engagements in other
productions in the United States and Mexico, but the actual
turning point came when Domingo was offered a permanent
contract at the New York City Opera beginning in October.

His official debut was scheduled for October 21 in the role of Don José in *Carmen,* but circumstances required him to substitute for the tenor who was supposed to sing Pinkerton in *Madama Butterfly* in the October 17 production but had fallen sick a few days earlier. The repertoire Domingo sang as part of the New York City Opera during the next fifteen months leading up to his engagement in Hamburg was a fairly traditional one, although it did include one modern work, *Don Rodrigo,* by the Argentinian composer Alberto Ginastera. Vocally this opera was almost impossible to master. Still, it was an important milestone for Domingo, because it was his first opportunity to collaborate with the director, the conductor, and the chorus on a work totally new for all of them.

Except for *Don Rodrigo,* the first fifteen months in New York brought few surprises. The routine was broken by interesting digressions, though, including learning the role of Andrea Chénier for a production in New Orleans within a period of three days because the famous Franco Corelli backed out at the last minute. Three months prior, which is to say, early in 1966, he made his Spanish debut in Barcelona by singing in three short Mexican operas: Luis Sandi's *Carlota,* Salvador Moreno's *Severino,* and Pablo Moncayo's *La mulata de Cordoba.*

On December 14, 1965, Domingo sang the role of the German poet E. T. A. Hoffmann in Jacques Offenbach's *Les contes d'Hoffmann* in Philadelphia. This was quickly to become one of his best roles and one to which we shall return in a later chapter. One month later, on January 15, 1966, Domingo was already in Toledo, Ohio, performing Cavaradossi in Puccini's *Tosca.*

Nevertheless, as I was later told, despite all the frenzy he

never lost his calm or composure. This particular trait continues to lure him into additional obligations as singer and conductor, whereas the mere thought of taking on such extra
duties would conjure up a nightmare of anxiety and stress for
other artists. And in spite of an appointment calendar just
about filled to capacity through 1997, Domingo is also scheduled to take on the role of artistic director of the Washington
Opera, starting in 1996.

Probably the most important digressions during this period
were those that took him to Boston, where he sang the role
of Hippolyte in Jean-Philippe Rameau's *Hippolyte et Aricie*
with the Boston Opera Company, a role that introduced him
to the style, not exactly easy, of the earlier French operas. His
partner was Beverly Sills, later to become director of the New
York City Opera. He also sang the role of Rodolfo in *La
bohème* opposite Renata Tebaldi's Mimì, and the memory of
the event has remained a particularly happy one for him. Although undoubtedly one of the greatest singers of the century, Renata Tebaldi demonstrated a great deal of personal
interest in the young Domingo family, especially in their new
arrival, Plácido Jr.

Domingo has less pleasant memories of the rehearsals for a
planned production of Arnold Schoenberg's opera *Moses und
Aron:*

> Meanwhile, we had begun rehearsing *Moses and Aaron,*
> which disturbed me very much. To this day I do not
> like the work and cannot understand it. Pity poor
> Aaron, who has to sing a terrifyingly difficult part while
> Moses distracts everyone's attention by reciting spoken
> dialogue! And Aaron's part is also cruel to the voice.
> Unfortunately for the company but fortunately for me,
> there were financial problems at the time, and, as this

particular production was very expensive and very risky as far as public attendance was concerned, it was set aside for a year. I was already engaged elsewhere. . . . I was not sorry in the least to give the whole project up. (AB, 56)

This remark betrays Domingo's attitude toward modern music as a whole, an opinion that has changed little over the years. However, it does not include the works of Gian Carlo Menotti or John Adams, which were composed later than Schoenberg's music. Menotti is completely in tune with the traditional style of Puccini, and Domingo supports him in this. With his minimalism, John Adams likewise harks back to traditional harmonies, even if his rhythmic structure is somewhat different. While thus not objecting to all modern music, Domingo does question those trends that emerged directly from Schoenberg's twelve-tone technique, such as serial music or, in general, experimental attempts that go beyond traditional harmonies, and even beyond "traditional" atonality. "I do not believe," Domingo writes in his autobiography,

that in fifty years the average human ear will have developed the ability to become familiar with the sort of music that most composers have been creating during the past generation or two. It is music for specialists. If that is what they want to produce, well and good, but they are fooling themselves if they believe that the public that wants to hear Bach, Schubert, Verdi, and Stravinsky will ever be able to cope with today's academic music. Even a truly theatrical work like Berg's *Lulu*, great though it is, has not entered and cannot enter the popular repertoire—I use the word "popular" in its finest sense—and *Lulu* is already half a century old. I think it is a pity that people like Menotti are discouraged from proceeding with their work, which is why I have asked him to write an opera for me based on the life of Goya. (AB, 154–55)

Not long ago Domingo told his music students at UCLA something along the same lines:

Since *Wozzeck* and *Lulu* and Britten's *Death in Venice,* which appear often in repertoire, only a few real operas have been written. I liked *Nixon in China* very much. But composers are loathe to write melodies anymore. They say that they're living in the twentieth, soon in the twenty-first century. But this attitude is wrong. If you have an appropriate story for an opera, you should write something melodic, between Britten and Puccini. Sometimes, when young composers send me a score, it looks like an electrocardiogram. They make it deliberately difficult. Cesare Siepi was once asked what he had against modern composers. His answer was, he had nothing against modern composers, but the modern composers had something against him. That's why I'd like to say, don't be afraid to write melodies.

In this same context he defended not only Menotti but also Ginastera's *Don Rodrigo,* a role that proved to be a great challenge for him at the New York City Opera in 1965. And as he assured me during one of our private conversations, he is currently planning to sing the title role in Britten's *Peter Grimes* in the near future.

During the time he had this discussion on modern music with his UCLA students, Domingo was hard at work directing the rehearsals for Bellini's bel canto opera *I puritani.* Not surprisingly, he enthusiastically defended its beautiful and passionate melodies. Evil tongues might be tempted to presume that traditional, melodic operas are easier for Domingo to learn and to interpret than serial or other modern music not written along the traditional lines of a Menotti. Yet it is more difficult today to interpret Mozart, Verdi, or Strauss in a way that will satisfy a sophisticated audience accustomed to recorded performances and the greatest singers in the world than it is to interpret an academic composer whose music the audience neither knows nor understands. If a singer makes a mistake with Mozart, Verdi, or Strauss, or gives a performance unequal to his or her highest standards, hundreds of thousands of listeners notice it immediately, but they do not notice such failings in the works of modern composers.

Two other side trips during the 1965–66 season in New York were also significant. In December 1965 Domingo sang in a performance of George Frideric Handel's *Messiah* in Boston, and in May of the following year he sang in Felix Mendelsohn's *Elijah* in Mexico City. Oratorios, masses, and requiems are among Domingo's favorite repertoire, which also includes Beethoven's Ninth Symphony. He participated in the latter for the first time in 1962 under the direction of Luis Herrera de la Fuenta in Mexico City, and he later perfected his performance under Karl Böhm in 1980.

Domingo has fond recollections of the 1970 performance of the *Missa solemnis* in Rome celebrating the Beethoven bicentenary in the presence of Pope Paul VI. Franco Zeffirelli was responsible for the visual effects, Wolfgang Sawallisch directed, and Ingrid Bjoner, Christa Ludwig, and Kurt Moll were his partners.

Equally memorable was the London performance of Verdi's Requiem under the baton of Carlo Maria Giulini. Domingo's memoirs recall: "In the *Dies irae* [Giulini] seemed to personify God the Father on the Day of Judgment. Not that he overacted or made pompous gestures: he simply *became* the music to an almost frightening degree. It was shocking to see someone who is so good and so gentle demonstrate such power, like God on the day of wrath" (AB, 75).

In 1985 Domingo sang in the world premiere performance of Andrew Lloyd Webber's Requiem, a work that owes its existence to Domingo's encouragement, and one that I hesitate to mention in the same breath with the other works discussed above. When the students asked him about Lloyd Webber, Domingo replied tactfully:

> He's one of the cleverest musicians of our generation. He integrates many of Puccini's ideas. I met him in London when he attended a performance of Puccini's *La fanciulla del West;* he was fascinated by the work, and you can really hear it in his *Phantom of the Opera,* just as you can hear a great deal of Rachmaninoff in *Sunset Boulevard.* But he's spectacular. If you think he copies here and there, just try to do it yourself. He was lucky in that he found the right and effective story line; after all, everyone can borrow ideas today. It's hard to be original, especially when you write melodies. The Requiem is a great piece; I like it a lot. It also contains many original passages.

The next important stage in Domingo's career was his engagement at the Hamburg State Opera. Rolf Liebermann, then general director there, heard Domingo sing in *Don Rodrigo* at the New York City Opera in late autumn 1966. Even though Domingo was suffering from a cold at the time, Liebermann asked him to audition and signed him on to sing in *Tosca* for the coming January. This was the beginning of a new experience for Domingo. In German houses, operas already part of the repertoire are rarely if ever rehearsed, even by the new singers, prior to repeat performances. Thus Domingo had only a single full production rehearsal, which was actually meant to serve the stage direction and was done without the orchestra. June Anderson, America's most famous Lucia di Lammermoor, happened to mention this in a recent press conference in Los Angeles; she gave it as her reason for refusing to sing in Germany. On the other hand, much longer rehearsal periods are usually set aside for new productions in Germany than is the case in America.

At any rate, Domingo had to sing the role of Cavaradossi without benefit of an orchestral rehearsal; the director, Nello Santi, gave him a few pointers before the performance and during intermissions, and everything went very well. Situations like these are not all that rare or unusual on the German opera stage. Even Helmut Berger-Tuna, currently the most popular Ochs auf Lerchenau and, like Domingo, an exceptional actor, told me that he once had to jump in on a performance of *Der Rosenkavalier* under the direction of Heinrich Hollreiser without any rehearsal whatsoever, and the performance turned out fine. Evidently, what can only be described as positive waves of concentration emerge between the singer and the conductor in such moments. Of course, it can happen only when the artists in question are consummate professionals.

Liebermann wanted to offer Domingo a permanent house contract like the one he had in Tel Aviv, but Domingo hesitated, and they ended up agreeing on individual contracts for the time being: *Aïda* in May, *La bohème* in December, and *Lohengrin* the following January. Nevertheless, the connection with Hamburg remained so tight that Domingo could write as late as 1983 that, with the exception of the Met, he had not sung anywhere as often as he had in Hamburg.

Although Domingo continued his engagement at the New York City Opera and still made his debut at the Vienna State Opera in 1967 as well as at the Deutsche Oper in Berlin that same year, the years in Hamburg have gone down as milestones in his career. That stage witnessed not only his first Lohengrin but his first Otello as well, and it was there that he taped several of the most interesting live recordings still available on CD today.

Lohengrin turned out to be a problem, though, and not only because the Wagnerian passaggio was bound to create difficulties for a still relatively young tenor like Domingo, even though he had already sung several veristic and four main Verdi roles. At that time, Domingo's command of the German language was still too tenuous to allow him to perform the role with confidence.

Many of Wagner's roles are difficult simply because they require extensive singing in the passaggio region. There is no question that this lends a Walter or a Lohengrin or a Tannhäuser a particular attraction, but many voices suffer precisely because of it—and this is true even for dramatic voices, not only the lyric ones—if they do not possess the requisite vocal structures and a proper technique. Regarding his initial Hamburg performance of Lohengrin, in January 1968, Domingo writes in *My First Forty Years:*

> Despite the successful outcome of the *Lohengrin* production, the role hurt me vocally. German is much more difficult for me than either Italian or French, and I required a substantial amount of coaching in the part. Normally, I teach my new roles to myself, sitting at the piano, singing only the tough parts and only when absolutely necessary. But I was nervous about my Wagnerian debut and about trying to make my German intelligible

to a German audience. Furthermore, much of the part
lies in what is called the passaggio, which means too
many Es, Fs and F-sharps. If a part lies basically lower in
the range, it does not matter that one has to go up even
as high as a B-natural now and again. What really taxes
a voice is a concentration of middle-high-register singing, and that is exactly what the role of Lohengrin—
which never goes higher than an A-natural—contains.
(AB, 67–68)

The result was that, for a while, Domingo had problems
when he tried to sing even a g^1 in other roles; in New York
he had to seek out an ear, nose, and throat specialist and
undergo sessions of vocal therapy. Nicolai Gedda had once
attempted to sing the part of Lohengrin as well, and it jeop-
ardized his voice to such an extent that Gedda finally dropped
the role completely from his repertoire. His decision had
nothing to do with his desire to sing a lyric Lohengrin—
earlier singers had also tried to do that, Leo Slezak and Franz
Völker, for example. Actually, the part has to be sung lyrically
anyway, because Lohengrin is a lyric role. Yet Gedda's voice,
too, wasn't built for Wagner, a fact he discovered after singing
Lohengrin three times in Stockholm. His decision dashed the
high expectations of the music world that surrounded his
planned debut in this role in Bayreuth.

Domingo's *Lohengrin,* on the other hand, turned out to be
a great success a few years later both at the Met in New York
and at the State Opera in Vienna.

In Hamburg, however, he still had problems with this role.
According to Marta Domingo, they were almost exclusively
due to her husband's difficulties with the language, even
though she admits that Domingo's technique has also
changed in the meantime. As she recently told me:

He has changed his technique and by doing so improved it considerably. But let me make something very clear: when he first approached the role of Lohengrin, his biggest problem was the language. As you already know, since he didn't speak German, he had to rehearse a great deal, and this tired him out. The problem was the language. If he had sung Lohengrin in Italian back then, these problems wouldn't have arisen. [In Hamburg] he was confronted with innumerable rehearsals as well as the need to constantly speak German in order to get the text under control. By the time he arrived in Hamburg, he had already rehearsed the opera too much.

One of the reasons for Plácido's enormous success is that he's such a great musician and knows both Italian and French, so that he doesn't have to use up his energy by spending hours and hours on exercises and rehearsals. He sits at the piano and feels his way through the score with his hands. He memorizes the music without using his voice. That's Plácido's great advantage. But with Lohengrin, everything was different. Because he didn't know the language, he had to practice and practice, mainly speaking the text, and this exhausts the voice. That was the problem.

Of course, it was Wagner himself who demanded that the singers of his operas—and this applied to his German singers as well—speak the text first; the singing of it came later. We will have more to say about Wagner's singing technique, as well as its debt to the Italian bel canto, when we come to speak of text and music in general and of Wagner and Domingo in particular.

Although Marta Domingo was certainly right in ascribing many of her husband's problems with his Hamburg Lohengrin to his problems with the language, his youth as well as his not yet perfected technique played their part, too, espe-

cially with regard to the way he dealt with the constant passaggio in Wagner's high tessitura. Listen to a cut from a
recording of that time and compare it with the later CD recording made in 1985–86; between the two renditions Domingo undergoes a clear change in technique and thus in
vocal production.

Wagner is not the only composer who creates problems
for tenors in the passaggio region. Bellini, for instance, the
master of Italian bel canto, isn't easy in this regard either.
The Italian school of bel canto singing repeatedly placed the
greatest emphasis on proper *messa di voce* (the swelling out
and ebbing off of a tone) in the passaggio region in order to
make the transition from the chest to the head register occur
without any audible break. The goal is to make both registers
sound as one as far as the voice is concerned. Although the
passaggio in Italian bel canto is easier to take, its tones as well
as the tones above it are produced in a completely different
manner than they are in Wagner's scores. In contrast to almost all Italian bel canto parts, in Wagner's music the passaggio receives much greater emphasis and thus has to be
"ex-pressed" with much more strength and energy than its
Italian counterpart, yet without sounding pressed. Wagner
wrote his roles for heroic tenors who were, ideally, also supposed to sound lyric; the Italian bel canto, on the other hand,
can be sung by lyric tenors who, ideally, ought to sound heroic as well.

Marta Domingo made passing reference to how easily her
husband manages to learn and rehearse his roles. He accompanies himself on the piano and sings only those passages he
feels he absolutely has to vocalize. Any particular difficulties
he leaves to the whims of chance onstage, on the grounds
that he has to give himself over to intense concentration dur-

ing a performance anyway. He explains this habit in his auto-biography:

> If there is a particularly difficult passage—so difficult that I find it frightening—I practice it very little. If I were to go over and over it at home and *not* achieve what I am after, I would be absolutely petrified before the public. I do study the passage mentally and sing it softly at re-hearsals, but I give it my all only at the performance. When the public is present, there is a strong psychologi-cal incentive for singing the passage well. The moment arrives, it's a matter of flying or falling flat on my face . . . and in the great majority of cases I succeed. (AB, 34)

This attitude clearly reflects Domingo's inner serenity and positive outlook. The latter will concern us rather more ex-tensively later on, for it lies at the core of his versatility and success as well as at the base of some problems.

Personally, I have yet to witness an instance when Do-mingo passes over difficult passages during rehearsal only to wait for the performance to sing them for the first time. Right now he seems to know and to be in control of just about everything, which is why he usually attends only the final rehearsals before a performance. Should he be unfamiliar with the production, he relies upon his ability to integrate quickly into the whole. Nevertheless, there are some produc-tions for which he still reserves a considerable period of re-hearsal time. One example was the Met's production of Verdi's *Stiffelio;* this opera had just been discovered and was being produced at the Met for the first time in the fall of 1993. The same holds true for new productions of such weighty operas as *Otello* regardless of how often he may have sung the part before.

Domingo can frequently be found at the piano before a performance and during the intermissions as well, completely immersed in intensive vocal exercises. Once again it is hardly fair to say that he steps out onstage without any vocal preparations; and this is true regardless of how often he may have sung the part in question. When rehearsing onstage, he rarely marks or mimes the role as so many other singers do. His vocal strength and energy seem almost inexhaustible.

World Fame: Vienna, the Metropolitan Opera, Teatro alla Scala, Covent Garden

Regardless of how one describes the quality of Domingo's voice, one thing is sure: it possesses a radiant vibrato independent of its bronze and highly textured warmth. Its penetration into the deep layers of a listener's musical experience has a lasting effect on many people. I have even been told that for some it has had a positive influence on their overall appreciation of music.

SINCE DOMINGO'S WORLD RENOWN IS COMMON KNOWL-edge even among non-operagoers, it would be tedious indeed to list all the places and houses in which he has sung. By 1984 he had already appeared in 1,753 productions in 106 cities and 24 countries. The man (of whom Birgit Nilsson is alleged to have said he knows every language except the one containing the word no)* once mentioned in an early video portrait (1984) that he has to refuse nine out of every ten offers that come his way.

Until 1984, the year he became one of the cofounders of the Los Angeles Music Center Opera, Plácido Domingo sang most frequently in five major opera houses: the Hamburg State Opera; the Vienna State Opera; the Metropolitan

---

*Nilsson quoted in Jens Malte Fischer, *Große Stimmen: Von Enrico Caruso bis Jessye Norman* (Stuttgart: Metzler, 1993), 526.

Opera in New York; the Teatro alla Scala in Milan; and the Royal Opera House, Covent Garden, in London. In his autobiography, Domingo dubbed all but the Hamburg State Opera "the four giants." This is not to say that Hamburg was incidental to his development, and of course the Met was then, as now, the high point of a career. However, Domingo has special feelings for the Teatro alla Scala and the Vienna State Opera. His autobiography describes his debut at La Scala in December 1969 with these words:

> It is true that I had already sung at the Met, the Vienna Staatsoper, and other great theatres. But when you stand on the stage of La Scala and look into that beautiful auditorium, you can't help thinking that nearly every celebrated singer from Mozart's day to our own has performed there. I would probably have had a similar feeling in New York had I made my debut in the old rather than the new Met, which had opened only two years earlier. The new Met will of course have its own history, but that will be for future generations of performers to appreciate. (AB, 80)

Domingo tempers all this praise for Milan's opera house with a few critical remarks; he mentions, for example, the noise behind the stage during performances, the organization of rehearsals, and even the rehearsal rooms themselves.

As far as the Vienna State Opera is concerned, Domingo recently told me that he still considers the opera company as well as the city and its audience especially friendly, warm, and culturally engaged and that he feels completely at home there. I do not believe for a minute that this remark springs from the fact that the Viennese audience to this day continues to shower him with his longest ovations, aside from the reception he has enjoyed at mass concerts in amphitheaters or following guest appearances in those opera houses where his presence counts as a rare event. I do believe, though, that the whole atmosphere as well as its cultural life is what makes this city one of Domingo's favorite places, even if he frequently spends more time in New York than he does in Vienna. Marta Domingo recently told me they spend an average of six months in the United States, with their home base in Manhattan (these six months include sojourns to Los Angeles as well as performances in other American cities) and that they spend the other half of the year outside the States, primarily in Europe. To quote his autobiography again: "Of these four giants, the one with the *potential* for consistently producing the best results is the Staatsoper" (AB, 93).

However, a few lines down he adds:

> But . . . the State Opera . . . has long been a breeding ground for intrigues and cabals worthy of the Habsburg court to which it once belonged. Austria is the country in which opera personalities are talked about the way that sports figures are discussed elsewhere, and the Viennese public is easily the most dedicated in the world. The pressure on a Staatsoper director is therefore enormous, and that explains why in the sixteen years since I made my debut there, I have already sung under five different administrations. Compare that to Covent Garden, for instance, where the administration has remained the same since before my 1971 debut. (AB, 94)

For all his love for Vienna and its Staatsoper, Domingo also has some sharp criticism of the system that makes it impossible for a larger number of first-class singers to appear in any one season. He also deplores the fact that new productions are rejected in favor of dusty old stagings despite the enormous operating budget the state subsidy makes possible.

Just how enthusiastic the Viennese audience can wax over Domingo is demonstrated by the fact that he once received a seventy-five-minute ovation and eighty-three curtain calls following a performance of *La bohème* there. This one event assured him a place in the *Guinness Book of World Records* as being the singer with the longest applause in the history of opera.

As far as the Royal Opera, Covent Garden, is concerned, Domingo's autobiography has both laudatory and critical remarks to make as well, but he does not devote as much space or as much interest to this house as he does to La Scala, the Met, and above all the Vienna State Opera. What he appreciates most about Covent Garden is the attitude of its employees: "There is no doubt that London's Royal Opera is one of the friendliest houses in the world. Everyone there, from the maintenance staff and telephone operators to the top of the administration, does everything to make life as easy as possible for the performers" (AB, 102).

It was on September 28, 1968, with his twenty-seventh birthday not far behind him, that Plácido Domingo made his Metropolitan Opera debut in Francesco Cilea's veristic opera *Adriana Lecouvreur*. This was the same year that Luciano Pavarotti, six years his senior, ascended the peaks of operatic aspiration. During the fifteen years between his debut and the publication of his autobiography, Domingo worked under four different administrations at the Met, but the reasons were not the same as those operative in Vienna. First Sir Rudolf Bing retired; then his successor was involved in an automobile accident and was followed by an interim administration until the new and permanent director was hired. As with the Vienna State Opera, La Scala, and Covent Garden, Domingo has both positive and negative feelings about the Met as well, but he defends the New York audience, so frequently reproached for being cold and showing little inclination to applaud. Domingo knows that, following the end of an operatic performance in New York, which is usually around eleven o'clock and sometimes even closer to midnight, most in the audience face more than an hour's commute in dangerous subways or unsafe streets. New Yorkers just do not have the time to sit around and applaud the way the Viennese do. At any rate, Domingo's observations attest to a growing appreciation and discrimination on the part of New York's operagoers over the past twenty years or so. And he assures us that the opera staff is marked by an attitude no less friendly than that of the staff in London.

In the meantime, Domingo has come to feel very much at home at the Met. Since his 1968 debut he has appeared in thirty different roles there in a total of between three hundred and four hundred productions. I recently visited Domingo in his comfortable and spacious apartment on New York's East Side. When asked about his current relation to the Met, he replied:

> It's a nice feeling to be part of this theater's tradition. Once you've spent a quarter of a century in this theater, you're part of the tradition. Today the Met really is my own house. I feel emotionally involved in every performance I do, and I am aware that we [he and his colleagues] are part of the history of this theater, and that makes [our appearance] very important, just like in every other great theater. Yes, I feel at home here. I will soon make my four-hundredth appearance here, and that's a long career.

Perhaps this is as good a time as any to turn our attention directly to Domingo's talent as a singer.

Has his artistry undergone a recognizable development in technique, in the sound of his voice and its ability to express various emotions and attitudes, since his Tel Aviv days and the early years in Hamburg? This question is equally as important as, and integrally related to, the next one: Exactly what is it that makes the quality of Domingo's voice so unique, and just what is his technique?

There are those who say that Domingo has undergone only a slight or even no development at all since the first recordings we have of him, which is to say, since the beginning of his international career. There are also critics who feel that he sang better, more beautifully, more leanly, and more subtly twenty-five years ago than he does today. Daniel Snowman, among others, tends to side with the first group, while Jürgen Kesting takes his stand among the second, at least with respect to a few specific roles.* I cannot agree with either judgment, although I too am of the opinion that in Domingo's case those qualities of voice that so fascinate us today were already discernible early in his career, and that much of what he sang then sounded somewhat fresher and more original than might be the case today. But that is far from saying that his "storm and stress" creations are better and more complete than the works of his mature years.

The following pages attempt to show how Domingo's voice has developed toward greater perfection and maturation since Tel Aviv and the early years in Hamburg. Marta Domingo notes that ever since the 1968 Hamburg *Lohengrin,*

---

*Daniel Snowman, *The Word of Plácido Domingo* (New York: Mc-Graw-Hill, 1985), 101. Jürgen Kesting, *Die großen Sänger unseres Jahrhunderts* (Düsseldorf: Econ, 1993), 902.

"he has changed his technique and improved it greatly. . . . My God, a musician who doesn't constantly improve, how could such a thing be possible? He truly has developed a great deal over the years, even as far as his breathing techniques are concerned."

Live recordings from the 1968 Hamburg *Lohengrin* production of two selections from the third act, "Mein Herr und König" and "Im fernen Land" (the story of the Holy Grail), are still available today and can be compared with the corresponding numbers on the 1985–86 CD under Sir Georg Solti. It is somewhat unfair, of course, to compare a live performance recording with one made in a studio, since the principal singer on a live recording is more exhausted at the end of the third act than he is on a studio recording, made with frequent, lengthy interruptions. One need only compare the simulcast version of "Im fernen Land" from a live performance of *Lohengrin* at the Met featuring Peter Hofmann with the same selection on a phonograph record, where Hofmann sings with less strain and occasionally even employs a *mezza voce,* something he was evidently incapable of doing on stage. Even when these circumstances are taken into consideration, however—and unfortunately we will have to proceed in this rather unfair way, for all the other early Domingo recordings were made during live performances as well—significant differences can still be discerned. First, the pronunciation on the older recording is much less satisfactory than on the later one, even though it is still not perfect there either. Domingo's inability to clearly and properly articulate the German language continues to plague his music. On the later *Lohengrin* recording, for instance, Domingo still struggles with the diphthongs, frequently uses *a* sounds that are too dark or very often confusing the open *o* with the closed *o,* and occasionally also produces slurred consonants. These problems are even more noticeable on the earlier recording. Moreover, the legato in the Hamburg performance—as in the line "ob ich an Adel euch nicht gleich," for example— still sounds somewhat tortured. During the story of the Grail Domingo's voice already possesses a great deal of his later "bronze" and "burnished" timbre in the high notes, but it does not sound very light. This, though, may be due to the effects of exhaustion at the end of the live recording. One also notices on the Hamburg version that Domingo occasionally abruptly changes over from a very dark timbre into the brighter sound he is known for, as for example in the line "alljährlich naht vom Himmel eine Taube." At "Taube" he goes into a brighter-sounding *mezza voce* but then becomes dark again in "um neu zu stärken sei-" and once again resorts to a brighter, heroic sound with "-ne Wunderkraft." What follows is certainly brighter in timbre for the most part, but it still possesses occasional short and abrupt transitions into the dark timbres. Although meant to be expressive, these transitions are not always appropriate.

On the other hand, on the 1985–86 recording of "Mein Herr und König," the listener is treated to what has become the familiar, beaming (if still somewhat covered), and radiant Domingo sound, and his legato phrases as well as all the other phrases are balanced and perfect in tone. In addition, some passages are taken in a wonderfully lyrical manner, such as the lines "Enthülle mein Geheimnis ich in Treuen. So hört, ob ich an Adel euch nicht gleich."

In the story of the Grail, Domingo does indeed begin with a baritone sound, but it is not the less-pleasing darkness we hear on the Hamburg recording. He frequently employs a tender *pianissimo,* but because it has an almost too artistic effect, it comes close to the mannered. This is followed in the line "alljährlich naht vom Himmel eine Taube" by his transition to a *mezza voce* with a technically perfect falsetto (whereby only the edges of the vocal chords vibrate, even though the note is totally balanced and well supported by the breath). We get another chance to admire this *mezza voce* with its supported falsetto in the line "dann muß er von euch ziehn." Domingo is very dark on these lines in the Hamburg excerpt, and with the exception of "Taube," he sounds almost gutteral.

All the positive improvements evident on the CD are also evident in a live videotaped performance of the Vienna State Opera made in 1990, except that here Domingo's voice sounds a bit more strained in the last scene of the third act. The following differences are equally noteworthy. Occasionally the articulation of specific words is a bit less clean here than on the compact disc. The word "Treue," for example, is completely botched, and the nondistinction between open and closed *o*'s is even more bothersome here than on the earlier CD recording. Certain musical phrases in the Grail story sound either a little weaker here than on the CD or else a bit shorter, as, for example, in the words "Macht," "Nacht," "entwendet," and "unerkannt." Moreover, in the videotaped version Domingo employs only shorter phrases with an accentuated head voice or falsetto. Instead of the whole passage "naht vom Himmel eine Taube," here we get only "eine Taube," or instead of the whole passage "wollt ich dich anders wiedersehen" (in the Swan Song), all we get here is "wollt ich dich." On the whole, the Grail story and the Swan Song sound a bit more tender and more lyrical on the CD than they do on the video, yet it is remarkable what differentiation in timbre, what balance in phrasing, and what power of expression are present in the dynamics even at the end of the somewhat abbreviated opera. Finally, just before this scene is the strenuous love and separation duet of the first scene of the third act. When compared to the live recording from 1968, the videotaped Vienna performance of 1990 demonstrates just about all the positive developments in the sound of the voice and in the shaping of expression that could already be heard on the 1986 CD.

All the differences discussed so far with regard to the Hamburg *Lohengrin* were possible only because Domingo's vocal technique had grown in security and freedom during the intervening years and because his further development of the overtone structures continued to enhance the quality of his voice. I shall return to this topic a little later on.

Let us now compare a few other recordings, starting with *La traviata*. In the 1966 live recording of the New York City Opera production, the high notes in the aria "De miei bollenti spiriti" of the second act still sound somewhat dark and not as clear as they appear on later recordings. The overall dynamics, on the other hand, sound more emotional and many phrases more genuine, even if they are not as balanced in tone and timbre as we know them, again, on later recordings. In one recording made twenty years later, for instance, the tones, and this includes the high as well as the low ones, are more radiant, the held notes have a more balanced effect, and the overall phrasing is more perfect, indeed, even more subtle, and most conspicuously more variable in timbre. Nonetheless, the whole performance sounds a bit more routine and less emotionally engaged. If we compare these two recordings, we get the impression that a genial young man was onstage in 1966, and that twenty years later we are listening to the singing of a mature but by no means graying or aged master. On the contrary. Still, the genial youth retains his own fascination vis-à-vis the later master; it is simply a matter of allowing one's ears to accustom themselves to the style.

We get this same impression when we compare the scene "Libiamo ne'lieti calici" up to and including the aria and the duet "Un di felice" from the first act of La traviata on a tape made in 1967 with the corresponding recordings made under Carlos Kleiber in 1977, only ten years later. By 1977 the high notes are already significantly more radiant than they were in 1967, where they sound relatively darker, especially in the duet. In addition, the phrases in the later recording give the impression of being sung more clearly and with greater security, the variation of tonal colors is more subtle, the *piano* seems to be softer, and Domingo's unique *messa di voce,* which I will explain later on, betrays considerably more skill and greater perfection, again particularly in the duet.

Although Domingo chooses to color "Un di felice" with a bit more of the baritone quality of his voice in this passage, it is still not that dark and almost gutteral sound we heard in the Hamburg recording of Lohengrin. Here everything sounds richer in tone, more skilled in phrasing; everything bears the masterful mark of his unique *messa di voce.* In fact, it almost borders on what could be considered too perfect in terms of technique.

I agree with the many critics who feel that Domingo's 1971 recording of Don Carlo ranks among the subtlest and best of his preserved performances. The date reveals its origin in the earlier phase of this great singer's career. His voice, then lean, was adequate for the role, for apart from his occasional trouble with high notes, he sets to the singing and phrasing with an unforgettable freshness and ease. This is a recording one is drawn back to time and time again.

Another interesting excerpt can be heard on a 1962 recording of the opera *Adriana Lecouvreur* made in Mexico City. The selection in question is the relatively short aria "L'anima ho stanca" in which the twenty-year-old Domingo is already using a good *mezza voce* in individual phrasings (especially at the beginning), where his high tones are very impressive and where, toward the end, the dynamic intensification is extremely convincing. A recording of this same aria made more than twenty years later is certainly no more convincing as far as the performance is concerned, even if the sound of the voice is brighter and more radiant. The dramatic intensification toward the end of the aria in the later recording still bears witness to a great performer, but for all his polish, we also get a slight hint of the routine.

Be that as it may, the earlier recording already shows that in the person of Plácido Domingo we are dealing with a great natural talent that went on to ever greater perfection. Yet his is a perfection that seems to shatter all the boundaries that have until now shaped the definition of a tenor. This is why I find it difficult to share Daniel Snowman's opinion: "Listen to recordings of arias committed twice to disc by Domingo over a ten- or twelve-year period and you will be hard pressed to tell simply from the voice which was the earlier and which the later" (Snowman, 101). This observation may apply to the period between 1980 and 1992 (though even here I have certain reservations), but it does not apply to the years between 1968 and 1980. Those years saw both a purely vocal as well as technical development.

So what are the secrets of Domingo's vocal artistry?

As with all singers, the characteristic thing about Domingo's voice lies in its overtones, as I have mentioned. Yet just how strongly and consciously Domingo stresses the higher overtones in his speaking voice became particularly clear to me through the following coincidence. Some time ago I had recorded a conversation and was now in the process of eliminating the disturbing high background noises. In doing so, however, I also eliminated the higher overtones of Domingo's speaking voice, with the result that the voice on tape was hardly recognizable as his any longer. A similar experiment with other speakers whom I had recorded on cassette (actors, less well known singers, other people), led to a less significant loss of vocal quality.

As already mentioned in my prefatory remarks, Domingo's voice has a strong projection, and though it does not seem as loud as that of other singers when one is relatively close to him, it projects all the more clearly the farther away one gets. I was able to observe this same phenomenon with Nicolai Gedda as well. The ability to project has to do with sine waves and the prominence of certain overtones. The closer the partials approximate sine waves, the farther they project. Noises, for example, that show no sine waves in the overtones (in the case of noise they are not called harmonics) very quickly fade away with increasing distance. This is why you can hardly understand two people who are talking to each other next to a running motor, even though you're standing next to them, but you can understand them much better when you move a slight distance away.

The development of Domingo's overtones is also related to the evenness of his voice, which several critics have praised and others have failed to perceive. It actually has to do with a uniformity of vocal sound possessing a wealth of vibrations within itself. Daniel Snowman describes the phenomenon this way: "The actual quality of Domingo's voice is astonishingly even. If you play a Domingo recording at low speed so that the voice sounds like that of a bass, the natural vibrato remains almost uncannily regular" (Snowman, 101).

The evenness of Domingo's voice has little to do with the actual timbre of his voice. The latter is due to the way his overtones are formed. They are produced in the larynx, of course, but are simultaneously intensified, filtered, expanded and shaped by the vocal tract (supraglottal cavities). And this, in turn, involves the interaction of different nerves, the structure of the larynx, the construction and flexibility of the vocal tract, proper hearing, and the proper control of vocal and formant kinetics. A number of elements are working together here. However, the final explanations as to why Domingo's voice sounds this way, Carreras's another, and Pavarotti's different again can be provided by neither anatomy, physiology, nor acoustics. Daniel Snowman strikes the perfect note when he says of Domingo's voice: "For all Domingo's power, it is the smooth, dark velvety sound that remains in the aural memory" (Snowman, 101–2).

Domingo's vocal color or timbre ranks among the most beautiful we know, yet this still does not explain why his singing has reached the highest levels of the *art* of singing. His artistry has something to do with his ability to extend his vocal material, which he has improved, expanded, and perfected over the course of years, equally beautifully over several octaves and through just about all phrasings. In addition, he knows how to create a context and a structure within these realms—and here I refer to the high tones above the passaggio. Domingo does not come by these tones naturally, but only with the help of his unique bridges and columns. It is this approach and context that renders less significant the question of whether the b^1 or c^2 or d^{b2} sound as clear and perfect in isolation as they do when sung by Gedda or Pavarotti. In Domingo's case, only when the c^2 or d^{b2} is filtered out—and on a day when he is somewhat rundown and weary at that—can his singing perhaps be described as dull, agonized, labored, or forced, as critics sometimes maintain.

Two examples of such evaluations should suffice: the first comes from the pen of Jens Malte Fischer:

> Not every tenor can be or has to be a C tenor (even Caruso, whom Domingo names as his most important recording model, was not). But apart from this fact, in Domingo's case one can observe an increasing but already rather old tendency to deprive the notes above the passaggio of their necessary point, that is, a tendency not to lead them into the "mask," the resonance chambers. The results are those sometimes agonized top notes that sound "broad" rather than centered because they are so labored, tones that remain within the bounds of the tolerable only because of this singer's unending routine as well as his other qualities. (Fischer, 527–28)

I happen to think it is not only Domingo's routine but his whole vocal context that render his high notes more than merely "tolerable"; as a result, they attain a quality we still perceive as expressive despite a less developed "mask" than can be heard in Björling's, Gedda's, or Pavarotti's singing, for example.

Jürgen Kesting, the author of an informative book about Pavarotti and a comprehensive study of Maria Callas, sees Domingo rather more negatively than positively: "Domingo possesses a velvety smooth, warmly timbred voice whose sound betrays little or nothing of the Italian stamp. It is not as bright and lean as the typically Italian voices of Bonci, Martinelli, Gigli, Lauri-Volpi, or Pertile, but rather of a dark, reddish-black tone, which is also not entirely devoid of throaty colorations. . . . Domingo's voice is clearly limited in pitch: there is no question that in the role of Manrico (in Zubin Mehta's 1969 production) his 'all'armi' radiated above and beyond the chorus, but the high C is not part of his everyday arsenal. Even in his best moments he is unable to take it *con attacca,* but prefers to ascend the arc of cantilena. Even then it sounds . . . forced or acoustically divorced from his voice" (Kesting, 899).

Kesting refers quite correctly to the "arc of an intensifying cantilena," for this is one of Domingo's vocal secrets. And yet, it takes a special ear to recognize the high C as being "acoustically divorced from his voice." Sometimes a bit forced, to be sure, but certainly not in the way Kesting assumes when he relates it to the cabaletta of an unidentified *La traviata* recording: "The author stakes all his Domingo recordings on his assumption that it [the high C] was recorded in isolation and then—all too clumsily—interpolated into the recording. I would not be at all surprised if the note hasn't been raised a notch by manipulating the speed" (Kesting, 900). Although I would not stake my Domingo recordings on the chance that the opposite were true, I cannot believe that such manipulations were undertaken, at least not in the 1977 *La traviata* under the baton of Carlos Kleiber. It is common knowledge, of course, that Kleiber did allow some passages to be retaken after the fact and subsequently edited into his famous *Tristan* production, but to manipulate a single note beforehand by increasing its speed and then inserting it into the flow of the performance seems highly unlikely for a professional like Kleiber, despite his predilection for ultimate perfectionism. The improbability only increases when one considers that Domingo would have to have sung the high C in isolation from any orchestral backing, just so a manipulated higher speed could thrust it to the heights. The recording shows clearly that the orchestra's pitch was not similarly raised, and the note would have to have been superimposed upon it. In those days there simply was no other way to do it. But how could Domingo have sung an isolated, clear high C with the intention of subsequently integrating it into the flow of the passage when we know he tends to build his high notes from below, as it were, producing his columnlike sound, or else makes use of vocal arcs? Of course, one might be tempted to consider another possibility, given today's modern technology (and I'm being facetious here): maybe the high C's are not from Domingo at all, but from his secretary, singing along with him during the recording sessions and over the loudspeaker during stage performances, while Domingo just stands there and marks the tone. Unfortunately, the fact that singers onstage merely mime to their own or to the voices of others has become a reality over the years, in both the classic as well as the pop repertoire.

In any case, the decisive element is Domingo's "arc of an intensifying cantilena," which he employs in a skillful and sophisticated way; the result is that the tone that rests upon these arcs has absolutely no need for a "necessary point" or "centering" as it does in the case of Gedda, Kraus, Carreras, or Pavarotti.

Yet another secret attaches to Domingo's growing artistry over the years: his vocal arcs as well as all individual tones, especially when they are held for any length of time, involve a harmonic vibrating and highly textured intensification of the voice. Even the shorter notes are "fed" by this singular swelling and subtle vibrato that borders on magic. It has nothing to do with the wobbling or fluttering of a voice, but rather with movements or vibrations that overlay the usual frequencies of a tone with pulsations of pitch, volume, and timbre. A wobbly or fluttery sound is bad and indicates an uncontrolled quavering or shaking due to insufficient support. Wobbly vibratos are the absolute opposite of Domingo's vocal mastery.

His secret, if it can be called that, is that Domingo lets the tonal frequencies vibrate "supplementally" and "morphologically"; yet this vibrato remains subtle and can be discerned only by a highly trained ear. It is this ability and quality that has frequently been described as Domingo's unique *messa di voce*. And since the upward swelling of the notes predominates, one could also call this type of artistry a "semi" *messa di voce*.

Regardless of how one describes the quality of Domingo's voice, one thing is sure: it possesses a radiant vibrato independent of its bronze and highly textured warmth. Its penetration into the deep layers of a listener's musical experience has a lasting effect on many people. I have even been told that for some it has had a positive influence on their overall appreciation of music.

I broached the topic of his vibrato in a somewhat challenging manner in an interview with Domingo. He replied by demonstrating how one sings a tone in a linear, normal way, which when sung by him, still sounded splendid; but he also demonstrated how he shapes that same note with his own special vibrato. There was a world of difference. He went on to explain: "It comes from my knowledge of music, from my knowledge of instruments. I know how to feed a tone. I feed a tone with [extra] vibrations. In these fractions of a second I use the greatest number of [dynamically differentiated] vibrations as possible, and to do that I use the diaphragm—that's why the tone sounds different. The audience doesn't know, doesn't understand, what's going on, but it does notice the difference. No tone a person sings should ever be boring. You have to shape everything in an interesting way.

"I approach [every note] with the feeling of an arc. The worst thing is when you have to sing every note with full strength. Vocally ideal is when you can create a note with diminuendo and crescendo. But I don't like diminuendo very much. Diminuendo is dangerous; voices can start to wobble with it. But of course, you have to sing what the composer dictates. I think all of this comes with feeling, with knowledge, with musicality."

And once again, Domingo explained the subtle, swelling vibrato of his tones and arcs with the comparison to a cello, where a good bow stroke has, or should have, this same effect.

The art of enriched, "fed" tonal phrasings sometimes tempts Domingo to combine certain passages with a portamento (a continuous glide from one tone to another) which other singers would shape with a less "forced" legato. This is most often his wont in passages in German operas, and sometimes in French as well. The problem as well as the criticism concerning an allegedly forced legato or portamento in Domingo's singing will be treated in another chapter.

Cavaradossi, Hoffmann, Otello

*In his interpretation of Hoffmann as well as of the
many other characters Domingo represents onstage, we
forget that this is a person portrayed through song and
thus removed from reality, and we experience
him as real.*

*Otello was very soon to become the role of his life. At
least, this is how even his critics see it. The critical
London Times even went so far as to say: "Ever
since Domingo sang his first Otello, all other interpreters seem little more than substitutes."*

IF ONE HAD TO REDUCE DOMINGO'S WORLD RENOWN TO
the two or three roles he is most identified with, those roles
would have to be that of the poet E. T. A. Hoffmann in
Jacques Offenbach's *Les contes d'Hoffmann* and Otello in Verdi's opera of the same name. The third in the list would
probably be that of Cavaradossi from Puccini's *Tosca*, since
this role has accompanied Domingo from Mexico City right
up to the present day. Although in a 1993 autumn interview
at the Met, Domingo said he felt close to the Chevalier des
Grieux from Puccini's *Manon Lescaut* because the character
seemed very genuine, and just recently he confided that he
really loves all his roles equally well, for different reasons, he
did go into some detail as early as 1986 in his conversations
with Helena Matheopoulos about his thoughts concerning

Cavaradossi, Hoffmann, and Otello, admitting that he identified completely with them. How could it be otherwise, when even his critics hail him as the most important Otello of our times, when Cavaradossi has been and continues to be a part of his repertoire ever since his Mexico City days (today he only rarely sings the two other brilliant roles of his early career, those of Rodolfo and Alfredo), and when he so skillfully masters the role of Hoffmann both theatrically and vocally that one hardly notices how inappropriate the role actually is for him?

Be that as it may, Domingo's portrayal of Hoffmann has become a medium for the expression of his own human and artistic charisma. The way he vocally and dramatically portrays the failure, the fantasy, the romanticism, the resignation, the cynicism, and, on top of it all, the staggering entry into the world of the muses of a poet just about completely destroyed by drink has elicited much more than compassion and empathy on the part of many audiences. In his interpretation of Hoffmann, as well as of the many other characters Domingo represents onstage, we forget that this is a person portrayed through song and thus removed from reality, and we experience him as real.

But first to Cavaradossi. The 1992 Los Angeles performance is but one instance among many of how convincing Domingo's portrayal of Cavaradossi has been and continues to be. Even though this role is one of the parts he has sung most frequently during his long career and is therefore in danger of sinking into mere routine, Domingo still manages to lend it a vocal and dramatic vitality. Moreover, he actually gave the role a totally new interpretation in a 1992 production of *Tosca* under the direction of Giuseppe Patroni Griffi. This was not the usual filming of an opera like Franco Zef-

firelli's *La traviata, Otello, Cavalleria rusticana,* and *Pagliacci,*
featuring Domingo and others, or like the 1976 filmed version of *Tosca* directed by Gianfranco de Bosio. The 1992 film
was sung "live" and on location, accompanied by an orchestra under the baton of Zubin Mehta playing simultaneously
from its position in a remote sound studio and transmitted to
the singers via television. In the Zeffirelli films mentioned
above, the music was recorded in advance, and the singers
lip-synched during the filming.

Domingo's continuing ability to portray Cavaradossi in an
artistically riveting way, so much so that even the two by now
overrecorded arias "Recondita armonia" and "E lucevan le
stelle" are not only dramatically but also acoustically moving,
is partly due to Domingo's personal understanding of the
part, an opinion not shared by all singers and directors. He
once told Helena Matheopoulos:

> Cavaradossi is usually portrayed as "Mr Tosca," just a
> pretty boy, "com' è bello il mio Mario," as Tosca sings.
> But this is utterly wrong in my opinion. The fact that
> Tosca commits the very brave act of murdering Scarpia
> doesn't mean Cavaradossi is a weak character. On the
> contrary; it is *he,* a committed revolutionary with Vol-
> tairian ideals and living on the dangerous edge of things,
> who is involved in politics and thus instantly reacts to
> the mention of Angelotti's name. Most of the time he
> has to humour Tosca and treat her like a child, with her
> jealousies and the dream world of her art. (*Divo,* 65)

It was the director Götz Friedrich who led him to this interpretation. "In Act III, in the Castel Sant'Angelo, he knows
perfectly well he is going to die, that this will be no mock
execution, but goes through the motions of believing it for

Tosca's sake. So, his behaviour throughout the opera makes it clear that he is the stronger character of the two, unlike *Turandot*, where both the hero and the heroine are equally strong" (*Divo*, 65).

Domingo's rendition of the third act is particularly surprising, since most actors and directors assume that Cavaradossi really believes he is going to live. Their portrayal reflects this assumption. But Domingo already interprets the first act of the opera in such a way that, for Cavaradossi, the day begins with a "strange premonition": "Without knowing why at the time, he begins this day—from the moment he arrives at the church to resume his painting—feeling this is going to be a strange, funny sort of day, and one should try to put across this vague sense of malaise" (*Divo*, 65).

Domingo included all these nuances in his 1992 stage performance in Los Angeles without resorting to merely reproducing his earlier portrayals. He never copies himself, although, as in the case of Cavaradossi, he does hold on to certain basic interpretations. This is evident in his Met performance from 1985, which is preserved on videotape and thus available to the reader for reference. Domingo is very manly here, but more of a victim than in the 1992 film: a victim not only of political circumstances, of doubts and premonitions, but a victim, too, of his passion for Tosca as well as of the power of Scarpia and his torture chambers. We realize he senses a "strange premonition" right from the start through his vocal and dramatic interpretation of the resemblance aria "Recondita armonia," but at this point he still relates it to the similarity of the two women, the unknown one he had painted the day before, and Tosca, his beloved. The audience gets a clear sense of how he struggles to overcome inner misgivings and pledges his love to Tosca alone.

In the third act, as Tosca tells him of the mock execution, he again has clear misgivings, for he knows what will happen (this too comes across through Domingo's singing and acting). He forces himself to hide his fears from Tosca, but the audience knows his outward bravado is but an act of love toward his beloved.

In the 1992 film Cavaradossi appears more superior and more mature than he did in the simulcast of the live performance at the Met. Here, too, he is manly and strong, but unplagued by doubt at the beginning of the first act and betraying no hint of a "strange premonition." When he sings the aria comparing the two women, he is certain he loves only Tosca; he is sure of himself with regard both to the situation and to his own passions. And even in the second act his shouts and screams from the torture chamber are the expressions of a man who refuses to be broken, with the result that he stands tall and triumphant when, as a tortured prisoner, he is brought before Tosca and hears the news that Napoleon as the herald of bourgeois freedom has won the battle against the regime to which Scarpia belongs. Not only does he triumph here with greater vocal strength than he did in the Met simulcast, where the effect is more passionate and he immediately falls to the ground after a deeply moving, long-held trimphant note, but the film version shows him an unbroken man as well. His physical strength and moral superiority are demonstrated again in the third act. Cavaradossi immediately doubts the reality of the mock execution on film even more than on the Met stage; once he clearly understands that the "fake" execution was only meant to deceive Tosca, he shows an increasing astonishment and almost pity for Tosca's naïveté. Tosca, though, is so completely caught up in her joy she cannot see it. Domingo's face ages from one minute to the next, so that the audience gets the impression that what we have here is ultimately a mature and fatalistic father who is merely playing a game with his child. Tosca, who jealously forced Cavaradossi as early as the first act to keep her "in a good mood," has reverted to childhood. He tells her he believes the execution is mere semblance and promises to fall down the way Tosca had so often practiced onstage, even though he knows it will be a fatal fall for him. This scene is a dramatic and vocal tour de force that has yet to be surpassed.

Ruggero Raimondi is also dramatically and in many details also vocally the best Scarpia one could wish for in this production of *Tosca*.

Domingo's marvelous rendition of the third act begins as early as the aria "E lucevan le stelle," which he vocally imbues with manliness as well as grief, melancholy, and fatalism—for me the most moving interpretation I have ever heard. In other respects as well, his voice can be said to have grown rather than diminished in 1992. No question but that his high notes are still constructed with the help of golden (or "burnished") bridges and are, if not radiantly golden in themselves, at least gilded. In light of all of this, one hardly notices that they occasionally sound somewhat labored, sometimes have too short a duration, or sound "sobbed." The overall impression made by the phrasing in each aria remains perfect and in this case, in the role of Cavaradossi, heart-wrenching for the spectator and the listener. Heart-wrenching, because manliness and fatalism combine in this third act in a particularly tragic union in this famous aria.

Domingo's identification with the figure of E. T. A. Hoffmann is even stronger than his identification with Cavaradossi or his Spanish compatriot Don José—the latter being another of Domingo's frequent roles and one he portrayed in a musically as well as aesthetically unforgettable rendition in Francesco Rosi's 1984 film version of *Carmen*. This is all the more remarkable considering that the other role that propelled him to world renown (and perhaps even more so than that of Hoffmann) is Verdi's Otello. Hoffmann and Otello are vocal opposites and are rarely sung by the same singer. Both roles are very difficult, and for Domingo they represented a relatively early challenge. He devotes a separate chapter in his autobiography to each of them, and this alone underscores the significance he ascribes to these two roles.

Hoffmann is meant for a great (and I mean *great*) lyric singer possessing a broad vocal range and an understanding of how to give shape to an enormous variety of dramatic and passionate nuances. It is a role made for Nicolai Gedda. And Nicolai Gedda is still the one who has so far given us the most unforgettable rendition, despite Domingo's enormous advantages in portraying this character.

In his interview with Helena Matheopoulos, Domingo underscores his reason for liking this role as much as he does: it allows his imagination its greatest freedom. For one thing, there's no definitive conclusion (Offenbach died before he was able to finish the music and arrange the scenes in their final sequence). For another, because of its episodic nature as well as its framed structure, beginning with a prologue and ending with an epilogue, there are the very different worlds of unrequited love and hope on the one hand and the self-destruction of a great genius on the other. In his autobiography as well as early interviews, Domingo compares Hoffmann's self-destructive bent with that of Beethoven. There is no question that Beethoven was greatly appreciated during his lifetime—just as was Hoffmann because of his stories—but as a person he was a difficult man to love. Like Hoffmann, Beethoven had a self-destructive streak in his personality.

In light of this, then, when talking to Helena Matheopoulos about the role of Hoffmann, Domingo was probably referring to the poet himself when he said: "By the end, he arrives at that certain cynical dimension characteristic of a man who, although completely defeated by love, yet pretends to be a great lover. But he is not, and his failure to find love is largely due to the presence of the devil inside him—not a real devil, of course, but Hoffmann's own self-destructive streak—who possesses him almost completely" (*Divo*, 70). A few lines down Domingo continues to describe his own interpretation: "In Hoffmann's case, the devil is pushing him in all the wrong directions, without his ever realizing it, so anxious and desperate is he to find love, real love. But in the end he is saved by his muse. His love of writing is so strong that, when offered another drink, he refuses" (*Divo*, 71).

This insight into the nature and character of the role is particularly apparent in John Schlesinger's Covent Garden production of 1981; I will come back to it again at a later point because I consider it the best production of Hoffmann I have ever seen.

Besides having written and been questioned as to his thoughts about this role, Domingo's analyses of it can be inspiring for other singers and directors as well, even if he might occasionally overinterpret to a certain extent. For example, he tries too hard to connect the historical poet and his real-life experiences too closely with Hoffmann's stories, even though the three stories that form the core of the opera—"The Sandman" (Olympia), "Rat Crespel" (Antonia), and "A New Year's Eve Tale" (Giulietta)—are only three of the many stories that E. T. A. Hoffmann actually wrote. Only the prologue and the epilogue in Lutter & Wegner's Wine Cellar (located in Hoffmann's day on Berlin's Gendarmenmarkt, today in the Schlüterstrasse) correspond to Hoffmann's historical existence. He did indeed drink a great deal there, and that not lastly in order to anesthesize the pains of a spinal disease. Domingo sees the Hoffmann in Lutter's wine cellar (in the opera it is called Luther's Tavern) as a fifty-year-old, in the Olympia act as a man in his early twenties, in the Antonia act, which Domingo has always felt should precede the Giulietta act but which rarely does, as a man in his mid-thirties, and in the Giulietta act somewhere in the neighborhood of forty-five. Hoffmann himself, by the way, died at the age of forty-six, and he wrote all three stories within the space of one year. The Giulietta episode actually originated before the Antonia story, and this, in turn, before the Olympia tale.

Domingo correctly realizes that the opera takes place geographically, intellectually, and emotionally in four different worlds: one is Luther's student tavern in Berlin; another the romantic self-deception of Professor Spalanzani and "Sandman" Coppelius in the Olympia act; yet another the courtesan/con artist society of Venice; and the fourth, the Antonia connection between art and death, in the house of Rat Crespel. Since the opera is written in varying tessituras, it demands different vocal colorations. The latter requirement presents a special challenge for a soprano when she, as often happens, has to sing all three featured roles—Olympia, Giulietta, and Antonia. "The role of Hoffmann has a high and uneven *tessitura* which demands different kinds of vocal colour," Domingo has said. It ranges "from light singing in the

Olympia Act, a pure lyrical sound for the Antonia Act, a rich, passionate voice for Giulietta and dramatic yet kind of destroyed tones for the prologue and epilogue" (*Divo*, 69). In his autobiography Domingo emphasizes still another element that burdens the role of Hoffmann: "I mentioned earlier that *Lohengrin* is a difficult role because so much of the writing is concentrated in the passaggio, the middle-high register, which puts a strain on the voice. The same is true of *Hoffmann*. . . . Certainly *Hoffmann* can be very dangerous for a young tenor" (AB, 159).

A number of *Hoffmann* recordings feature Domingo in the lead role. The following observations are based on the videotaped version of the 1981 Schlesinger production of the Royal Opera Covent Garden and on a 1989 CD recording on the Deutsche Grammophon label. In what follows, I will compare these two renditions with the Gedda interpretation taped in 1964–65, which is also available on compact disc. In the Schlesinger production the Giulietta act precedes the Antonia act, whereas on the CD this sequence is reversed. Obviously Domingo was able to exert his influence here, for on the Gedda recording the Antonia act follows the Giulietta act, as it does with Schlesinger and in most of the other productions of this opera as well. It's worth our while, then, to hear Domingo's arguments concerning the Olympia-Antonia-Giulietta staging. The following are only a few of his reasons:

> Olympia, the first beloved, is the symbol of naive, idealized love, unreal to the point of illusion. She is a doll, a symbol of superficiality. Then comes the very real, passionate love for Antonia—perhaps a bit on the platonic side, but still very intense. For Hoffmann, Antonia

is not just a woman—she is Woman; and when she dies, his ability to love dies, too. Finally, there is Giulietta, a whore, to whom Hoffmann comes with a cynical attitude. . . . It is true that all Hoffmann's love affairs are unbalanced: he never manages to combine the ideal, the passionate, and the carnal aspects of love; and in that sense the order of the tales does not matter. But I think that psychologically and dramatically, Olympia-Antonia-Giulietta is the most effective sequence. It is not enough that this man has suffered disappointment and disaster: in the end he is also deceived, and by a whore. How *could* he proceed to Antonia after that destructive resolution? It would not make sense. (AB, 165)

Domingo does not justify the Olympia-Antonia-Giulietta sequence from a psychological and dramatic point of view alone, but from a vocal perspective as well. The beginning of the Antonia act is unquestionably strenuous for Hoffmann, but then the music of the Antonia-Mother-Miracle trio dominates, and Hoffmann reappears only at the end and sings only eleven words. The transition to the epilogue, which once again takes place in Luther's tavern, is thus unnatural, physically as well as emotionally. "But after the 'Giulietta' scene I feel exhausted, finished—which is exactly what the Epilogue requires. In addition to having the tenor's most difficult music, it has four of his most magnificent vocal moments: the couplets, the aria, the duet, and the septet" (AB, 166).

Hoffmann's first appearance in the prologue (occasionally designated as the first act) is interesting, for it very quickly moves into the extremely difficult "Legend of Kleinzack." In the Covent Garden video Domingo appears sharper and already more bitter (his expression of a devastated or "destroyed" tone) than Gedda does in this scene, and thus also more trenchant. Gedda, on the other hand, sounds more lyrical and more nuanced. In the CD recording of 1989 Domingo emphasizes the lyrical, with the loss of some nuances, so that in this comparison the great Swede actually sounds more trenchant and sharper (the word "sharper" here refers to the vocal characterization of the role and the situation, not to the pitch). As far as dramatic acting and characterization are concerned, I prefer Domingo's rendition in the video version to that of Gedda on disc, but when it comes to vocal nuancing, I prefer the Gedda recording. If I compare both CDs to each other, Gedda's is the superior, especially when it comes to the "Legend of Kleinzack." This is not only because he sings the high notes more clearly than Domingo does (and this holds true for the video as well as for Domingo's CD, where Domingo actually lets his high notes resonate more distinctly but cuts them off too abruptly) but also because Gedda succeeds in relating the first two stanzas of the Kleinzack legend with an ironic distance born of different vocal colors, accentuations, and nuances. When he comes to the passage recalling his beloved, Gedda changes from an initially reflective to a passionate and engaged man. The way his musical nuances return from a certain distance to the realm of personal experience is so unique that the listener really does not have to understand the text at all. Finally, in the third verse of the Kleinzack song, Gedda identifies with the dwarf out of pure disappointment and desperation. His sharp accentuation of certain syllables combined with his strong emphasis on certain melodic phrases and high points tranform Gedda into the very embodiment of this drunken monster.

The sharpness of the sound of his voice as well as his unforgettable dramatic portrayal of this scene on the video version makes Domingo's performance memorable in its own way.

Neither on film nor on disc, however, does Domingo succeed in establishing the clear contrast between an ironic narrative distance in the first two stanzas of the Kleinzack legend and the final personal identification with this little monster in the third, at least not as clearly and as distinctly as Gedda does. In the video version Domingo seems to identify with Kleinzack right from the start, whereas on the CD recording he seems to maintain the narrative distance right to the end.

And what about the different shadings in the individual acts? In the video's Olympia act, Domingo's fundamental color is brighter, more youthful, more legato than it is in the prologue, where severity, harshness, and a kind of cynical resignation as well as bitterness (the latter primarily in the epilogue) dominate. In this same act, on the other hand, his vocal quality is carried by dreams, illusions, idealism, and naïveté, which make it brighter; the upward arcs are more radiant, more glowing, whereas the vocal coloration in the prologue and epilogue is not only more severe but darker as well, without reaching the baritone-like quality so evident in Domingo's Otello. On the 1989 CD recording a frequent *mezza voce* intrudes into this act and adds a daydreaming quality to the sound. The voice, too, seems leaner, sometimes even more cutting than on video. On the whole, one gets the impression that the higher overtones are emphasized here and that Domingo now and again interpolates the tiniest pinch of nasality.

Offenbach set the overall vocal position, or tessitura, higher in the Olympia act than in either the prologue or the epilogue, and Domingo, in turn, adds expression through his own vocal color to produce what I consider an incomparable rendition.

As far as the Giulietta act is concerned (which is the second episode on the videotape and the third on the CD), Domingo's voice on the video is once again harsher, more manly, more cynical, and somewhat darker in its coloration. He adds an intermediate sound to his coloration, which certainly expresses cynicism and even anger but does not yet betray the resignation so pronounced in the prologue and epilogue. Although still evident, his passion is now more of the flesh than of the heart, as in the Antonia act, or of romantic dreams, as in the Olympia act. And again, because he is adding a cynical color to his voice, the higher notes present a certain problem for Domingo. He occasionally breaks off abruptly, though the upward arcs are still convincing and thrilling. The CD, too, delivers a voice that is sharper, harsher, maybe even a bit more sarcastic in this than in the other acts. One even has an aural impression of additional, emphasized overtones, although in a lower register than in the Olympia act. The very sound of his voice, combined with his theatrical interpretation, imbues this act with a greater desire and passion than are evident in the two other episodes. Take for example the duet "Je le veux. Oui, sagesse ou folie." Even though Domingo could have sung his part a bit more aggressively than he does vis-à-vis his partner, Gruberova, everything is still pitched to the sensual. And when it comes to the point, as in the scene "O Dieu, de quelle ivresse embrasses-tu mon âme?," when the listener begins to believe that his passion does indeed come from the heart (for the heart is not completely expunged from this act), Domingo's portrayal is that of a man of advanced age or perhaps someone disappointed early on in life, a man who has abandoned his romanticism to purely sexual fascination and superficiality.

The Antonia act is something else again. In the video, Domingo's vocal coloration can only be described as lying somewhere between that of the other two acts; his voice has a more balanced, more natural effect. Also lacking is any trace of forced expression in his singing. The tone here seems to correspond best to Domingo's "base color," to the unique sound of his voice. Domingo actually confirmed this impression during a recent conversation. Nevertheless, it still has a different sound from, for example, that in *Tosca*. In this act the audience is vocally convinced that the person standing before them is a youthful suitor who loves Antonia "naturally" if not passionately, with all his heart and soul, but one who is neither inordinately wrapped up in romantic dreams nor cynically sensual. On the CD, Domingo's voice sounds more like his normal voice—a golden bronze tenor with a somewhat dark coloration—with the result that the passions expressed come from himself and thus from the heart.

If we now compare these recordings with Gedda's CD, we hear less variety or differentiation in the principle vocal coloration from one act to another in Gedda's voice. His fundamental colors within the individual acts remain more uniform than Domingo's. One reason may be that Gedda sings everything, even his passionate pieces, with a certain artistic distance. Everything, be it ever so perfectly sung, is infected with a certain coolness, a slight stepping back or withdrawal. Gedda sings more with his head, Domingo more with his chest; this is meant metaphorically and has nothing to do with register. Gedda, however, also produces a certain subtle difference between his ground colors; this is particularly evident when one compares the Giulietta act with the other two and against the prologue and epilogue. In Gedda's case, too, this difference is not solely due to the various vocal positions and melodic lines that Offenbach created for the individual acts. The Swedish Gedda produces these different colorations much less deliberately than does the Spanish Domingo. Gedda's basic timbre in the Antonia act has a more youthful, lyrical, more devotedly concerned effect than it does in the Giulietta act, where, in contrast to Domingo, Gedda seems much more romantic, honest, even occasionally tenderly affectionate and avoids the sensual and cynical as a matter of principle. As always, though, he remains a bit too noble, a bit too courtly. Gedda's strength and intentions thus lie less in the expression of certain basic attitudes and timbres than in his nuanced interpretations of arias, musical situations, and scenes.

We must also remember that Gedda's acting is no match for Domingo's. Gedda's vocal modulations, shadings, and nuances are truly more delicate and hence more expressive than Domingo's, even if he sometimes runs the risk of crossing the line to affectation or of exaggerating his perfect technique (probably the most perfect of all) to the point of *l'art pour l'art*. This is as true in general as it is in particular with regard to Gedda's interpretation of Hoffmann. However, in his duet with Antonia, for example, Gedda lets the notes on the syllables "l'â-me" during the repetition of "fleur de l'âme" float, hover, and reach a diminuendo followed by a crescendo on "-me," so that this single note encompasses tenderness, love, and devotion as well as a premonition of pain to come. In this, his genius has yet to meet its match. Domingo doesn't even sing this phrase on his CD recording.

On the other hand, when Gedda sings the solo section from "O Dieu de quelle ivresse embrasses-tu mon âme!" to

"Tes regards dans les miens ont épamché leur flamme!" in the duet with Giulietta, unlike Domingo he fails to imbue the scene as well as the whole act with an underlying marked and sustained timbre of cynicism and lust most appropriately centered below the belt. And yet, as if in compensation for this shortcoming, Gedda renders the individual passages of this scene with most impressive shadings ranging from the tender, the lyrical, and the musing all the way up to an expression of passion and then back again to the tender and devoted. The effect, which was probably Gedda's intention all along, is as if Hoffmann at this point is taking his love for Giulietta just as seriously as he does his love for the other women because, as a poet, he remains lost in his dreams even here. Gedda's performance with the courtisan in this act naturally contains passages rendered very cynically as well, but they are to be found elsewhere in this act and only in certain details. As I've already mentioned, Domingo manages to imbue the entire act with a cynical attitude bordering almost on indifference, even when he then, as in the solo mentioned above, abandons himself to something like heartfelt love and dreaminess, which then also infuse his delivery. Gedda, on the other hand, creates the moods and the colors out of the situation at hand as well as out of the musical phrase of any given moment. From this we can see that Gedda's abilities to create different shades of color, dynamic modulations, and other vocal nuances are superior to those of Domingo.

In one of our personal conversations Domingo spoke extensively of his interpretation of the Hoffmann role. What he said is approximately the same as what was quoted above from his autobiography and his interviews with Helena Matheopoulos. By way of supplement, then, I should only like to add Domingo's reply to my question as to whether his vocal rendition of the Antonia act most closely approximated his actual vocal color: "Yes, absolutely, because of the lyrical and the romantic aspect of it. Even though I perform a lot of the dramatic repertoire, I think that my voice is basically lyric. I just color it in such a way that I pass over from a light, lyrical flow to the dramatic and heroic; to do this you have to color your voice."

"September 28, 1975, was one of the most important dates in my career. In Hamburg that evening I performed the role of Otello for the first time," Domingo tells us in his autobiography (AB, 132), and he follows it up with a complete chapter on "The Moor of Venice." Otello was very soon to become the role of his life. At least, this is how even his critics see it. The critical *London Times* even went so far as to say: "Ever since Domingo sang his first Otello, all other interpreters seem little more than substitutes." On the other hand, not all critics are equally enthusiastic about Domingo's Otello, though they have to admit that Domingo is at least the best Otello of our time, even if several of them cannot resist comparing him to the great Otellos of the past. Even so, agreement concerning Domingo's interpretation so dominates among the critics that we may allow ourselves to quote excerpts from two of the rather more negative reviews, always with the caveat that I should not like to be identified with their judgments. First, here is what Jürgen Kesting has to say in his book on great singers: "Domingo conquers the role with more security, a more beautiful sound and more flexibility than does Ramón Vinay, who sings expressively but with too much shading . . . , than does Mario del Monaco, who rarely produces less than a shriek, than does James Mc-Cracken, who sounds shaky and unsteady. . . . But there is

no nuance, no detail, no interpretative insight, no vocal attack that might remain in one's memory like"—and now
come the comparisons with Francesco Tamagno, Enrico Caruso, Jussi Björling, and other greats of the past (Kesting,
904).

Jens Malte Fischer devotes a complete chapter of his book
on the great voices to various Otello interpretations, probably
because Verdi's *Otello* seems to be the opera of all operas for
this critic. In writing about Domingo's Otello, Fischer refers
specifically to the sound track of the Zeffirelli film, which to
his mind hardly deviates from the earlier recording of 1978
either in musical artistry or in interpretation:

> Domingo is without doubt the most impressive Otello
> of our times; his enormous talent and the quality of his
> voice triumph here, too, but when one reviews the
> whole "Otello legacy" of our century, as we have just
> done . . . one cannot help but notice a certain disap-
> pointment while listening to him, . . . [a disappoint-
> ment] that results from the fact that, in light of
> Domingo's maniacal consumption of roles, this role is
> just one among many for him. . . . His interpretation
> comes across as "streamlined"; it is painted with a broad
> brush. The listener can detect all the great predecessors
> and is carried away by his voice, but his is a relatively
> impersonal rendition of the role; it lacks a willingness to
> take on a vocal or a dramatic risk. Domingo's intrinsic
> amiability is incapable of losing himself in a character, of
> driving his portrayal to a radical intensification."
> (Fischer, 112–13)

I shall contradict much of this, even though I do consider as
valid some of the things Kesting and Fischer say. As I see it,
they're only partially true.

When Domingo sang his Otello in Hamburg in 1975, his partners were none less than Sherill Milnes as Iago and Katia Ricciarelli as Desdemona. August Everding directed, and James Levine was the conductor. Domingo's own description suggests that Everding's staging must have stressed many psychological elements and relations between Otello, Iago, and Desdemona, elements that are frequently overlooked or else reduced to meaningless short shrift. Everding tried to keep Otello's mistrust and jealousy spurred by Iago's intrigues from erupting too soon, which is defensible. A general who has just returned from a successful military campaign and who has just spent an intimate night with his wife does not let himself be brought round very easily by a third party. Moreover, his doubts about Desdemona have to have a chance to work on him before he can take Iago seriously. And finally, he makes everything dependent upon proofs that are revealed only much later in the misguided dialogue with Cassio and the handkerchief. "In short, we tried to delay the full impact [of Iago's intrigues] as long as possible, to make the sequence of events seem at least slightly less hurried than it often appears to be," Domingo writes in his autobiography (AB, 133). A few pages later he goes into great detail about another *Otello* production, by all accounts no less interesting: the 1976 Paris production by Terry Hands.

We will address the 1986 Zeffirelli film later, since it is one of Domingo's most recent recordings as Otello and because it is also available on videotape. As a film, this is not one of Zeffirelli's best, but it does give us the opportunity to review several principal aspects of the vocal rendition of the Otello role and how they contributed to Domingo's overall development.

When it became known in the opera world in 1975 that

the then thirty-four-year-old Domingo would be singing the
role of Otello that very year, many critics—as well as
friends—felt this might be rushing things a bit. Some even
felt Domingo should not sing Otello at all, because it would
jeopardize his lyric or lyric-dramatic roles, primarily those of
Alfredo and Rodolfo. As Domingo reports in his autobiography, even Rolf Liebermann, at that time no longer director
of the Hamburg State Opera, told the members of the ensemble on September 14, the day Domingo sang his last Rodolfo prior to the *Otello* premiere in Hamburg: "Keep your
ears open as you listen to Plácido, because this will probably
be his last *Bohème*" (AB, 135).

Liebermann's was a false prophecy. Domingo survived
Otello gloriously. He had studied the role intensively, including several weeks of complete, full-length stage rehearsals.
Not only did it not damage his voice, it helped it enormously.
His tones, and primarily the higher ones, became more radiant, more brilliant, wider, lighter, but also broader—a fact
that may take some of us by surprise, for he sings Otello with
a baritone-like, rather dark, almost purple coloration to his
voice. Although no one would rank this role among the
higher lyrical scores, the high notes in *Otello* (and there are
enough of them) have to be attacked differently from those
of Alfredo (*La traviata*) or Rodolfo (*La bohème*) or Nemorino
(*L'elisir d'amore*) or even the Duke (*Rigoletto*). Hence I agree
with those critics who feel there is a pre- and post-Otello
period in Domingo's vocal development. Even the lyric roles
sounded better after Otello. For me they have not only ma-
tured in brightness, radiance, and brilliance but have also attained overtones previously unknown to Domingo, at least
when compared to earlier recordings and taped excerpts. Domingo himself admits: "Far from harming me vocally or in

any other way, *Otello* gradually revealed to me a new way of singing that has made the rest of my repertoire much easier for me" (AB 135).

During one of our conversations Domingo confirmed the distinction between his pre- and post-Otello periods. He felt that his post-Otello development made his voice richer in brilliance as it enhanced his overtones and rendered his high notes lighter and more open. The effects of all this, he believes, were particularly evident in his lyric roles.

What does Domingo consider some of the difficulties of the Otello role? Most of them are concentrated in the strenuous second act, which for Domingo is "an opera in itself" and thus "tremendously intense." He told Helena Matheopoulos:

> You start off with the tense and vocally demanding scene with Iago; this is followed by what I consider the most difficult section of the entire opera: the quartet, which has a hideously taxing *tessitura* with a top line of B flats, requires a "covering" kind of sound, never a *forte,* and has an almost *a cappella* ending. . . . without this quartet, *Otello* would be a much, much easier opera to sing! At the end of it, you have the exclamation "tu fuggi, m' hai levato alla croce," and from that moment on until the end of Act II you are constantly involved without any chance to rest. (*Divo,* 62)

And what about the criticisms of Domingo's Otello cited above? True, one can get the impression from the *Otello* film that Domingo's vocal interpretation seems to be "painted with a broad brush" (Fischer). And surely some past interpreters have performed certain parts of the score, the "nuances," "details," "interpretative insights," "vocal attacks"

(Kesting) more impressively and more movingly. I can remember how, as a teenager in a concert in Dresden, I heard
Franz Völker sing the love duet from *Otello* with a soprano
of the Dresden State Opera. To this day I have never forgotten the initially passionate and then, glancing up at the evening star (Venus), the tender and yet still sensuously erotic
tones of this greatest Lohengrin of his time. For me it was
vocally the most erotic experience I have ever had. I do not
know if the memory would have remained so indelible if, at
the same age, I had heard Domingo sing this duet. And I say
this in full appreciation of the fact that his purple, which is to
say baritone-colored, tones in the love duet are just as perfect
as are his dynamics in the higher regions. He expresses passion convincingly if perhaps at times a bit reservedly; but then
again, his gestures remain reserved throughout this scene as
well.

It is important to remember that he is portraying Otello
the exotic general, and not Turridu (*Cavalleria rusticana*) or
Canio (*Pagliacci*). Besides, in some scenes Domingo's Otello
lets his feelings erupt more passionately than they do even in
the love duet. The only difference is that they do so in such
a way that his voice, with its glorious mixture of baritone and
tenor, of bronze, purple, and velvet, somehow gets in the
way of the individual expression of situations and musical
phrases, as paradoxical as that may sound. The members of
the audience are so transported by the beauty of his voice
that they are unable to concentrate on individual nuances.
Perhaps one has to possess a less perfect voice and be a less
perfect singer to portray individual scenes more convincingly.
At least that way the audience will be less enamored of the
voice and can concentrate its attention on the high points,

on which many less glorious singers than Domingo concentrate their efforts.

In some individually recorded arias from *Otello* Domingo seems more direct and differentiated than in the film. This impression is heightened by the fact that, when listening to a recording in contrast to watching a video or film, one is not completely captivated from beginning to end by the unique intensity that emanates from this great artist, to the point of losing one's critical distance.

I also have heard Otello's final scene sung in a more desperate, more lamenting, "more heart-rending," and therefore perhaps also more moving way than in Domingo's *Otello* film. Yet I have to say that I have also heard Domingo himself sing more wrenchingly in stage performances than he does in this film. In the 1989 simulcast production from Covent Garden he appears more convincing in this scene (although less perfect in a vocal sense) than he does in the film. In fact, Domingo's stage performances usually are better and more convincing, for there he does not have to divorce his theatrical interpretation from his vocal expression of the role.

Nevertheless, I do believe that Domingo's relatively restrained agitation as well as his vocally controlled intensity in the final scene of his performances were absolutely intentional from a musical as well as a theatrical point of view. After all, Otello does not end up like Turridu and does not kill like Canio; instead, he dies like a wounded lion, like the Lion of Cypress and San Marco. In dying as in killing he remains the great African general who had already endured mortification in the north before he became a hero. Thus death itself still retains aspects of greatness and nobility for him. It is certainly a painful death, for he lost his Desdemona through deceptions to which he fell victim all too quickly simply because of his mistrust—in fact, he actually becomes her murderer—but he meets his death with a degree of nobility and a certain religiosity that simultaneously reveal the last trace of his tragic pride. This is also how he sees Desdemona's death, which he now mourns. Such a lion cannot call after his Desdemona as heart-renderingly as the poet Rodolfo cries out the name of his beloved Mimì at the end of *Bohème*. That's why Domingo's rendition (particularly in the London excerpt) of his "Niun mi tema" is colored with the somewhat proud, fatalistic tone of lament and grief. Despite all the baritone-like qualities of his voice, his singing remains relatively bright in timbre and he introduces a soft, even a tender, lyrical tone at the point in question. Naturally, he also displays his anger, but no melodramatic desperation. Whoever misses this distinction (and in this group I do not mean to include those serious critics cited above) understands neither Domingo nor his Otello.

I'll return to Domingo's theatrical portrayal of Otello in the next chapter. For the moment let me conclude by saying that, whether in the film and video versions or in the stage performances I witnessed in Los Angeles in 1989, Domingo's perfect technique, including his support, comes into full play precisely in his role as Otello. And this is what makes me confident that he will continue to take on or sing many a difficult role in the future.

Versatility: From Rafael Ruiz to Tristan, but Little Mozart and Still No Bach

In spite of his heavy schedule, in spite of his popularity and the diversity of his repertoire, Domingo seems to have remained a religious man who finds or at least seeks solace and strength in church and in prayer.

PLÁCIDO DOMINGO HAS THE MOST VARIED REPERTOIRE of all the great tenors of our day. Not surprisingly, then, it also includes what is called "light" entertainment: operetta, musicals, folk songs, and pop tunes. José Carreras, Luciano Pavarotti to a somewhat lesser extent, Richard Tauber in days gone by, and later even Fritz Wunderlich have been at home in this genre under the auspices of the "light" muse. Domingo's onstage operatic repertoire ranges from Rafael Ruiz, a zarzuela figure, to Parsifal. And if we add to these roles those productions recorded in studios and not yet seen onstage, his repertoire swells to include what are for him such difficult roles as Hüon von Bordeaux in Carl Maria von Weber's *Oberon* (whose "dramatic-coloratura" aria "Von Jugend auf" is a source of particular anxiety for him), or Tannhäuser in Wagner's opera of the same name, to Walter von Stolzing in Wagner's *Die Meistersinger,* as well as the emperor in Richard Strauss's *Die Frau ohne Schatten.*

The sum total of the roles Domingo has sung to date both onstage and in studio production comes close to an astonishing one hundred. He does not intend to continue singing all of his earlier featured roles—Rodolfo or Alfredo, for example—for his age is beginning to be a mitigating factor. Undaunted, Domingo is constantly learning new parts, including the title role in Verdi's *Stiffelio* in 1993 at the Met. He had already sung Siegmund in Vienna in 1993, and Tristan is planned for Vienna in the near future and thereafter in Los Angeles.

Where does Domingo get his energy? When I visited him in New York late last March, we first met backstage at the Met. It was right after the annual Metropolitan Opera National Council Winners' Concert for young singers in and around New York. He greeted every participant in his amicable way and congratulated all of them on their performances. Then he, his wife, and I drove in their large black limousine to Saint Patrick's Cathedral, where the cardinal was celebrating mass. It was Palm Sunday. Domingo donated a generous sum for palm fronds, a few of which he also gave me. Then he chose an inconspicuous spot for the three of us, where he and Mrs. Domingo could kneel for some time in quiet prayer and meditation. He had tears in his eyes. Not only was the pew inconspicuous, but he too was hardly recognizable. This was the time he was singing Otello at the Met, so he was still wearing his stage beard and his hair had been dyed black. In spite of his heavy schedule, in spite of his popularity and the diversity of his repertoire, Domingo seems to have remained a religious man who finds or at least seeks solace and strength in church and in prayer.

After mass I accompanied Domingo to his elegant and tastefully decorated apartment on the twentieth floor of an East Side high-rise with its adjoining office space. The view overlooks the East River in the vicinity of the Queensboro

Bridge. It was here, in this apartment, that we engaged in a very relaxed conversation.

This was the year Domingo was working on the zarzuela *El gato montés* for Los Angeles, his role being that of the tenor Rafael Ruiz. Although he no longer gave the impression of a young torero onstage, his voice was clear and warm, displaying a bright acoustical spectrum and youthful vitality. Rafael Ruiz is a young torero embroiled in a lover's rivalry with a basically sympathetic bandit, who was outstandingly portrayed by Justino Diaz. Domingo's singing was perhaps a bit heavier, more vigorous (but certainly not sluggish) in its dynamics and phrasing than it might have been more than three decades ago in Mexico when he sang the role for the first time. Even so, his notes still bore the mark of that velvety golden mellowness so appropriate for a zarzuela. This only goes to prove that neither Verdi's Otello nor Wagner's Parsifal and Siegmund did any damage to the brilliance of his voice, not even in the lighter roles. Domingo has lost none of his ability to differentiate between Otello and Lohengrin on the one hand and the more open, highly textured (golden) vocal colors of a zarzuela role on the other. For we have all witnessed how Lerner and Loewe or Lehár can sound like tortured heroes from the Nibelungen: too full, too thick, too heavy and, above all, too clumsy, when a portly Brünnhilde suddenly decides to portray Eliza Doolittle in *My Fair Lady* or a Wagnerian tenor suddenly decides to sing Count Danilo in *The Merry Widow*.

Although nothing in his voice would hinder Domingo's continuing to sing the role of Rafael Ruiz, his physical stature as well as his facial features and movements render it no longer a role for the future. Of course, Siegmund and Parsifal are supposed to be quite young, too, but for these legendary figures the music and the story carry their own weight in that they are heavier and more mythical in themselves. The portrayal of a realistic everyday life with folkloric elements is not the main focus in Wagner, nor is the influence of Italian verismo (of which Domingo is a masterful interpreter). Moreover, the purely vocal and technical demands of Wagner's music rule out the inclusion of younger singers, with the result that everyone expects a somewhat older performer in these roles; Rafael Ruiz, on the other hand, is a role ready made and perfectly appropriate for a twenty-year-old.

This brings us to the question of how Domingo sings Wagner's music. I have already discussed his interpretation of Lohengrin, and he once told me a few things about his portrayal of Siegmund, including the following observation:

> Siegmund is the hero par excellence. I think his is one of the most beautiful of all roles. It's so incredible, especially the first act (of *Die Walküre*). . . . I think it's difficult to find a better act than this one. . . . The text is the most important thing in the first half of the first act. And yet, when you begin the "Winterstürme," the melody dominates to the end of the act. The melody dominates everything, and the text is no longer so important. It goes without saying that you have to enunciate clearly, but the melody dominates. Earlier on, the discussions with Hunding, the report about persecutions, and the killings—all of that is very important as text. [The scene] "ein Schwert verhieß mir der Vater" is also important as text. But starting with "Keiner ging, einer kam, siehe der Lenz lacht in den Saal," it's another story. The melody becomes more important. Naturally it's always good if the audience understands what's going on. In the beginning [of the act] you have to be sure your dic-

tion is clear, but after that it's all bel canto. Maybe not bel canto, but there are these glorious, beautiful [melodic] lines.

Obviously Domingo gives a great deal of thought to his interpretations of Wagner's works. For him, not only is every role and every opera different from all the others, but the differentiations and developments within a Wagnerian role require different vocal colorations and shadings as well. Domingo illustrated what he meant by describing Parsifal:

At the beginning you have a youthful, almost wild character, but then he grows and matures, and in places this development poses problems for one's voice. One danger zone is the very youthfulness of the character, which has to be very clearly expressed. One senses this extreme youth [in the music] from the very start of the piece. But then comes the act with the flower girls, and Parsifal is kissed by Kundry. This kiss transforms him into a different, a totally different tenor, not only because he's now beginning to understand pain, love, and death as a result of Kundry's monologue, but because of the kiss itself, for Parsifal himself is suddenly transformed into a mature man. When he then sings "Amfortas!—Die Wunde!—Die Wunde!," he's a completely different character. And this is the one that continues to the Easter scene in the third act, when Good Friday comes and Gurnamanz tells of the spell and Parsifal experiences it. At this moment Parsifal's voice changes back to its original youthful color, to a youthful tenor. By the end of the scene, though, he's once again his mature conscious self. All of these changes in vocal color, these changes in shadings, make Parsifal such a very difficult role to sing. It's not a long role, but an extremely demanding one.

And it's precisely these demanding roles that Domingo loves so much. He once told me: "Singing Parsifal and Siegmund

improves my high register. Maybe because I color them in a
different way, and since I never use the extreme registers to
the hilt [for Domingo, the role of Siegmund is almost baritone-like in the tessitura of the first act of *Die Walküre*], I feel
very good after Wagner and even sing my romantic repertoire better."

One of the most demanding tenor roles ever written by
Wagner is that of Tannhäuser. Thus, if for no other reason,
this role is of particular interest here. Domingo sang the role
only once, on a 1988 recording (released in 1989 on the
Deutsche Grammophon label), and he has no plans ever to
perform it onstage. He told me all the problems that keep
him from doing so.

To come right to the point: I consider Domingo's Tannhäuser interpretation, like his other Wagner representations,
in general and in certain particulars more Wagnerian than
many of the renditions more "Germanically" trained Wagner
singers have produced.

The opening scene on the Venusberg is the decisive factor
in anyone's appreciation of a Tannhäuser interpreter. Right
from the start the singer must lend clear vocal differentiation
to the two worlds between which Tannhäuser is torn: the
sensual world of Venus and the almost platonic world of Elisabeth, who is first revealed to him in his yearning for the
purity of nature. We are thus presented with a Faustian con-
flict, except that Goethe's Faust never dove so deeply nor for
such a prolonged period into the world of the purely sensual.
Domingo succeeds in giving complete expression to this
wrestling match between Venus and the revived yearning for
"heaven's comforting vault" as well as for summer, spring,
and song. This yearning begins "Im Traum war's mir" with
a beauty of voice and lyric that has never been matched,

except that in places the legato is a little too extended and the pronunciation in what follows is occasionally unclear. Nevertheless, as said before, the voice is full of beauty and lyricism right from the start, except that here and there Domingo uses a somewhat forced portamento from one syllable to another and thus, to a "Germanic" ear, "swims" through the notes and syllables a bit too much. We can find this rather excessive swimming and floating in other individual legato lines in this Tannhäuser interpretation as well.

In contrast, Domingo sings his song of praise "Dir töne Lob!" with great energy—so much so, in fact, that in several places he almost forfeits his mellowness. Occasionally he even assumes a vocal diction more suitable for Verdi than Wagner. Here I am thinking of the line "Doch sterblich ach, bin ich geblieben." In the duet with Venus (sung by Agnes Baltsa) Domingo begins in an equally manly and energetic manner, but his projection occasionally fails him because of his pronunciation problems. His vocal coloration is also too dark at times and thus again sacrifices some of its mellowness. All of this is of little significance, however, for starting with the line "Stets soll nur dir, nur dir mein Lied ertönen" he rises to a perfected expression that unites a proper degree of legato with its appropriate stress. Even his high notes are steady and strong. This is ideal Wagnerian singing in keeping with Wagner's own definition. Moreover, we can clearly perceive how Tannhäuser's yearning for earthly pleasures, for freedom, becomes all the more urgent and persistent the more he unconsciously senses how very much Venus still binds and fascinates him.

It is astonishing how strongly Domingo's voice projects over the chorus during the reunion scene with the Landgraf and the other singers. But we cannot attribute this to Domingo alone; the electronics of amplification probably did their share in reducing the other male singers somewhat, for what tenor can project so strongly and so dynamically against a half dozen strong voices, including the bass of a Matti Salminen? Even the best overtone spectrum cannot do this.

At the beginning of the scene with Elisabeth, Domingo's voice seems rather lackluster, too baritone-like, too matter-of-fact. Despite these drawbacks, however, his expression is convincing, and he soon regains his tenor's brilliance. In the actual duet with Elisabeth, Domingo does not seem passionate enough to me, even though I realize we are dealing with the phenomenon of pure love now. I have heard this love scene sung more dynamically and more thrillingly elsewhere. Later, in the song contest, Domingo begins his reply to Wolfram, "O Wolfram, der du also sangest," in a tone devoid of the requisite agitation, anger, and sarcasm. Yet shortly thereafter, in the line "Zu Gottes Preis," his voice unfolds to its most sublime vocal perfection. This, in turn, is followed by a more passionate and fervent performance, despite the occasional signs of strain in the high notes. Domingo sings several passages with a rather exaggerated legato, but once again, it is not that distracting because, beginning with the line "Dir, Göttin der Liebe," we are treated to the full display of his extraordinary talent for singing Wagner, which includes his ability to produce the expression and vocal perfection Wagner demanded. To my mind, this adoration of Venus in the competition with Wolfram ranks both vocally and theatrically among the most outstanding and most thrilling examples of recorded singing. Only with the line "Zum Heil den Sündigen zu führen" do I once again begin to sense a little too much of the legato mellowness, although the singing is still full of energy. Several passages in the duet with Elisabeth, however, come across as slightly constricted or weary. Domingo's voice holds its own better against the men in the chorus than it does against Elisabeth (sung here by Cheryl Studer). Nevertheless, in these scenes, too, Domingo manages to change and to shape his vocal colorations in such a way that all other weaknesses fade into insignificance. As if one could speak of weaknesses at all at this sublime level of artistry!

Were I a singer in my own right and a Wagnerian heroic tenor at that, I would never cease to dread the Rome episode in the last act. For me this scene is one of the most difficult and most frightening within the whole body of Wagner's operatic works, not only because it makes extraordinary dramatic and vocal demands on the singer (I am thinking of the passaggio and the high notes), but also because it is the culmination of hours of difficult stage performance. Domingo's rendition of this episode is a studio recording, and we do not know how and whether he could have mastered it as well onstage after three hours of live performance. Yet the way he shapes his entrance as well as the Rome episode is very impressive on the CD. He begins his appearance after his excommunication with a kind of "speech song" ("Ich hörte Harfenschlag") containing equal measures of statements, questions, echoes of home, exhaustion, and astonishment, until the voice becomes cynical, sarcastic, and even a bit melodramatic in "Wolfram bist du, der wohlgeübte Sänger."

The Rome episode represents the high point of vocal theatricality. In the first half, up to "dann Gnad / und Heil verhießen sie der Menge," the voice retains a highly lyrical quality. This is achieved by means of many legato lines as well as a deeply moving *messa di voce*. Where other singers employ, among other things, dynamically sharper glottal stops to express their bitterness and their pain in this episode, Domingo's anguish is instead borne on an emotionally moving legato and his unique "swell notes" on the words and syllables that Wagner deliberately designed for the purpose: "*In*-brunst," "*Bü-ßer,*" "*je,*" "*Weg,*" "*Rom,*" "*Eng*-el," "*Stolz,*" "*Ü*-bermütigen." His manner of swelling the notes by "feeding" them with a subtle vibrato is shown to perfection here, for he also seems to combine it with a skillfully applied rubato that enhances the elegaic character of the scene. Domingo follows this up with increased vocal strength and dynamics, so that the eight lines of the papal damnation assume their own cynical double coloration and dynamic intensification that only an artist of Domingo's caliber can convey. In the next few lines he once again returns to a kind of baritone-like speech song before concluding the scene with a tone that is once again heroic but still painful.

Domingo's rendition of Tannhäuser, as well as of all the other Wagner roles in his repertoire, differs from what we have come to expect from German singers. He introduces more legato, more portamento, more arcs, and more swell tones so uniquely enhanced by his own special type of vibrato. This results in some beautiful legato phrasings borne on a "single well-apportioned breath" (Wagner) that delight the ear of the listener. Sometimes, however, he overuses such smooth phrasing, so that the clarity of his spoken dialogue and thus Wagner's music-drama effects, where language and music are supposed to be "of equal worth," suffer a bit: the result is too much bel canto. This is particularly noticable in the first act of a *Walküre* performance broadcast from the Met as well as in his Metropolitan Opera interpretation of Parsifal.

When I say too much legato and too much bel canto, I

mean just that, for it was Wagner himself who advocated a mixture of Italian bel canto and German elocution for his operas and then personally rehearsed the roles with his singers. It was Cosima Wagner who later prevailed in requiring the purely German element in Wagnerian singing. What Wagner understood as "speech-song" (*Sprachgesang*) was a good legato with a clear articulation of word and sense. I shall come back to this again in the chapter on text and music; what Cosima understood by this term was intensified spoken articulation. To her way of thinking, it was a "spoken song," which meant there was little or no legato and, above all, absolutely no bel canto in it.

Wagner, on the other hand, dreamed of a "German" or "national" bel canto. Important to him was the acoustically pleasing phrase that made full use of the consonants as carriers. He gives a detailed explanation of what he means by this in his fundamental and comprehensive essay *Opera and Drama,* written in 1851. We learn, for instance, that he demanded a great deal of legato, especially for *Lohengrin.* The Bayreuth school under Cosima's direction put an end to all of that. Domingo, on the other hand, ranks among those Wagnerian singers who once again strongly emphasize the legato in Wagner's works. Yet he tends toward the other extreme, so that the linguistic flexibility Wagner demanded occasionally gets short shrift. Of course, even during Cosima's lifetime Franz Völker was already singing Wagnerian parts with a greater legato, as was Leo Slezak with his lyrical *mezza voce.* But these two did not belong to the Cosima circle that reigned in Bayreuth for as long as Cosima actually wielded the scepter. Son Siegfried, in turn, set out in different directions again.

Wagner's relation to Italian bel canto was always ambivalent. He truly hated the bel canto of the castrati, though he admired Bellini and the way tenors (not castrati) sang his music. He also agreed with his friend and singing coach Julius Hey in believing there was no vocal technique and appropriate singing discipline in the Italian school that could not be applied to German singing instruction. Cosima Wagner, on the other hand, loathed all Italian and French bel canto music and their schools, and this attitude had a disastrous effect on her interpretations of the master's works after his death. In her diary entry of February 12, 1871, she wrote: "*Faust, Le Prophète, Les Huguenots,* Bellini, Donizetti, Rossini, Verdi, one after another, I feel physically sick, I pick up and seek refuge in a volume of Goethe (*Paralipomena zu 'Faust'*). But nothing helps, I suffer and suffer."★ When Wagner stopped talking to his friend Hans Richter about Gounod, Bellini, and Meyerbeer and started analyzing Bach and Mozart instead, she wrote: "Thus R. continues for a long time to speak, and the Italian and Jewish ghosts are dispersed—but the feelings of nausea remained!"

On the other hand, she felt compelled to enter the following remark about Wagner himself on August 3, 1872: "R. sings a cantilena from *I Puritani* and remarks that Bellini wrote melodies lovelier than one's dreams. The melody recalls Rubini to him, how wonderfully he sang it, and he observes: 'Our German singers have to go about it in an entirely different way, because they have not got this gift. Because of what is denied them, they must aspire to unheard-of things, like Wieland, who came to fly on missing feet." Giovanni Battista Rubini was Italy's most famous bel canto tenor

★*Cosima Wagner's Diaries,* ed. Martin Gregor-Dellin and Dietrich Mach, trans. Geoffrey Skelton, vol. 1 (1869–1872) (New York: Harcourt Brace Jovanovich, 1977), 335–36.

around the middle of the nineteenth century, and Wagner admired him greatly.

Besides the essay mentioned above, there is another short piece with the title "Bellini: A Word in Season" that dates from 1837; here the young Wagner waxes downright enthusiastic about the composer of *Norma* when he writes:

> That *Bellinian* Song enraptures Italy and France, is natural enough, for in Italy and France men hear with their ears . . . but that even the German music-scholar should have . . . given himself for once to reckless delight in a lovely song, this opens up a deeper glimpse into the inner chamber of his heart,—and there we spy an ardent longing . . . to throw off all the fumes of prejudice and pedantry which so long have forced him to be a German music-scholar; to become a Man instead at last, glad, free and gifted with every glorious organ for perceiving beauty, no matter the form in which it shows itself.★

He continues a bit further on: "We then shall find, especially with *Bellini,* that it was the limpid Melody, the simple, noble, beauteous Song, that so enchanted us. To confess this and believe in it, is surely not a sin; 'twere no sin, perchance, if before we fell asleep we breathed a prayer that Heaven would one day give German composers such melodies and such a mode of handling Song. Song, Song, and a third time Song, ye Germans!"† And then, on March 7, 1878, Cosima noted in her diary: "Before that R. played various Italian themes, from Bellini's *I Capuleti ed i Montecchi, La Straniera,* and *Norma,* and said: 'For all the poverty of invention, there is

---

★*Richard Wagner's Prose Works,* trans. William Ashton Ellis (New York: Broude Brothers, 1966), 8:67.
†Ibid., 68.

real passion and feeling there, and the right singer has only to get up and sing it for it to win all hearts. I have learned things from them which Messrs. Brahms & Co. have never learned, and they can be seen in my melodies."★

Wagner's prose works contain additional observations about Bellini, several of which judge the Italian composer as more important than Weber for the Germans.

So what is Domingo's relation to Carl Maria von Weber, Wagner's predecessor, and for that matter, to Richard Strauss, Wagner's successor? The great Spaniard has performed in one opera by each of these respective composers.

Let us start with Domingo's role as Hüon in Weber's *Oberon*. It was recorded in 1970. Without dissecting it completely, one can say that Domingo's voice in this opera is certainly leaner than we know it today, but it still lacks the radiant brilliance and fullness of the later years. With his first entrance—"Sei ein Führer mir, holder Geist!"—Domingo's voice has a lyrical, heroic tone, which is exactly what the role calls for, and it carries over the chorus as well, but he occasionally employs too many legatos where a portato (a tonal glide between legato and staccato) or a clear separation of syllables would have been more appropriate, as in the line "Kann ich meinen Augen traun." He begins the famous aria "Von Jugend auf" equally well, holding the listener spellbound with his various shadings, which include a supported falsetto on the word "Liebe" and a solid baritone-like coloration in the line "welch düstrer Trauerflor." He frequently tries to darken some of the deeper and higher notes to lend them expressive power, but his attempts backfire a bit when they produce a guttural sound as, for example, in the last line,

★C. Wagner, vol. 2 (1878–1883), 35.

"doch Sein ohne Ehre." This somewhat guttural darkening is gone for good in the post-Otello Domingo. Today, all his acoustic colorations are free and mellow.

As far as the other scenes with Hüon are concerned, the fundamental expression remains a heroic-lyrical one, enhanced by much legato, skillful portamento, a trained *mezza voce* (however sparingly employed), occasional extra accentuations, and portato. Of course, one's personal taste determines one's ultimate judgment on how Domingo uses this vocal arsenal in *Oberon*. I find it more than successful, despite the already mentioned, occasionally somewhat guttural attempts at darkening a note as well as the sometimes imperfect pronunciation of isolated words. On the whole, though, he did not sing the role of Hüon in 1970 nearly as perfectly and satisfactorily as he did that of Don Carlo the same year, even though there is a certain kinship between the freshness of the portrayal and the leanness of the voice. Still, Hüon is simply a different role from that of Don Carlo, even if it is equally difficult to sing and certainly more difficult than many of Verdi's other tenor parts.

With regard to Richard Strauss, on the other hand, Domingo writes in his autobiography: "Strauss, generous as he is with female singers, is rather stingy with tenors, and Bacchus [*Ariadne auf Naxos*] would have been both an ungrateful and a vocally dangerous part for me" (AB, 156). His reservations notwithstanding, between 1989 and 1991 he recorded the part of the emperor in Strauss's *Die Frau ohne Schatten* under the direction of Sir Georg Solti.

The emperor has to sing a total of three arias (a challenge in themselves) as well as a duet with the empress, followed by a quartet with the empress, Barak, and his wife, in which the voices of the unborn children can also be heard.

Because of its passaggio, the first aria is the most difficult. Domingo masters it impressively, but it, too, frequently betrays a much extended or drawn-out legato and a specific *messa di voce* contrived specifically for this purpose. The portamento and Domingo's own masterful vibrato on the swell tones help him deal with the difficulties of pitch ("und höhnte" with its a¹ is a good example) as well as with the passaggio as a whole. Also admirable are the arcs or bridges that Domingo so skillfully constructs when approaching the high notes; these he then adorns with his glorious vibrating crescendo, as in the word "rankte" with a 5/4 beat on an a¹ on the syllable "rank-" and a 1/4 beat on a g-sharp¹ on the syllable "te." At the end of this scene he produces a portamento on the words "aller Beuten ohn' Ende" with a 4/4 beat on the b-flat¹ on the syllable "En-," producing an effect that does Strauss proud. The deeper positions sound glorious as well.

Everything in the second act's next aria, "Falke, Falke," also sounds close to perfect, even if once again an occasionally too extended or drawn-out legato or portamento pushes to the fore. Here and there a legato seems a bit forced to me, as at the beginning of the aria between the passages "Das Falknerhaus" and "einsam im Walde," as well as within the passage "soll die drei Tage"; it happens again in the second part of the aria when, thinking his wife has been unfaithful, he sings a bit too elegiacally and lets his voice float a bit too much despite the lyrically masculine sound of his voice. In my opinion, a singer such as James O'Neil, who certainly possesses neither the overtone qualities nor the technical sophistication of a Domingo, sings all three arias of this opera with more expression. O'Neil's rendition of the second

"Falke," with its bound 10/4 note on the syllable "Fal-," is more moving than Domingo's rendition of the same passage.

On the other hand, Domingo's arcs, portamentos, and portatos are and remain unique, even for Strauss. This is especially evident in the last aria, which comes in the third act. The quality of Domingo's tone fits the message of the text particularly well here, although I cannot deny that in this aria too the occasional legato and portamento are excessively drawn out. Even so, they do not tip the scales to any significant degree. Instead, and especially in this aria, the listener is impressed by how masterfully Domingo constructs the rising tonal phrases such as that on the word "leben," where the syllable "le-" rises chromatically from f to b-flat[1] for a total of six steps and three measures: perfect in the vocal phrasing, perfect in the legato arc, and perfect in the portamento. Many of these musical miracles are repeated in his duet and in the concluding quartet, which extends up to a 9/4-beat long c^2 at the end. Unfortunately, there are other places in the quartet where Domingo's voice has a rather soft effect, but this may also be due to the recording technology.

Another striking aspect of Domingo's interpretation of the emperor, and one we find quite frequently in his other portrayals as well, is how very high he drives his chest voice and how, while in the head register region, he creates a strong mixed register with the greater part dominated by the chest voice. There are other singers who prefer to let the head register dominate in such a *voix mixte*. For my part, I find Domingo's mixture extremely effective and expressive.

Part of Domingo's reputation for versatility rests on his Russian roles, as well. While still in Tel Aviv he and his wife, Marta, had both sung in Tchaikovsky's *Eugen Onegin*. Moreover, while still early in his career he planned to expand his repertoire with the addition of the role of Hermann from Tchaikovsky's *Pique dame.* Although Domingo is featured neither in an *Eugen Onegin* nor a *Pique dame* performance, he has sung Lensky's aria "Kuda, kuda, kuda vi udalilis" from *Eugen Onegin* on several of his recordings. What follows refers to a 1991 open-air concert under the direction of Mstislav Rostropovich; in addition to a videotape of the performance, there is a cassette recording from 1993 featuring Randall Behr, the resident conductor of the Los Angeles Music Center Opera. On both recordings one is once again impressed by the brilliance of Domingo's voice. The masterfully constructed high tones come through loud and clear. His subtly vibrating crescendo on individual tones and phrases, hardly perceptible and yet present all the same, are incomparable. Domingo seems to be having absolutely no problems with the piece. The live recording has a stronger tone, whereas the cassette version sounds more lyrical. This may have something to do with the different environments in which both concerts were sung.

Of course, if we compare these two recordings with Nicolai Gedda's interpretations of the same piece, we are immediately struck by two things: the first is the fact that Gedda's clearer articulation of the language stands out in greater relief, which should not surprise us given that Russian is his native tongue (his adoptive father, Mikhail Ustinov, was a Russian soldier and singer in the Don Cossack Choir). Secondly, however, Gedda gives the piece a totally different interpretation—one can almost say worlds apart from Domingo's. Gedda's modulations of dynamics and timbre, his transition from a powerful lyrical to a tender *mezza voce,* the different registers he uses—the chest register, a pure head voice, a mixed register, and a trace of supported falsetto as defined elsewhere in this book (that is, not a "pipe" voice but a gentle vibration of the edges of the vocal cords in the head voice region), as well as a kind of combination between a pure head voice and a supported falsetto—all of these components are apparently inimitable. This is not to say that Domingo's rendition lacks differentiating shadings, but it must be said that the cassette recording is richer in these than is the open-air concert, the latter leaving the listener with the general impression that Domingo was singing by rote because of his difficulties with the text. Clear dynamic nuances are also lacking on the video version. Nevertheless, Domingo's unique and peculiar crescendo and diminuendo on individual notes or phrases have lost none of their charm, even on this recording. About the Lensky aria we can also say that everything Domingo touches still turns to gold or textured brocade—but with Gedda, the Lensky aria turns into a delicately polished diamond.

Although he had already sung the role of Ferrando in Mozart's *Così fan tutte* in Mexico City in 1962 and frequently took to the stage in Tel Aviv during the 1963–64 season in the role of Ottavio in *Don Giovanni,* Domingo has never recorded a complete Mozart opera. As a matter of fact, apart from his interest in singing Don Giovanni, he has neglected Mozart rather badly ever since the Tel Aviv days. One CD from 1991 features Mozart arias, and it confirms Domingo's assessment that there is no more difficult composer to sing than this one. In matters of technique, Mozart is actually more difficult even than Wagner. On the one hand, it is common knowledge that an immature tenor or one lacking the proper technique can come to complete ruin in his attempts to master such roles as Lohengrin, Walter, and Tannhäuser. On the other hand, everything has to be perfectly clear with

Mozart, whose music also has difficult passaggios. A singer has to show his colors when performing one of Mozart's works. There is no hiding behind the orchestra or taking the easy way out by dampening or covering one's high notes, as one sometimes can in Wagner. The audience will notice it every time, because the voice peals out in clear and unimpeded isolation. Moreover, Mozart writes arias (e.g., the Don Ottavio arias) in which the change in register from the chest to the head voice has to be made clearly without forfeiting the harmonic transition; if not, the singer inevitably chokes up. Domingo's recording of Mozart's music lacks this clean transition. Instead, he either drives his chest voice up to the high pitches or lets it dominate in a *voix mixte.*

If we listen to Domingo's rendition of Mozart's arias and duets, there is no doubt that his current voice is best suited to the role of Idomeneo. Here, in the recitative and aria "Qual mi conturba / Fuor del mar," Domingo's energy and all-around perfection of tone is perfectly appropriate, and here too he succeeds in producing perfectly satisfying shadings. The situation changes, however, with the aria "Che beltà, che leggiadria" in *La finta giardiniera.* To my ear, Domingo sounds too energetic here, and not lean enough. I also miss the shadings of Mozart's early (rococo) period.

In contrast, Domingo's individual renditions of Don Ottavio's recitatives, arias, and duets from *Don Giovanni* are interesting. The following appraisal is based on the 1991 recording he made of these selections, and since I have yet to locate an allegedly existing concert recording of the aria "Il mio tesoro" from Domingo's early years, I have no basis for comparison. In the 1991 recording, at any rate, Domingo tries to introduce more spirit and theatricality into the role of Don Ottavio, who, compared to Don Giovanni, is a rather conventional and insipid character. The music is beautiful, but nowhere near as thrilling as that of the seducer. Domingo's interpretation is less lyrical than expected, especially in the first of the two famous arias. In "Dalla sua pace" he hardly ever uses the *mezza voce* and never the falsetto. In other respects, too, he is not as nuanced in his shadings as is Nicolai Gedda, for instance, in his *Don Giovanni* recording of 1966. There Gedda fashions his alternating chest and head voice, his mixed register, and brief falsetto passages into one of the most beautiful and most ingenious color palettes ever heard. Domingo, in contrast, lends this role a dynamic all its own and a vocal presence that almost competes with that of Don Ottavio's opponent. I say almost, because Domingo cannot add to the music and the libretto what simply is not there. At any rate, he shapes the role more dramatically and the character more precisely than is usually the case.

Domingo also sings two of the more humorous roles of Mozart's creation: Pedrillo from *Die Entführung aus dem Serail* and Basilio from *Le nozze di Figaro*. Although Domingo tries to bring out the light and humorous side of Pedrillo's aria "Frisch zum Kampfe," he does not quite succeed. The heroic and courageous elements of the first and second lines are more convincing. What he does manage to convey in between by means of distant hints of a pure head voice (perhaps better described here as a somewhat nasal *mezza voce*), though quite successful as far as the changes in vocal coloring are concerned, still does not come across as light and youthful enough. Nevertheless, though the youthful and truly comic elements may be missing, we are entranced by Domingo's modulation of vocal coloring between belligerence on the one hand and timidity on the other.

The coloration in Basilio's recitative, on the other hand, is very well done. Here the comic element comes through and is even maintained for a few lines in the aria. And yet Domingo is inconsistent in his coloration here and regains a buffo tone in the line "ecco le membra coprir mi giova" only with the help of a sort of darkened falsetto. In other respects his interpretation of this aria sounds almost like a Don Giovanni scene with all its dynamics and colorations. It fascinates, but it somehow misses the essence of Basilio. Buffo parts are no longer Domingo's métier, at least not for the present.

And this brings us to the three great lyric arias. There are marvelous phrasings in "Konstanze, dich wiederzusehen." They begin right away with the first "Konstanze" and its captivating portamento. The color modulations at the beginning could serve as a model, but the aria suffers a bit later on under a coloration that remains too static and seems to lack vitality. Some of this is the fault of the music—Mozart did not have a Da Ponte as librettist here, and it was Da Ponte who knew how to arouse Mozart's dramatic (Shakespearean) genius for depicting characterization through music.

Among the selections from *Così fan tutte,* the famous aria "Un'aura amorosa" is sung less lyrically by Domingo than by other Mozart singers, so much so, in fact, that one even gets the impression Domingo is singing it a bit too quickly. But here too, the tones are glorious with their proper, that is, inobtrusive portamento. Nevertheless, I could have wished for a tender and leaner sound; also, several of the high tones seemed somewhat pinched to my ear.

The recitative "In qual fiero constrasto" is powerful and convincing, and this quality carries over into the aria "Tradito, schernito." But here, too, several of the high tones seem strained, despite the fascinating rendition. This aria is followed by the duet "Fra gli amplessi," in which once again the high tones sound a bit too labored (and there are real problems with the repeated "più non tardar"). Even so, the lower notes are phrased masterfully. One can see, however, that with Mozart's music, the upward bridges are not easy to climb.

We get a similarly mixed impression of Tamino's portrait aria from *Die Zauberflöte,* even though this selection contains unforgettable modulations with coloring as well as with phrasing choices. From the very beginning of "Dies Bildnis" one can clearly hear how masterfully Domingo lets his voice swell up to the g^1 on the syllable "Bild-." Yet this upward swell, combined with a sort of portamento from the b-flat on "Dies" to the g^1 on "Bild" is a bit too artificial for many ears, perhaps even a bit blurred. Instead of freely striking the g^1 in "Bild-," Domingo enlists the aid of a concave acoustical arc to create a kind of upward crutch, which he then no longer needs during the stepwise descent from the f^1 on "-nis" down to the a-flat on "schön." Domingo's descent as a single phrase becomes a model of a Mozart portato. As for the rest, several successive high notes in this aria sound a bit labored. After a rather light beginning the remainder of the aria actually sounds somewhat ponderous.

The fact that Domingo is planning to sing the role of Idomeneo is welcome news indeed. Unfortunately, he has never given us either a recording or a stage performance of Tamino, Belmonte, or Ferrando (and in essence also no Ottavio), and this is hard to forgive. (He sang the role of Ferrando only once, in Mexico City, and portrayed Don Ottavio at the very beginning of his international career in Tel Aviv.) It is too late for these roles today. Although Domingo's voice has gained a lot through experience, through his singing of Otello as well as through his Wagner interpretations, the leanness and lightness required for Tamino and Belmonte are simply no longer there.

Domingo has never sung a Bach Evangelist, either; in fact, unlike Mozart, there are no recordings of Domingo singing Bach at all. This is regrettable. Of all interpreters, I would imagine that Domingo could have lent new dimensions to Bach's *Passions*. Since Domingo is a master of recitative singing (part of this is due to his talent as an actor, which he carries over to the musical shaping of the recitative), his Evangelist would surely be a memorable event. I can just imagine how he would use his unique and artistically vibrant swell tones to phrase the "und sprach" or "und sprachen" at the end of a recitative. This in itself would surely produce a musical event of unparalleled magnificence. Moreover, like Peter Schreier before him, Domingo is also capable of conducting the *Saint Matthew* and *Saint John Passions*. He has told me how much he would like to do this, so we may yet have an opportunity to enjoy Domingo's interpretation of Bach.

Toward the end of his autobiography, under the heading "Future Plans," Domingo included the following statement: "I love the German Lied repertoire—so much so that I would not dare to attempt any of it without extremely careful preparation. That is another project for the future" (AB, 210). Many have read into this an eventual recording or live performance of works by Schubert, Schumann, Wolf, Brahms, Strauss, or Mahler. It looks as if we will have to wait a bit longer, though. Trying to learn "Die Winterreise" or "Dichterliebe" on a flight from Los Angeles to Tokyo strains even the intelligence and musical genius of a Plácido Domingo. And he is very aware of that fact.

On the other hand, he has given a few other reasons why

he is still not yet planning an evening of exclusively Schubert, Schumann, or Brahms lieder:

> I've sung a bit of Schubert, Bach, and Brahms. But I live on the stage, and when I give concerts, the audience wants to hear the great arias. [Lieder singing] will be something that, when I have the time, I would gladly discover for myself. But I am delaying it and delaying it. . . . Maestro Solti is always asking me to give a lieder cycle at some time. But I'm too busy with my [stage] characters, and the little time I have left I have to devote to these concerts with the great arias. But maybe later. When things get so far that a part of my voice begins to suffer from the passage of time and I give up singing opera, maybe then. After all, the tessitura of lieder is lighter, but they make up for it with the enormous difficulty in [musical and artistic] expression, and you really have to pronounce each and every word properly. But vocally they are much less demanding. I'll probably do it some day, I just don't know when.

Domingo and His Critics

To this day the many-sidedness of Domingo's career has done nothing to destroy his sense of human and especially family ties, and despite his heavy schedule he never gets anxious in extreme situations, at least not outwardly. This has the effect of helping all around him maintain their calm as well.

Regardless of what the reviews say about Domingo the artist, in the end it is Domingo's own opinion that matters.

Much has been written about plácido domingo, most of it positive, admiring, and respectful. In saying this I am referring not only to critical reviews of premiere performances, but to what has been published about him in magazines, newspapers, journals, and books as well. Naturally there are critical remarks, too, as, for example, the one Rodolfo Celletti made in his *Voce di tenore* (1989): according to Celletti, despite Domingo's unquestionably spectacular voice, his technique and singing style leave much to be desired. Again and again, and Celletti is not alone in this, people find fault with what they consider too much versatility and a calendar that is simply too full. Such criticism has and continues to elicit frequent and annoyed reactions from Domingo, a characteristic otherwise lacking in his personality. In his book about great voices, Jens Malte Fischer writes:

The reproach of a routine interpretation hits a nerve. John Steane's book *The Grand Tradition* had already hinted at this problem twenty years ago when Domingo had reached the first peak of his career. In my discussion of *Otello* I cautiously sided with Steane. It cannot be otherwise. Whoever decides at one time or another to sing in more than two thousand performances over the course of thirty years instead of only five or six hundred, whoever has approximately eighty different parts ever at the ready instead of eight or ten (parts, by the way, which he constantly hones and perfects), such a man, if he is no *Übermensch,* simply has no choice but to arrive at a standardization. (Fischer, 528)

And Jürgen Kesting writes in his book on the great singers: "With his ascension to the dizzying heights of a tenorissimo currently disporting himself in the studios of four different recording companies, [Domingo] was obviously forced to devise something like a uniform stylistic approach" (Kesting, 902).

The problem seems to be that many feel Domingo sings too many roles too frequently, resulting in a "standardization" or a "uniform stylistic approach," and that this approach, in turn, stands in the way of the ultimate profundity and individual interpretation of any particular role. Jürgen Kesting again: "The uninspired precipitate is rendered so painful by the mere fact that he does possess such a superb instrument" (Kesting, 903).

Domingo addressed the question of his many-sidedness and the assertions that he gives too many appearances and honors too many recording engagements in his autobiography and rejected it out of hand:

My heavy schedule brings up a thorny issue. Singers today are accustomed to hearing two main criticisms with boring regularity: we allow ourselves to sing too much and we sing the wrong roles. At my home in Barcelona I have a book about the famous Spanish tenor Francisco Viñas, who was in his prime at the turn of the century, and it contains a list of his performances. In one month, for example, he sang *Parsifal* twelve times; in another he sang seventeen performances of such light-weight trifles as *Lohengrin, Tannhäuser, Le Prophète, L'Africaine,* and *Aida.* Doing three *Tannhäusers* in four days was not unusual for him.

Viñas was by no means an exception in this respect. Caruso's schedule was often equally full, and many of the best-known singers, in the days before jet planes, sang a great deal more than most of us do today. "Ah, but you travel so much farther nowadays," people say, conveniently forgetting that it is less strenuous and takes less time to go from Milan to New York in 1983 than it took to go from Milan to Rome in 1903. Perhaps we do not sing enough today! (AB, 126)

Following up on this thought, Domingo concludes that in 1983, he was already singing less than he had been ten years earlier—only every fifth day, on the average—and that if he were to accept all the offers made to him, he would have to deliver three performances a day, 365 days a year. In another part of his book he explains that a respite that lasts too long (two to three weeks, for example) actually does harm to his voice. He knows this from a personal experience in Vienna after a seventeen-day hiatus in his singing schedule. He walked onstage without any preliminary warm-up exercises because he thought his voice had recovered sufficiently, and the result was the exact opposite. He was hard pressed to sing the part of Pinkerton to the end, and this is not an especially strenuous role. Domingo likes to use an advertisement for watches made for *Time* magazine to indirectly refute the assertion that he works too much. The slogan reads: "Unlike me, my Rolex never needs a rest." This slogan and Domingo's picture grace a rather lengthy blurb on his successes and his obligations.

Confronted by both sides of the issue, I have to say that I agree with them both. When Domingo says he spent less time a year onstage in 1983 than he did ten years before, this must be viewed in the proper perspective. He also had numerous studio engagements, film contracts, and conducting obligations at that time, and they have only increased during the following decade. He therefore was and is still busy on more than just every fifth day. I have personally witnessed times when he had professional engagements not on a daily but on an hourly basis. On the other hand, I also know that he does build in rest periods and vacation days during which he engages in no professional duties whatsoever.

Domingo's rather wry observation that a journey from Milan to Rome took longer in 1903 than a flight from Milan to New York does in 1983 overlooks an important consideration: the difference in time, the altitude changes, and the unnaturally dry air in an airplane physically stress the body. "Thank God we like flying" Marta Domingo told me.

> Picture it: we get on the plane and relax immediately. We settle into our covers and our pillows, eat very little, and try to sleep for the most part. If Plácido has to study, he studies. But completely isolated from everybody and everything. I tell you, sometimes we get on a plane and don't speak a word to each other. We separate and go our own ways. We float along in the clouds. We really like it very much. . . . Sometimes he's tired. I mean, if he didn't get all the sleep he needs. But he is

blessed—he can fall asleep quickly and is just as quickly awake again. He recovers very quickly.

This ability brings us to the second frequent criticism, the one concerned with his so-called uniform stylistic approach or routinization that supposedly results from these numerous professional obligations and deadlines.

At times one certainly does get the impression that Domingo is not giving his best, his utmost, in the vocal rendition of a role and that he sometimes could give it more of an individual stamp. He also seems to sing a number of selections during mass concerts or on sound recordings either too routinely or too superficially; one wonders if he might not have taken on or refreshed a role too quickly or might not have had the time to prepare for the concert sufficiently. He has no problems as far as technique is concerned, for he masters everything very quickly.

Nevertheless, I must repeat what I said in an earlier chapter: if one listens to the same recording of a particular interpretation of one of Domingo's roles a number of times, one continuously discovers new individual touches and new depths. Initially it is his extraordinarily fascinating voice, with its uniquely burnished, richly textured fundamental timbre sometimes described as purple in its darker colorations, that detracts the listener's attention from the details. Paradoxically, were Domingo to sing with a voice that went less "to the ear" and penetrated less deeply into our musical subconscious, we would pay more attention to those details. In such a case, he would need only to shape his renditions exactly as he does now, and we would find in his singing that individualization and depth in places where we might occasionally fail to hear them today. The bewitching sound of this voice is sometimes its own worst enemy.

Despite his extremely heavy schedule, Domingo always tries to give his best. Robin Thompson, the artistic administrator of the Los Angeles Music Center Opera, who is in constant touch with the singer, has said: "I have never known [Domingo] to take [any one] performance, a matinee for example, less seriously [than others] and only give 50 percent. He always wants to give all or nothing." And Christopher Harlan added: "Lately Domingo is sometimes exhausted backstage. But onstage he still puts out 100 percent."

With the exception of the Hamburg Lohengrin and an occasional case of laryngitis or sore throat, Domingo has never had problems with his voice. The only really critical threat came after the severe earthquake in Mexico City in 1985, which killed four members of his family. Marta Domingo revealed that

the son and grandson of a dearly beloved aunt who helped raise Plácido died in the building that collapsed. So did one uncle and his wife.

Plácido was in Chicago when the earthquake hit. We tried to communicate with them [our family members], but there were no phones. So finally we rented a private plane because we sensed that something terrible had happened. When we got there, no one had heard anything about our relatives. And when he got to the building and saw the ruins, Plácido immediately took the initiative and said we had to do something right away. The first step was to find out whether anyone was still alive. Many people in solidarity came to help. Everything happened very quickly, and everyone was involved because Plácido was there reminding them they were working against time, against every minute. After he found [the bodies of] his relatives, the [other] people thought he would leave the rest and wouldn't bother about anybody else. But Plácido stayed. And he was very active. He stayed another ten days. He wore a chemically coated mask as protection against the dust, but even so, he breathed in too much of it. During the next three or four months, every time he sang his vocal chords suddenly began to rasp. The doctor said that his throat, his larynx, even his lungs were so full of dust there was nothing he could do. The body would have to gradually get rid of it itself. It took several months. It was nerve-racking. Each time Plácido started to sing, his voice sounded glorious at first but then suddenly started to scratch. That's when we learned just how self-controlled he was, for we kept asking ourselves: Okay, the body is getting rid of the dust, but will the vocal chords ever function properly again? Have they been permanently damaged by the dust and the rasping? Thank God, they weren't.

Domingo's even-temperedness surely contributed to the fact that his vocal chords suffered no additional damage. Had he given in to impatience and attempted to sing too soon, had he decided to force himself to train, he might have permanently ruined some muscles, cartilege, or nerves in his larynx. As it is, though, he continues to call upon 100 percent of his vocal strength, and the critics need not stop arguing among themselves about him and his artistry for a long time to come.

I had a chance to observe Domingo's poise and equanimity in the face of danger myself a while ago. Domingo had just flown to Mexico City to visit his mother when Los Angeles was shaken by a fairly strong earthquake on January 17, 1994. It did a great deal of damage and took the lives of more than sixty people. Even so, they continued the rehearsals for *El gato montés* on the nineteenth, just two days later, as scheduled. While Domingo was standing with the other singers onstage, a significant aftershock made the stage floor shake and the chandeliers swing on their chains. Naturally, Domingo as well as the others stopped singing, but after a few jokes, his humor and poise were conveyed to all present, and the rehearsal could be resumed where it left off a few minutes later. We were all still laboring under the psychic shock of the previous quake, a fear that lasted for months for most people and continues to haunt others even today. Add to this Domingo's fresh memory of how the Mexico City disaster had buried his family alive (a tragedy he still avoids talking about today). When I broached the subject during my visit in New York—we were driving through the city in his limousine—his voice and his manner took on a sad and depressed tone.

To this day the many-sidedness of Domingo's career has done nothing to destroy his sense of human and especially family ties, and despite his heavy schedule he never gets anxious in extreme situations, at least not outwardly. This has the effect of helping all around him maintain their calm as well.

But back to Domingo's critics. Regardless of what the reviews say about Domingo the artist, in the end it is Domingo's own opinion that matters, and he frequently emphasizes the responsibility lurking behind this fact. He is the only one inside his skin, and he is the only one who knows what he still can and cannot do. Should he take on too much, he is the one who must answer for it and bear the consequences. I am convinced that he has always known his limits in any given stage of his life and that he also knows when and where he could have done better or made a deeper impression. In the end, just about every singer knows this; not everyone, however, is willing to admit it.

The Los Angeles Music Center Opera

Although Domingo is able to shut out everything around him when concentrating on the role, the staging, and the music in front of him . . . in the intermissions he is equally able to shift back to his amiable self just as quickly and just as thoroughly. I have never known him to be preoccupied during the breaks or intermissions of a rehearsal or a performance. . . . Nor has he ever shown signs of nervousness, irritability, or arrogance.

ALTHOUGH DOMINGO STILL SINGS IN THE TEATRO ALLA Scala in Milan as well as in the Royal Opera, Covent Garden, in London on a regular basis, his actual permanent engagements are with the Metropolitan Opera in New York, the State Opera in Vienna, the Washington Opera, and the Music Center Opera in Los Angeles, whose very existence is due in great measure to Domingo's personal involvement.

Although one of the largest cities in the world, until now Los Angeles has only once had its own permanent opera company of national and even world renown. Between 1924 and 1933 such prominent artists as Elisabeth Rethberg, Claudia Muzio, Lily Pons, Benjamino Gigli, Tito Schipa, Friedrich Schorr, Lawrence Tibbett, and Ezio Pinza all sang at the Los Angeles Grand Opera. The musical scene was supplemented by such local institutions as the Civic Light Opera for musicals and the Los Angeles Opera Company, founded in 1948 by the Italian Franceso Pace. The latter was initially housed in a church, but starting in 1951 and continuing for more than a decade it played six weeks a year in the Wilshire Ebell Theatre. In 1965–66 it played its final season in the Dorothy Chandler Pavilion under the direction of Henry Lewis and Peter Ebert. The Dorothy Chandler Pavilion is part of the Los Angeles Music Center, first established in 1964. Although that 1965–66 season saw only three productions, none less than Marilyn Horn sang in one of them. A former student of the University of Southern California in Los Angeles, she ranked even then among the leading female singers on the international opera stage.

Also important were the opera performances directed since 1945 by the legendary German director Carl Ebert featuring music students from the opera department of the University of Southern California as well as guest productions of other prominent opera houses, including the San Francisco Opera, the Metropolitan Opera of New York, and the New York City Opera. Starting in 1966 the latter regularly performed three or four weeks a year in the Dorothy Chandler Pavilion. Plácido Domingo participated in several of these early guest performances. Part of the Olympic Arts Festival that took place during the 1984 Olympic Games were guest productions by the Royal Opera Covent Garden as well as the 1985 productions of the Deutsche Oper Berlin; Plácido Domingo was among the featured soloists at both performances.

Nevertheless, the fact remains that, since 1933, there had not been a resident opera company of world renown in Los Angeles that performed the whole year through—and this in a city where Otto Klemperer directed the Los Angeles Philharmonic for many years, Bruno Walter conducted the Columbia Symphony Orchestra, and such famous composers or soloists as Igor Stravinsky, Arnold Schoenberg, Erich Wolfgang Korngold, Sergei Rachmaninoff, Ernst Toch, Hanns Eisler, Mario Castelnuovo-Tedesco, Jascha Heifetz, Vladimir Horowitz, Gregor Piatigorsky, Artur Rubinstein, and Jacob Gimpel spent many years of their lives.

There was, as well, the Los Angeles Civic Grand Opera Association, also founded by Pace, which was renamed the Los Angeles Music Center Opera Association and given its own board of directors after the Los Angeles Opera Company moved into the Music Center; but from 1966 on its main contribution was to organize guest performances like those offered by the New York City Opera. The daily administrative duties were handled by one secretary equipped with a desk and a telephone. All major financial decisions as well as income passed through the Music Center of Los Angeles County Board of Governors, associated with which were also (and still are) the other institutions of the Los Angeles Music Center: the Philharmonic, the ballet, the theater, and the Master Chorale. Except for maintaining the buildings, which are owned by Los Angeles County, by far the greatest bulk of expenses must be covered by private donations and ticket sales. In the early years, almost all donations were funneled directly into the Music Center Unified Fund and were distributed from there to the individual units. The opera, for example, received between $750,000 and $800,000 annually in the early 1980s. Today these individual units have to raise additional funds for themselves, and for the opera this responsibility devolves not lastly upon the board of directors.

Toward the end of the 1970s attendance at the guest performances of the New York City Opera fell further and further behind because the quality of the New York productions no longer corresponded to the expectations of the Los

Angeles audience. In 1983 the guest performance program was eliminated altogether.

It was during this period that the attorney Don Erik Franzen, who had gotten to know Plácido Domingo through his law partner, Peter Funsten, aroused the singer's enthusiasm to help establish a resident Los Angeles opera company. In 1984, together with Peter Funsten and Carl Princi, a well-known radio announcer for opera productions, Franzen advanced the project of an independently producing Los Angeles Music Center Opera. Another pivotal moment in all of this was the collaboration of Bernard A. Greenberg, now president of the board of directors of the Los Angeles Music Center Opera. He soon began to bring the members of the rather skeptical Music Center board around to the idea of an independent operation. With the help of Michael Newton, who was then the new president of the board, as well as that of the oil magnate Tom Wachtell, they finally succeeded in establishing an independent opera.

Domingo, who actively supported the project, dedicated his 1984 guest performances with the Royal Opera, Covent Garden, as well as those with the Deutsche Opera Berlin in Los Angeles to the cause. The success convinced even the skeptics on the Music Center board, and additional benefactors were soon won over. As it happened, since the New York City Opera performances were no longer being offered, the significant savings from the year 1983 realized by this turn of events became the basis of the initial financial backing. In 1984 Peter Hemmings, former director of the Scottish Opera as well as of the Australian Opera and the London Symphony Orchestra, was named general director. Assisting him right from the beginning was Plácido Domingo as artistic consultant—a function he still performs today. In 1986 the Los

Angeles Music Center Opera opened with its premiere production of *Otello*: the featured singer was Plácido Domingo, and the director was Götz Friedrich. Since then there have been six to eight annual productions, each with six to eight performances. A significant number of local singers fills out the international team that is put together for each production.

Despite occasionally arbitrary decisions, Peter Hemmings has proven to be a successful manager thus far. The opera has no financial difficulties to speak of, and the Dorothy Chandler Pavilion, with its thirty-two hundred seats, is just about sold out even for such operas as Alban Berg's *Wozzeck* or John Adams's *Nixon in China,* works that do not rank among the traditional auditory feasts. Under the management of Hemmings and Domingo, the Los Angeles Music Center Opera continues to prove that opera is anything but dead: in fact, just the opposite is true. Greater Los Angeles, with its multi-ethnic population, also includes since 1979 the Long Beach Opera and its many avant-garde productions, as well as the Opera Pacific, offering a markedly traditional repertoire. Neither of these institutions is currently under life-threatening financial constraints.

As far as the programming and the goals of the Los Angeles Music Center Opera are concerned, Peter Hemmings recently told me: "Plácido Domingo shares my conviction that we ought to offer a mixed repertoire: operas of all descriptions and periods, and that we should maintain this policy even in difficult times. We should not concentrate solely on the sure thing." In addition, both men reject the idea of a repertoire theater in which one or two dozen operas are performed alternately during the course of a single season. This policy will continue even after 2001, when the Music Center

Opera will no longer have to share the Dorothy Chandler
Pavilion with the Philharmonic Orchestra, since the latter
will acquire its own concert hall across the street. Hemmings
continued: "Even then we won't introduce a repertoire theater. The concept of a repertoire theater is dead. Even in
Germany. The system was good when each opera had its own
permanent ensemble. Today all the big names sing in many
different opera houses."

Up to now, Hemmings and Domingo have held to this
policy consistently, and it has proven to be the right one.
Even such a difficult opera as Strauss's *Frau ohne Schatten* has
increased its audience share, from an 80 percent ticket sale in
the beginning to the last performance, which was sold out.

Since I was in the position to observe Domingo's work in
Los Angeles for a number of years, I speak from experience
when I say that Domingo the man and Domingo the artist
are one and the same person.

He has an intuitive grasp of the musical as well as the theatrical intentions of a particular production, a talent that never
ceases to amaze many renowned and experienced conductors
and directors. When learning a new role, Domingo feels, a
singer should rehearse as much as possible and preferably with
the orchestra, in order to match the color of his voice with
the sound of the orchestra. This is essential, since the composer makes his own statement concerning the ambiance of
a scene, the emotions of a situation, and so on, by means
of specific instrumentation, and the singers "have only to
condense" this mood with their voices.

On the other hand, Domingo considers it a waste of time
when directors spend hours rehearsing the staging of a scene
with extras or members of the chorus while the principal
singers sit around doing nothing. He knows such rehearsals

are necessary, simply because everyone has to be thoroughly prepared, "but not at the expense of the music, which is often neglected" (AB, 211). Rehearsal time for the singers, then, ought to be better distributed. After all, to Domingo, rehearsals are not meant to be a time to relax and sit around. He enjoys it most when he is learning a new part; then he is ready to take the time to rehearse (there were 150 hours of rehearsal time for his first *Otello*) and is forced to concentrate all his attention on the score: "Because to *really* sing, you have to delve into a score deeply and meticulously and seek to unravel all the secrets it contains, all the little things behind the notes and between the lines. For example, whenever there is a change of key, usually there is also a change of mood—from bliss to wistfulness or whatever—and you should modulate your voice accordingly," he once told Helena Matheopoulos. He went on to give an example of how the voice has to adjust to orchestral colors: "For instance, after the celli solo before the love duet at the end of Act I of *Otello* the atmosphere is set for us so perfectly that we *have* to colour our voices like a cello" (*Divo*, 59, 60).

In my experience, as I have said before, Domingo usually attends only the last rehearsals; but this was when he was performing roles he had often sung before or whose staging he was familiar with or when he knew that he could very quickly adjust.

I have always been struck by his total concentration on the role, even during the rehearsals, by the way he rarely marks, and by how little time he needs to apprehend the theatrical elements. As far as staging is concerned, he only needs to be told something once to be able to explain it to others who have rehearsed much longer but who had perhaps forgotten one instruction or another. He has been known to correct his fellow singers in this way long before the director or the director's assistant has a chance to interfere. And he always does it in a well-meaning and amiable way. Domingo's musical as well as visual memory is phenomenal, and should anything go seriously awry during a rehearsal or lead to confusion, people count on him and his humor to calm the waters, even when the singers and the orchestra fall out of synch. Before stepping in, however, he always makes sure the director or the conductor has nothing against his suggestions or that all he has to do is reinforce their instructions. He never argues with the director or the conductor, nor does he ever play the role of star. On the contrary, he is always unpretentious and friendly. He often expresses his respect for the conductor and the director of a particular production, which is not to say, as we shall see, that he agrees with every arrangement or sees in every conductor the genius of a Carlos Kleiber, whom he admires so greatly in his autobiography.

To his mind, there is only one authority, one chain of command during a production. I once overheard Domingo, after a rehearsal in which he was conductor, say to the stage director: "I tried to conduct so that everything would correspond to your intentions onstage. I tried to accommodate you as far as I could. I hope you're satisfied." A strong sense of self-discipline vis-à-vis the director is very important to Domingo. When the students in his UCLA seminar asked what a singer should do if a director demands the impossible, he replied: "It sometimes happens that some roles are assigned to the wrong singer or that a director doesn't know what he can demand of the singers, because so many directors come from the theater or from film and don't understand very much about singing. But here too one should be disciplined and should try to discuss the problems calmly. Communication is important, because it reduces tension."

Although Domingo is able to shut out everything around him when concentrating on the role, the staging, and the music in front of him (how else could he have mastered so many roles in a short period of time with often only a few rehearsals?), in the intermissions he is equally able to shift back to his amiable self just as quickly and just as thoroughly. I have never known him to be preoccupied during the breaks or intermissions of a rehearsal or a performance; he was always able to focus completely on the people around him and joke with them, whether in Spanish with members of his family or in English with colleagues and whoever else might be there. Nor has he ever shown signs of nervousness, irritability, or arrogance, and whenever there was a buffet for the performers and stage hands during a pause in rehearsal (which was usually the case since it is so awkward to go out to eat in costume), he usually brought up the rear. Too many people along the way had held him up, but he usually stayed at the end of the line even when others encouraged him to go to the front and even if those people ahead of him were extras whose obligations during the rehearsal were less taxing than his own.

But to return to Domingo's ability to grasp things quickly—General Director Peter Hemmings once told me: "When Domingo arrives, he immediately adjusts to the staging as well as to his respective partners. He's very bright. I've never seen him give a purely routine performance." And director Christopher Harlan added: "[Domingo] has such an extraordinary memory that you only have to go over something with him once for him to know it. Say a production is revived after a number of years and you make several changes in the staging—he recognizes them immediately. And then he even corrects the other performers. If his memory should fail, which is rarely the case, he immediately knows how to compensate for it."

Just how important rehearsals have always been for Domingo despite his heavy schedule can be seen in the remarks he made in his autobiography concerning the short preparation period prior to a recording:

> In recent decades, a high percentage of operatic recordings has been made in London, not only for economic and contractual reasons but also because British orchestra musicians are outstanding sight-readers. In a work that is not part of the standard repertoire . . . a typical three-hour session will begin with an orchestral reading of a segment of the opera. They will rehearse alone for a while and then with the singers. An hour after that bit of music has been played by the orchestra for the first time in the musicians' lives, it is recorded for posterity. This is a frightening way of working because of the pressure, and a frustrating one because it does not allow the work to ripen naturally. (AB, 182)

Under conditions like these it may be possible to produce an outstanding recording of works familiar to the musicians. But these undesirable conditions deprive Domingo of his interpretorial depth, no matter how highly he admires the musicians—particularly the British—who can so rapidly learn a piece, just as Hollywood studio orchestras have also developed the ability to learn a score in record time.

Domingo would certainly prefer to have two or three selections taped in succession over two or three days after appropriate rehearsals, so that the tension of a "live" performance could be maintained in each instance. This

would have the additional benefit of allowing the best renditions or the best segments to be spliced together instead of,
as so often happens, recording them piecemeal over a period
of months.

When you talk to people who know Domingo, the general and genuine consensus of opinion is that he is the friendliest and most even-tempered man imaginable. He makes the
same impression on me. Even on a very hectic day—with
vocal rehearsals in the morning, administrative business during lunch, conducting rehearsals in the afternoon, and production consultations in the evening—he never loses his
equanimity. The challenge is to catch him with only one
foot out the door. The name Plácido ("tranquillity") fits his
personality very well. When in his company, one never has
the sense of bottled-up anger and frustration just waiting to
explode. At worst he avoids those people who tend to put
too much pressure on him; if that proves impossible, he
makes sure the conversation is brief.

"He's very even tempered and generous," says Marta Domingo, "and blessed with incredible perseverance, patience,
and understanding. Of course, sometimes there is too much
impertinence and people think they have the right to abuse
or demand too much of him, those are the only moments
when he says: 'Stay back. Don't push.' But he is usually generous and says: 'Okay, one more minute.' "

Many interviews dwell on Domingo's warm and caring
nature, and I could add a number of personal observations as
well, but I would rather turn to Robin Thompson, the artistic administrator of the Los Angeles Music Center Opera,
who frequently has to deal with Domingo continents away:

> Domingo is polite, friendly, relaxed, open, kind, atten-
> tive, considerate, caring, warmhearted. Only twice have

I seen him even slightly angry, and that was not because of the people involved but because of the situation. He's never unpleasant or hateful toward others, as the stereotypical image of the opera singer frequently assumes. He actually takes great care to learn and then remember the name of every person with whom he comes in contact and he can still remember them later on.

This last attribute is particularly appreciated. Years later, Domingo can still recall the names of stage hands he has worked with in various theaters and productions.

Topper Smith, the music administrator of the Los Angeles Music Center Opera, adds:

I've been waiting nine years for [Domingo] to show his other, his true face, but his true face is the one he always shows: he doesn't know anger and that's why he doesn't repress any that might explode at some later time. And he never says, "Don't do that" or "I won't do that." If he doesn't agree with something, all he says instead is: "I'd like to try it this way sometime." . . . Naturally he knows he's talented and wields great power in the music world, but he doesn't abuse his authority. He doesn't use his influence as a power play. He lives for music and treats everything and everybody with respect. He's a real mensch.

Without Domingo the Los Angeles Music Center Opera would never have come into being as an independent, resident institution, and without his presence it would have a difficult time maintaining the worldwide reputation it currently enjoys.

Peter Hemmings once mentioned something along these same lines: "Domingo knows how opera companies work in this country and how they're kept alive. That's why he helps us with fund-raising. He attends the necessary receptions, conferences, parties, or gala events following premiere performances just to encourage private benefactors, corporations, and foundations to make a contribution. His personality and presence alone bring in at least 25 percent of the needed capital."

Plácido Domingo's first German benefit performance, on Easter
Sunday 1986, in the concert hall of the Munich Philharmonic, to
help victims of the earthquake in Mexico City. Domingo and
the soprano Teresa Berganza were celebrated enthusiastically.
(dpa/Düren)

Plácido and Marta Domingo on April 27, 1986, in Munich.
(dpa/Bajzat)

Plácido Domingo as Otello, one of his greatest roles, at the Los Angeles Music Center Opera in 1986. (Frederic Ohringer)

Plácido Domingo and Julia Migenes in Jacques Offenbach's *Tales of Hoffmann,* in a performance of the Los Angeles Music Center Opera in October 1988. (Frederic Ohringer)

Plácido Domingo with Maria Ewing in a scene from Puccini's
Tosca, in a performance of the Los Angeles Music Center Opera in
November 1992. (Ken Howard)

Plácido Domingo as Otello at the Los Angeles Music Center Opera
in March 1989. (Frederic Ohringer)

Plácido Domingo in Puccini's opera *La fanciulla del West (The Girl
of the Golden West)*, in a performance of the Los Angeles Music
Center Opera in June 1991. (Frederic Ohringer)

Plácido Domingo kicking the ball. The profits of the celebrity game went to the "Plácido Domingo SOS Children's Village" in Mexico. (dpa/Bajzat)

Plácido Domingo during a rehearsal session for a benefit performance at the State Opera in Berlin in August 1993. (Ullstein/Olaf Müller)

Plácido Domingo as conductor with the Hessian Radio Orchestra
in Frankfurt's "Old Opera House" in January 1989.
(dpa/Brakemeier)

Domingo as Rafael Ruiz in Penella's *El gato montés (The Wildcat)*,
in a performance of the Los Angeles Music Center Opera in January
1994. (Ken Howard)

Plácido Domingo as Gustavus III with soprana Leona Mitchell as Amelia in Verdi's *Un ballo in maschera (A Masked Ball)*, at the Los Angeles Music Center Opera in September 1993. (Ken Howard)

A scene from Verdi's *Otello*, in a Götz Friedrich production of the
Los Angeles Music Center Opera in April 1989.
(Frederic Ohringer)

THE
ACTOR

The Stanislavsky Method

Domingo's acting bears the strong stamp of the Stani-
slavsky method. . . . In the world of opera, which just
about owes its existence to the idea of alienation, the
Stanislavsky method is an advantage, at least the way
Domingo interprets and applies it. He is convinced
that the naturalistic or realistic representation of a role
is what attracts audience interest today, especially since
the libretti are often "a little primitive." Moreover,
this approach lends a vitality and credence to the story
line, and this in turn helps attract the younger genera-
tion who are yet to be won over to the world of opera.

ONE OF DOMINGO'S GREAT ADVANTAGES AS AN OPERA
singer is his acting ability. In fact, he could base a successful
stage career on it alone, without having to sing a single note.
A few examples of his talent in this field include the roles of
Canio (*I pagliacci*), Turriddu (*Cavalleria rusticana*), Dick Johnson (*La fanciulla del West*), and Des Grieux (*Manon Lescaut*):
he could portray these characters as convincingly on the traditional theater stage as on the operatic one. This assertion is
prompted for the most part by his portrayal of veristic roles,
but I can also see him in the dramatic role of Shakespeare's
original Othello. It goes without saying, of course, that it
would have to be a Spanish-language production.

Just how great an actor Domingo really is can be demonstrated by comparing him with Benjamino Gigli. A Holly-

wood film that dates back to the early years of the "talkies," 1927 to be exact, features Gigli in the role of Turiddu in the final scene of *Cavalleria rusticana*. If we compare this effort with Domingo's performance in Zeffirelli's 1982 filmed version of the same opera, we are immediately struck by how realistically and convincingly Domingo portrays the innkeeper's son. Every movement, every expression, every passion is genuine and credible even without benefit of the music. Gigli, on the other hand, plays his part almost like an amateur; he is stiffer in every respect and has an overwhelming tendency to strike attitudes. He uses certain clichéd head movements and much too many dramatic hand movements, all of which Domingo rejects for today's operatic actor, for these stock expressions render the person onstage more a marionette than a living and breathing individual. If one turns off the sound in Gigli's performance, his acting comes across as extremely unnatural. His vocal expression, especially his *mezza voce,* however, still retain their unique power of fascination.

Domingo is not the only singing actor, even if he is without doubt one of the best; the list also includes Teresa Stratas, Renata Scotto, Justino Diaz, Frederica von Stade, and many others. It is becoming increasingly important today for singers to perfect their acting skills as well as their vocal talents, simply to introduce and win over the younger audience to the joys of opera. Just listening to a beautiful voice onstage is no longer sufficient.

To Helena Matheopoulos Domingo said: "Opera, when done in the right way—a great production with great singing actors and a great conductor—is the most exciting artistic experience imaginable. But when badly conducted, or acted in an old-fashioned way, nothing could be worse! I mean, one would walk out after five minutes!" (*Divo,* 58).

Domingo's acting bears the strong stamp of the Stanislavsky method, as is evident in his portrayal of veristic roles. Stanislavsky's "naturalism" (Stanislavsky himself preferred to call it "realism") is a perfect match for the verismo works in the operatic repertoire. Domingo's craft also employs other Stanislavskian precepts, such as (1) the actor should be thoroughly familiar with the external circumstances impinging upon and determining to a certain extent the psychic makeup of the stage character; (2) all external physical movements have to correspond organically to the intrinsic character of the person being portrayed; and (3) the stage character must be portrayed with total naturalness and psychological credibility.

Lee Strasberg added to and modified Stanislavsky's original precepts, and it is his version of the method that continues to dominate the American stage today. This dominance is also due in great part to the significance and influence of the film industry in the United States. Hollywood actors tend to portray their characters in a psychologically naturalistic way rather than in a style reminiscent of Piscator or in line with Brecht's ideas of alienation, even though several of the great American film stars did indeed emerge from the Erwin Piscator school in New York. The Stanislavsky approach goes a long way in explaining the popularity of works by Anton Chekhov and Henrik Ibsen in America, for both of them wrote plays that cry out for the Stanislavsky approach to dramatic realization.

Domingo learned the Stanislavsky method early in his career and has remained true to it ever since. He writes in his autobiography: "Constantin [a person involved with the theater in Mexico City] taught me to study the background of whatever part I was doing in accordance with the Stanislavsky method. One must think about the psychological make-up of every character one interprets, not just through his words but also by considering what his family background would have been, his manner, his bearing, and so on" (AB, 26).

I recently realized just how significant these Stanislavsky studies continue to be for American actors. A short while ago I met the man who was to play the role of Ill in a stage production of Friedrich Dürrenmatt's *The Visit*. He virtually pumped me for information: how did I picture Ill's parents and grandparents; could I describe for him the precise physical movements and psychological attitudes of a Swiss shopkeeper in a small Swiss town during the 1950s; did I know of any documentary films on the topic—as if Dürrenmatt would have deemed any of these details essential to the message of his parable.

Yet in the world of opera, which just about owes its existence to the idea of alienation, the Stanislavsky method is an advantage, at least the way Domingo interprets and applies it. He is convinced that the naturalistic or realistic representation of a role is what attracts audience interest today, especially since the libretti are often "a little primitive." Moreover, this approach lends a vitality and credence to the story line, and this in turn helps attract the younger generation who are yet to be won over to the world of opera. Helena Matheopoulos quotes Domingo as saying:

> We have to make all those characters inhabiting different centuries and civilizations relevant to *today*; we have to find a way of conveying the *feeling* of their period,

while interpreting them with the insights of the [present time]. . . . For when singing Cavaradossi, for instance, you shouldn't walk as we do today because everything about him—the costume, the boots, the posture—is different and instantly conveys a different "feel." Similarly, when singing Roméo you have to walk the way they did in the Renaissance: on your toes and sort of floating. And in *Otello* you have to move like a panther, with strong yet gliding steps. (*Divo*, 58)

Marta Domingo shares these Stanislavskian tendencies in her role as director and as Domingo's advisor. While we were talking about the way Domingo researches his operatic characters and their background, she said: "It's a lot of education. Nothing is casual, nothing is coincidence. By no means. He really studies, and I do a lot of research to make things easier for him and to save him some time. But he does all the work. Moreover, and I have to tell you this again, he has this extraordinary intuition."

Role-Interpretation and Vocal Phrasing

Domingo explained how his theatrical characteriza-
tion of a role affects his vocal expression: "I just can't
produce a sound without thinking about the character's
real background and then of the style, first of all of the
composer, and then of the character. The age as well
as the characteristics of the character are important. . . .
I really need a palette that contains all these
different colors."

A COMPARISON BETWEEN HIS INTERPRETATIONS OF Turiddu and Canio will demonstrate how Domingo gives a different shape to each of his roles. Much of this casting, because it involves adjusting the coloration and phrasing of his vocal expression along Stanislavskian lines, is reminiscent of Chaliapin. Domingo ranks among the few singers who have portrayed both roles onstage on the same evening. If these roles are to be sung properly and acted convincingly, to perform both on the same evening severely strains a singer's concentration and energy, especially since they are both intense roles possessing a tragedy all their own. Some might point out that the role of Tristan, which will soon be on Domingo's schedule, is longer than that of Turiddu and Canio put together. True, but Tristan is *one* character involved in *one* tragedy, regardless of how many different acoustical colors Domingo has to employ in the various situations. Turiddu and Canio, on the other hand, are two different characters with two different tragic fates.

Zeffirelli's 1982 film versions of *Pagliacci* and *Cavalleria rus-*
ticana inform the following discussion, even though *Cavalleria*
rusticana wasn't released until later. When Domingo climbs
out of his circus cart at the beginning of *Pagliacci,* he looks
like he is stepping out of a Fellini film: realistic, comedic,
someone who knows how to change his expression from
anger and threat to laughter and playfulness at a moment's
notice. And he succeeds in making these changes between
threats and seriousness, laughter and play, right up to the end,
when tragic sobriety finally dominates all of Canio's behavior. The audience perceives this double-sidedness of the comedian in Domingo's vocal presentation as well. Domingo
threw himself so completely into the role of Canio during
the sound recording that his musical phrases have a corresponding effect. The vocal coloration alternating between
humor and challenging invitation in his opening song betrays
a slightly "aged" radiance (in other words, they are not nearly
as open as in the Mexican folk songs or in the zarzuelas)
and are well balanced and centered in their crescendos and
occasional decrescendos, all of which underscores the comedic side of Canio's personality. These colors abruptly change
to anger when the conversation turns to Nedda, only to return immediately to the radiant tone of superiority.

The crescendo and decrescendo phrases in the great aria
he sings after he has learned of Nedda's unfaithfulness, as well
as many of his vibrato-enhanced swell tones, convey a pained
and grieving mood; the vibratos become more and more ir-
regular and finally end in a sob. This musical rendition is
supported by his facial expressions as well as the whole dramatic context. If we compare this rendition of the aria with
an isolated one made for a CD recording, we find that Domingo sings the aria on disc considerably more lyrically,

where all the phrasings are concentrated on the aria itself and less on the overall dramatic context. The aria turns into an opera in itself. In the film, on the other hand, all his phrasings grow out of the dramatic background, and this in turn leads, particularly in the tragic conclusion, to a masterful alternation of vocal colors and phrasings ranging from a tortured game (where the tones sound piercing) to desperate gravity. On the whole, extended phrases and swell tones predominate in *Pagliacci* as expressions of the clown's character: he must appear to his audience as the superior actor, even though he is ultimately shattered by his fate.

In contrast, Domingo's Turiddu seems to be more of a peasant's son right from the start: he is more direct, perhaps also a bit coarser, and unlike Canio, does not need to ingratiate himself with anybody through long extended, radiant, and bright tonal phrases. His entrance song is thus more lyrical in its phrases, the transitions from one melodic phrase to another are more passionate, and the alternation between *forte, mezzo forte,* and *piano* comes across as the genuine expression of his emotions. There is no need for pretense here. In the duet with Santuzza his tonal phrases and swell tones seem a bit shorter because he is singing with more intensity and greater emotion, with greater variation in color and dynamics. The vibrato sounds more passionate right from the start. This Turiddu is intent upon defending his guilt over against Santuzza, and he does so by assuming an air of self-protective aggression that is also a part of his character. Once Lola enters the scene, Domingo's swell tones become even more passionate, and his phrases are fraught with inner tension: the high notes are sung intensely and directly (although in terms of technique, sometimes more hinted at than actually sung out) and the portamento expresses strong emotion.

Later, in the famous final aria "Quel vino è generoso," Domingo's vocal colors and phrasing choices are marked by fear, self-incrimination, bad conscience, and fatalism. He alternates between crescendo and decrescendo and moves from a *piano* into a desperate *forte* as he recounts the laments of a guilty man and a loser. After all, Turiddu, in spite of all his aggression and inconsideration toward Santuzza, is in the end a loser, someone whom fate has defeated and whose behavior borders on the self-destructive. Domingo conveys all of this very genuinely and convincingly through his music and his acting. Zeffirelli, on the other hand, as Domingo tells us in his autobiography, had a totally different vision of this character in mind.

Domingo explained how his theatrical characterization of a role affects his vocal expression:

> I just can't produce a sound without thinking about the character's real background and then of the style, first of all of the composer, and then of the character. The age as well as the characteristics of the character are important. I don't say that that should apply as a general rule. There are singers who have such a God-given, glorious sound to their voices that they don't need anything else to play a role. I don't want to judge my own voice, how good it is or isn't, but I do know that as an artist, I need to feel like a painter with my voice. I really need a palette that contains all these different colors. . . . And the same holds true for the concerts I give. I sing Nemorino, Otello, Vasco da Gama, Cavaradossi, Edgardo, Alvaro, or zarzuelas, and every piece is more than just a vocal aria. I believe I really can interpret [the selection] in keeping with what it really means, and that the listener can distinguish the difference between the characters [behind them].

It might be instructive here to compare the initial scene of Radames (*Aïda*) with that of Vasco da Gama (*L'africaine*), as well as Lohengrin's with that of Calaf (*Turandot*), in terms of Domingo's theatrical and musical interpretation. The first comparison deals with heroic characters in two operas not entirely unrelated as far as the music is concerned, and the second deals with two legendary figures in musically very different works, even if Puccini's *Turandot* is closer to Wagner's music drama than *La bohème,* for example.

Domingo portrays Radames (in the premiere performance at the Houston Grand Opera in 1987), although a bit corpulent, as rather more like a big child or an adolescent: in his very first appearance, eager to fight and actually joyful at the very mention of battle. And yet, he moves about the way the figures on ancient Egyptian frescoes appear: occasionally heroically abrupt, as one would expect from a mere youth, but stylized, and thus frescolike, at the same time. In the famous aria "Celeste Aïda" Domingo's more heroically than lyrically sung phrases are completely in keeping with the dramatic portrayal of the character, even if the lyrical passages, at least as far as they refer to Aïda, come across as quite evocative. In all other respects this aria has an overall dramatic effect with a pronounced variation in timbre. There are some extended phrases and swell tones (which is also true for the dialogue between Ramfis and Amneris) as well as shorter, intense portamento phrasings. On the whole, the coloration of the voice is bright: belligerently challenging, youthfully excessive, and dreamy, all at the same time.

In contrast, Domingo portrays Vasco da Gama in Giacomo Meyerbeer's *L'africaine* (San Francisco Opera, 1989) as an impatient but more mature man in the early years of middle age marked by adventure, conquest, and exploration. Despite his excitability, he uses many expansive and rather slow arm movements to convey the sense of the Renaissance poses we all know from pictures and portraits of the period. When he bows before the members of the royal council, he does so nobly, slowly, and briefly. On the other hand, his vocal coloration and phrasings betray more of an agitated, aggressive, and challenging attitude. His tonal phrases and swell tones underscore the power of eagerness, self-consciousness, and conviction; there is nothing of the dreamy quality here. This is why the timbre is also a bit darker and sharper here than in the portrayal of Radames. The dynamic phrases as well as the vocal colors change much more rapidly, thus expressing the impatience and conviction of a man fully conscious of his historic mission and absolutely ready to rebel against the Portuguese authority. Radames, in contrast, is no rebel; he "betrays" Egypt because he is in love.

In Domingo's portrayal of Lohengrin (Vienna State Opera, 1990), his scenes with the Brabants have a transcendent quality, and only in the bedroom scene with Elsa do his movements become more direct and take on a more humanly vulnerable appearance. The overall impresson is that of a hero plucked from another world, which is, in fact, what he is. He almost seems to be the son of a divine father, and Domingo uses body language to convey this idea—he usually holds his sword in the same rigid arm position, close to his body, and his arms and head move only in conjunction with his whole body. Not only are his movements kept in check, but his vocal phrasings are also restrained and somewhat detached, with much legato, portamento, and portato. The sound of his voice is bright and lyric. Only in the bedroom scene do the phrasings become more passionate and more direct. This mortal also reemerges in the story of the Grail, for now the divine son can expose himself as human to the Brabants as well and can deliver his reproaches against Telramund und Elsa directly throughout the final scene. He no longer has to veil his statements, although he does reassume the frozen and statuesque quality of a distant messenger of the Grail by echoing his body language of the first scene.

Calaf is a Persian rather than a Germanic fairy-tale figure. Despite his noble character, Domingo portrays him (Metropolitan Opera, 1988) as more barbaric in his movements, grimmer in expression, and essentially more uninhibited in his passions. Moving about much more freely and naturally here than in *Lohengrin,* he even clenches his fists and in general behaves as we might imagine a noble prince from the time of Ghengis Khan. As one would expect from such a character, Domingo's vocal colors are sharp and pointed, and they convey a rather exotic sound by means of their strong, bright, open arcs and pitches. Into these colors, reminiscent of Spanish or Mexican folklore, Domingo mixes darker colorations. Unlike his Lohengrin, Domingo sings several high notes in a very direct way, as befits Calaf's character; thus he omits any climbing arcs or portamenti. Dynamic adjustments result in briefer and more pointed phrasings than the ones that characterize *Lohengrin,* even though Puccini's phrases (especially in his other operas) are usually rather shorter anyway (or at least more peaked or pointed) than many of the rather linear phrases in Wagner. Domingo emphasizes this difference, for regardless of the music, he could have sung Wagner's longer phrases in a way that made them seem shorter and more pointed and Puccini's shorter phrases in a way that made them sound extended and more epic. But to do so would contradict his theatrical interpretation of the respective roles. In any case, Domingo's voice seems more piquant in tone and phrasing in *Turandot* than it does in *Lo-hengrin,* even in places where he employs a distinct porta-mento and, as he did in *Lohengrin,* lets the high notes swell their way up to the heights.

Text and Music

*No matter how much time his daily professional obli-
gations claim, and this includes the memorization of
new parts as well, Domingo never neglects or ignores
his interpersonal relations and concerns.
On the contrary.*

*Plácido Domingo is one of those singers who place
enormous value on the text of an opera or a song. He
. . . is very aware that opera and lieder composers did
not simply write musical poems for the voice, but
rather set texts to music.*

ONE OF THE GREATEST PROBLEMS FOR OPERA AND LIEDER
singers is finding the proper relation between the text and
the music. This task encompasses much more than the clear
and distinct articulation of the vocalized text, for it also involves learning and understanding the inflections characteristic of each language, which are essential not only to musical
phrasing but also to communicating the text's meaning to the
audience. Perhaps the best way to approach this topic is to
progress from general to more specific observations. Before I
begin, however, I should like to add to what has already been
said about Domingo's characteristic warmth and concern for
others. No matter how much time his daily professional obligations claim, and this includes the memorization of new
parts as well, Domingo never neglects or ignores his interper-

sonal relations and concerns. On the contrary. The following episode will more than illustrate my point.

I had an appointment with Domingo in New York toward the end of March. Our meeting was scheduled for a Sunday, Palm Sunday, as it happened. That meant I had to leave California the day before. But that Saturday was burdened for us because our son, who was living in Berlin at the time, had set out on a journey and was supposed to get in touch underway. We were still waiting to hear from him. Moreover, he had an appointment in Berlin on the very same Saturday that I had wanted to fly to New York; the person in question had gone to Berlin especially to meet him. But my son did not show up. I was concerned and called Domingo's secretary, Nicholas Marko, to tell him I might not be able to come as scheduled and would he please pass the reasons on to Domingo. In the end I did make the trip upon Mr. Marko's suggestion that, should there be an emergency, I could fly to Berlin from New York much more easily than I could from Los Angeles.

When I met Plácido Domingo the next day at the Met, surrounded as he was by a throng of other artists, his first question was whether I had heard anything from my son. Marta Domingo asked me the same question a short time later when I met with her as well. Fortunately, the whole affair ended well: my son did arrive in Berlin that very Sunday, but there was no way for him to get in touch with me or with Berlin from where he had been in Poland at the time. The Domingos had been genuinely concerned even though they did not know my son at all and I did not belong to their close circle of friends or acquaintances. When it comes to family or friends, all such situations assume top priority in

Domingo's thoughts. Examples and stories from others have confirmed this for me time and time again.

Plácido Domingo is one of those singers who place enormous value on the text of an opera or a song. He has frequently bemoaned the fact (as in connection with the *Meistersinger* recording where he sang the role of Walter von Stolzing) that his German pronunciation is still not adequate. He also stresses how important it was, when preparing his Otello, to study both the Shakespearean as well as the Boito text so as to integrate it all properly into Verdi's music. As he explained this habit to Helena Matheopoulos in 1986: "A great proportion of my singing is based on the interpretation of what I'm saying. As Verdi never tired of saying, 'la parola regna suprema' [the words reign supreme], because the composers wrote their music to the text. Therefore *what* we are singing should determine *how* we sing it" (*Divo*, 66). His autobiography is also full of admiration for those who pay attention to linguistic details: he relates, for instance, how the conductor Nello Santi insisted on the proper pronunciation of vowels and how Toscanini used to practice one or two words with his singers, sometimes for hours on end.

All of this goes to show that Domingo is very aware that opera and lieder composers did not simply write musical poems for the voice, but rather set texts to music. Especially in the late romantic music dramas of Richard Wagner and Richard Strauss, the text is theoretically on equal footing with the music, although the text is often more difficult to understand in the works of precisely these two composers than it is, for example, in that of Mozart. This is due to their tendency to overload the orchestra harmonically and to break up traditional kinds of musical phrasing. Yet even in the case of Wagner and Strauss, the texts could come across more clearly and more understandably than they do in most opera houses today; the problem is that artists are simply paying less and less attention to their study of phonetics.

A good phonetic approach frequently requires modification both in the articulation of individual sounds as well as in the overall prosody of a performance (intonation, dynamics, emphases), and this is no longer a common practice even among most German singers. The voice teachers, directors, and conductors are in large part responsible for this development. Voice teachers concentrate almost exclusively on the vocal technique they consider proper, conductors are almost exclusively interested in the mere musical rendition of a score, and directors frequently do not understand a word of an opera sung in its original language. I have known British directors, for example, to rehearse German operas without any knowledge of German at all. If the singers happen to be Americans who do not know any German either, the relation between language and music suffers badly.

Moreover, the extensive traveling of international singers from continent to continent has induced many general directors to completely ignore their singers' linguistic qualifications. A great voice from overseas will be engaged for Wagner or Strauss even if that singer's German leaves much to be desired. Even worse, when it comes to a singer of great renown and popularity, he or she is frequently excused from those rehearsals concentrating on the articulation of the text; in fact, they may be excused from just about every rehearsal.

We must also keep in mind what Domingo said to Helena Matheopoulos, "*what* we sing should also determine *how* we sing it." This "*what* we sing" refers not only to the text of an opera but to the respective scenic and textual representation of an aria or a duet as well, regardless of how "primitive" or incredible it might be. A clearly articulated pronunciation of the sung text not only serves a better understanding of that text but serves the subtlety of the musical score as well. When Richard Strauss, for example, in the prologue to *Ariadne auf Naxos,* frequently places the musical stress of a word in direct contradiction to its normal stress in the spoken language, or when he has the musical intonation of a phrase work against the expected intonation of ordinary speech, he is employing two levels of conversational technique that have a mutually intensifying effect simply because of the tension they create. The difficulty arises for the singer who must keep the proper stress on the word and the intonation of the text as written in Hofmannsthal's libretto "in his ear" while he simultaneously sings Strauss's setting, for if he does not, he loses the tension between the two levels that Strauss intended. In contrast, in Mozart's *Zauberflöte* the stresses and intonations of the score coincide almost perfectly with the conventions of everyday spoken speech. This was deliberate on Mozart's part, for he wanted to make his vocal and orchestral music understandable to a large audience, despite the complexity of the music, which unfortunately is frequently underappreciated as a result. *Die Zauberflöte* is actually a *Singspiel,* and though its music sounds simple enough, it was conceived in the spirit of the greatest musical subtlety.

What follows are two specific examples from Strauss and Mozart. When Tamino sings his aria "Dies Bildnis ist bezaubernd schön," Mozart lets the music phrasing follow the melody of the spoken language to a great extent and thus strongly connects the musical rhythm with that of spoken language and its conventional stress structure. One only need read the text to sing it. Many such correspondences in the *Zauberflöte* determine the basic tone of the relationship of language to music in the opera. In contrast, when the prima donna in the prologue to Strauss's *Ariadne auf Naxos* sings, "Was gibt es denn da für Erscheinungen?" and pushes the final syllable "-gen" to remarkable musical heights, this certainly does not correspond to the normal stress patterns of spoken language, but it does allow Strauss to characterize the highly strung nature of the prima donna. Strauss is known for such characterizations, which rely on musical deviations from traditional diction in many other operas as well. Hence a singer must have both levels in mind (and in ear) to convey the proper psychological tension between the music and the language.

Another almost constant problem contributes to the difficulty in understanding the text of an operatic performance, and this has to do with ensemble singing or background orchestral accompaniment. There are too many overlapping overtones, including vocal formants. One way to distinguish the individual voices and render the text understandable is to have the singers alter the dynamics on otherwise unstressed end syllables or more strongly accentuate initial and end consonants. Vowels combine, whereas consonants separate and differentiate, even in the case of unstressed end syllables, so that the words are less likely to get lost in each other. Even the otherwise hardly understandable voices of the unborn children in Strauss's *Frau ohne Schatten* can be understood over the orchestra and the solo voices when they sing their "Mutter, Mutter, laß uns nach Hause" if they place greater stress on the end syllable of "Mutter" and more sharply articulate the final consonants both there as well as on the words "laß uns."

Moreover, when given a sharper accentuation, consonants can underscore the rhythm of sung texts. When the comedians in *Ariadne auf Naxos* sing, "Es gilt, ob Tanzen, ob Singen tauge, von Tränen zu trocknen ein schönes Auge," in their lighthearted way, a sharper accentuation of the consonants emphasizes the dancing quality and lets the four comedians distinguish themselves one from the other even while they overlap each other vocally. A considerably softer articulation of the consonants is appropriate when Ariadne sings her lament so as not to disrupt the legato and the proper portamento; here the consonants are more likely to appear in the portato.

These are only a few indications as to how language has to be articulated differently in keeping with the musical score. But we have not yet even mentioned the problems posed by the proper separation of syllables, the treatment of caesurae between textual and musical phrases, and the concept of softer and sharper (but never too hard) glottal stops. We must also keep in mind that different languages have different linguistic "roots" (to borrow a concept from Richard Wagner).

Domingo, who sings in many languages though his articulation and diction are not as clear as that of Nicolai Gedda, said to Helena Matheopoulos:

> In Italian singing *legato* means cutting neither the musical line nor separating the words, while French singing requires that one marginally separates the words while retaining the continuity of the musical line. If one fails to do this, one immediately sounds un-French. Yet singing French roles *too* correctly and *too* perfectly, with absolute tonal beauty and an impeccable accent, can make them lose some of their dramatic impact. So, one should compromise a little and strive to have as perfect an accent as possible while letting the voice go a bit. (*Divo*, 68)

Domingo knows that in German-language operas the consonants, the so-called glottal stops, and the separation of syllables are considerably more important than they are in Italian
operas, for instance. Moreover, he also knows that singers can
no longer feature vocal ornamentation the way Caruso did,
even if they sing in Italian. Such florid singing is simply no
longer acceptable. Nevertheless, as I have mentioned before,
he does try to insert much more legato and portamento in
Wagner and Strauss than we are used to hearing from most
of the "Nordic" singers. And although he puts in a bit too
much at times for my taste, this technique does get him closer
to Wagner than many other singers who put too much of a
one-sided stress on the consonants and glottal stops. Wagner
was in any case against a singer's employing vowels and consonants "as mere sensual material to chew in their mouths."
Besides that, he always favored the all-encompassing arc of
melody and breath. In this way he lent his consonants and
vowels equal weight while still maintaining their differentiating function. In this regard, Wagner's *Opera and Drama* is a
very important work for librettists, composers, linguists, singers, and phoneticists alike, but unfortunately it has received
too little attention (perhaps because this "essay" has the bulk
of a book and is very difficult to read). Without delving too
deeply into the details presented there, I would like to discuss
certain essential points. In doing so I will concentrate on the
use of consonants and vowels and shall omit such topics as
Wagner's ideas on end rhyme, metrics, the melody of speech,
and so on.

The bearer of the melodic arc as well as the melodic phrase
is, in every instance, the vowel. "An understanding of the
vowel, however, is not based upon its superficial analogy
with a rhyming vowel of another root; but, *since all the vowels*

are primally akin to one another, it is based on the *disclosing of the
Ur-kinship* through giving full value to the vowel's *emotional
content, by means of musical Tone.* The vowel itself is nothing
but *a tone condensed . . .* which . . . becomes an immediate
outpour of the Feeling."* The consonant, on the other hand,
borders and lends the vowel tone a certain color.

> The first function of the *consonant* consists in this: that it
> raises the open-sound of the root to a definite character-
> istic, by firmly hedging-in its infinitely fluid element,
> and through the lines of this delimitation it brings to the
> vowel's colour, in a sense, the drawing which makes of
> it an exactly distinguishable shape. This function of the
> consonant is consequently the one turned *outward* from
> the vowel. Its object is to definitely sever from the
> vowel whatever is to be differentiated therefrom, and to
> place itself as a sort of boundary-fence between the two.
> This important position the consonant takes up *before*
> the vowel, as its initial sound. . . . In this situation the
> consonant shews us, in a sense, the countenance of the
> root, whose body is filled by the vowel's warmly
> streaming blood, and whose hinder side is turned from
> the eye, in the terminal. (Wagner, 267)

Throughout all of this the consonant retains its decisive
function as springboard for the melodic shaping of a "rhythmic word-phrase knit according to the breath's necessity"
(Wagner, 268). This, in turn, leads to the musical and melodic
significance of alliteration, for alliteration (or *Stabreim*) likewise combines musical phrases, elevates the musical attention
and then, through the inclusion of differing vowels, can still
change the sense, the melody, and the tonality. Accordingly,

*Richard Wagner's Prose Works, vol. 2, "Opera and Drama," p. 275.

then, the phrase "Liebe gibt Lust zum Leben" would be set to music differently than would "Liebe bringt Lust und Leid." In the first example, "as a like emotion is physically disclosed in the Accents' stabreimed roots, the musician would here receive no natural incitement to step outside the once selected key, but would completely satisfy the Feeling by keeping the various inflections of the musical tone to that one key alone" (Wagner, 292). In the second example,

> here, where the Stabreim combines two opposite emotions, the musician would feel incited to pass across from the key first struck in keeping with the first emotion, to another key in keeping with the second emotion, and determined by the latter's relation to the emotion rendered in the earlier key. The word *Lust* (delight)—which, as the climax of the first emotion appears to thrust onward to the second—would have in this phrase to obtain an emphasis quite other than in that: *die Liebe gibt Lust zum Leben*. (Wagner, 292).

Obviously, there's a clear difference even in the melody of speech here.

Wagner also comes to the following important conclusion: "Just as the consonant hedges the vowel from without, so does it also bound the vowel within: i.e. it determines the specific nature of the latter's manifestment, through the roughness or smoothness of its inward contact therewith," and he continues in a footnote:

> The Singer, who has to get the full tone out of the vowel, is acutely sensitive to the difference between the effects of energetic consonants—such as K, R, P, T—, or indeed, strengthened ones—such as Schr, Sp, St, Pr—, and softer, weak ones—such as G, L, B, D, W,—

upon the open sound. A strengthened terminal—nd, rt, st, ft—where it is radical—as in "Hand," "hart," "Hast," "Kraft"—, so definitely lays down the nature and duration of the vowel's utterance, that it downright insists on the latter's sounding brief and brisk; and, being thus a characteristic token of the root, it fits itself for rhyme—as Assonance (as in "Hand und Mund"). (Wagner, 271)

As the previous section has demonstrated, vowels and consonants were of absolutely equal importance for Wagner, so much so that he was as much against a mere vocal (that is, composed of vowels) ornamentation as he was against an unmusical and noncontextual consonantal "spitting fest." A clear articulation was thus a prerequisite for him. Singers had first to read the text clearly out loud (an exercise that should be done today as well!), then they had to enunciate the text clearly while singing it, until finally, under Wagner's direction, the actual musical line and shape was worked out on the basis of this "word-tone-phrase" progression with the help of proper breathing techniques. A good accentuation had to be maintained throughout, but it was now combined with a beautiful sound and cohesive, breath-supported, "inspired" phrasing. Jens Malte Fischer calls this a "cautious middle road between 'speech song' (Sprachgesang) and bel canto" (Fischer, 234). Of course, Wagner also placed great value on a proper portamento as well as portato whenever it was more important for his purposes than a sharp accentuation. And in the end, he certainly did require legato as well, whenever this fit in with and was an integral part of the dramatic presentation. Dramatic presentation in all its musical variety thus remained the foundation of Wagnerian music drama.

As far as Domingo's German is concerned (and I do not dare comment on his Italian or French), there are individual recordings, such as that of Florestan's prison scene from *Fidelio* in the videotape *Homage à Seville,* where his German is very easy to understand, especially in the slower parts, and where it becomes indistinct only with the quicker tempi toward the end. Domingo is also very easy to understand on the already-mentioned CD recording of the portrait aria from *Die Zauberflöte.*

On the other hand, there are arias from Viennese operettas in which Domingo's German is neither quite accent free nor sufficiently differentiated in articulation—a disturbing factor in this type of song. With their relatively simple melodies and rhythms, they follow the articulation of everyday speech much more closely than does Florestan's aria, for example, where the orchestra has a much more dominant and complex role than it does in the works of Lehár or Kálmán. The text of an operetta song, as banal as it might be at times, comes more strongly to the fore than in the musico-dramatic alliterations of a Wagnerian *Ring* opera or the subtle poetry of a Hugo von Hofmannsthal libretto in a composition by Richard Strauss. Singers like Domingo who still have an accent in German will betray themselves immediately when they sing an operetta song. Domingo has this same problem when he sings selections from American musicals.

Nevertheless, there is no question that Domingo's command of German has improved since his first *Lohengrin* performance in Hamburg. Of course, a few of the typical problems with diction that date back to that 1968 *Lohengrin* and to the 1970 production of Weber's *Oberon* still exist today. In addition to, and disregarding for the moment, his tendency to produce unusually extended legatos, portamentos, and portatos or his own unique *messa di voce* while singing works of Wagner and Strauss, these problem areas include a frequently soft to non-existent accentuation of end, and sometimes even initial, consonants. This improper articulation can no longer be described as a "Wagnerian bel canto" in Domingo's style. It results in the absence of the accentuated consonant within a word or a phrase, "whose body the vowel fills up like warmly flowing blood" (Wagner).

The following few examples document those places where Domingo, so very aware of his language skills, still has difficulties in singing German. He still has trouble with the *ch* sound, often shapes the diphthongs, especially the *au* and *ei* combinations, with a wrong vocal coloration, or else all too frequently sings an open *o* where a closed one is called for and vice versa, a mistake that just about every foreign singer makes. He confuses the closed, or long, *o* by singing it like an open, or short one, and this can be very disturbing. In many cases the listener can write these inadequacies in articulation off as being little more than unpleasant pronunciation mistakes, but there are too many instances where they change or interfere with tonal phrasing intended by the composers. In these instances the language problem becomes a musical problem as well. Thus we find on the *Oberon* recording, for instance, a very frequent "diphthongization" of vowels, so that "Liebe" becomes "Luiebe," "Vater" "Vuater," "jetzt" "joetzt," "hat" "huat," and so on. This, in turn, darkens the color of the tone and the overall sound of the voice at precisely that point where Weber did *not* want that effect. In addition, Domingo often fails to separate syllables correctly, especially those that are produced by a slight glottal stop or a barely audible hesitation; "ge-endet," for example, should not be articulated in such a way that comes out as "goendet," for this changes the differentiation within the musical phrase itself.

This omission of slighter or stronger separations between syllables, or glottal stops, becomes even more problematic when it leads to the agglomeration of several entire words. This no longer has anything to do with legato, the acoustical connecting of vowels in phrases and combinations characterized by a corresponding portamento. Even in a legato line a slight, even if very slight, separation of words or syllables has to be maintained, for it is essential that the singer guard against eliminating initial consonants or merging initial vowels with the end of a previous word or syllable by completely ignoring a glottal stop.

With very few exceptions, Domingo's later recordings show that he has just about completely overcome his tendency to transform vowels into diphthongs, but he has yet to conquer his other difficulties in German: his consonants. They are either too weak or are missing altogether ("bedören" instead of "betören," "Dannehrte" instead of "Dann kehrte"); he sings a short *o* where a long *o* is required ("Nott" instead of "No:t," "grosser" instead of "gro:ßer"), *a* sounds that are too dark (as in "dahin," "Art," "Ritterschaft," "unerkannt"), and improper articulation of umlauts ("mächte" instead of "möchte," "Känig" instead of "König"); and he occasionally uses the wrong emphasis, which affects the musical phrasing. False diphthongs ("moin" instead of "mein", "boi" instead of "bei," "A/uge" instead of "Auge," a too dark *o* sound in "scheun") and the elimination of word and syllable separation caused by the insufficient accentuation of initial consonants or a complete lack of glottal stops before initial vowels still abound in his German singing. In such instances Domingo sings "überalle" instead of "über 'alle" (*Lohengrin*), "zurErde" instead of "Zur 'Erde" (*Tannhäuser*), "dieAugen" instead of "die 'Augen" (*Die Fledermaus*). Sometimes these slurred portamenti also serve him in building the upwardly climbing vocal bridges that are so important to his technique, as in "überalle" (*Lohengrin*), "nunerwachte" (*Tannhäuser*), "undhöhnte" (*Die Frau ohne Schatten*) or "Beutenohn'Ende" (*Die Frau ohne Schatten*). As mentioned before, these bridges, especially in the last example, can produce a very sophisticated sound. When talking about these bridges, then, one can by no means describe them as an "indistinctly intoned chain of tones blurred by a portamento," as Franziska Martienssen-Lohmann describes a "false" legato. As far as musical intonation is concerned, Domingo's "tonal chains" remain extremely precise despite the occasional neglect of consonants and initial vowels.

What on earlier recordings may still have been a genuine problem, having to do with an insufficient command of the German language and its phonetic structure, becomes in the later recordings a problem of the occasional lack of linguistic and textual comprehension, since Domingo has the text and the score in front of him during studio recording sessions, thereby facilitating his articulation. And his stage performances in German as Lohengrin, Siegmund, or Parsifal could be improved by more intensive work on "Wagnerian diction," though Domingo's Wagnerian diction already surpasses that of some German-speaking Wagner singers. Nevertheless, additional study would surely enhance his Wagnerian bel canto and lend more depth to his musical interpretation.

Domingo once told me: "I am keenly aware that the language [in Wagner's works] is one of my greatest problems, since German is the last language [I learned], and I wish it were easier for me. It's not easy for me, but I prepare very well. And I think I can be very satisfied with the audience's reaction, which is very important to me, following my performances of Parsifal and Siegmund in Bayreuth and Vienna."

Stage Performances, Live Telecasts, and Film

Domingo's idea of good stage direction is closely re-
lated to his conception of a historical presentation in
the Stanislavsky sense. He feels, first and foremost,
that a stage director "would do well to avoid interpre-
tations that are so intellectualized and abstruse that
the audience needs a book to understand what
is happening."

For Domingo, the future of opera lies in the possibility
that people will simply be able to tune into an opera
production on cable television.

THE PROFESSIONAL ACTOR IN DOMINGO HAS DEFINITE
ideas about stage settings; he is also well aware of the advantages and problems involved in making a recording, broad-
casting a live telecast, or filming an opera.

We have already seen that, as an operatic actor, Domingo
adheres to the precepts of the Stanislavsky approach, which
is to say, he takes great pains to familiarize himself with the
familial, historical, and psychological background of each
character he portrays. What makes it all come alive for him
lies precisely in this awareness of the historical and psychological perspective of a role—his fascination with the whole
context of a work allows whatever relevance the work has

for today's audience to be brought to the fore. The suffering of an Otello in the Venice of Shakespeare's day is more alive for us than if we should turn it into an everyday event of our own era, which is what we usually get in a thousand different forms in contemporary films and news broadcasts. This last observation is probably as accurate an extension of Domingo's thoughts on the subject as any other. What he aims to convey through his portrayal of a role is a historically oriented naturalism. And since, for Domingo, opera is supposed to entertain, the historical ambience of a staged event can be at least equally as entertaining as the reproduction of an event that happened in our neighbor's backyard.

Domingo's idea of good stage direction is closely related to his conception of a historic presentation in the Stanislavsky sense. He feels, first and foremost, that a stage director "would do well to avoid interpretations that are so intellectualized and abstruse that the audience needs a book to understand what is happening." For "the art of interpretation in the theatre is the art of clarification; and if any detail of a production has confused rather than elucidated the substance of a work for a reasonably intelligent person, it has failed in its function" (AB, 200). This is the basis of Domingo's criticism of Patrice Chéreau's controversial 1976 staging of Wagner's *Ring* in Bayreuth, for in the end Chéreau mixed up the historical and the mythological levels. For Domingo historical validity, and if not that then at least historical consistency, is absolutely essential. Put another way, historical logic is more important than adherence to historical truth.

Thus in 1993 Domingo conducted a staging of *La bohème* in Los Angeles that took place in the Paris of 1895 rather than the Paris of 1830, and he has also sung in a *Pagliacci* film in which the clowns arrive in an automobile instead of the usual circus cart. Verismo episodes such as these can be moved about in time without destroying the inner logic of the work or its contextual relation to reality. Thus Domingo would surely also be amenable to the idea of transposing a Greek tragedy, for example, to the present day. The event is so far removed and the text so abstract that the action itself can be moved up into our own century.

The situation is not the same with the operas of Verdi, however. A *Don Carlo* or an *Aïda* still needs its historical context in order to maintain its vitality and logic. "There are operas," Domingo once told me,

> that one can easily transpose into another time. I greatly admire what Jonathan Miller has done with *Rigoletto*, and one can surely transplant *La bohème* to Greenwich Village. You can cast *Bohème* with today's bohemians. But you will have to translate the text into English and use all the characterizations of today. You can't speak about Louis Philippe [the king at the time of *La bohème*] in Greenwich Village and shoot heroin at the same time or do whatever else is characteristic of our times. That's why you have to be very careful if you want to do this. When you transpose an opera to a different time period, you have to make the transposition completely and convincingly. . . . Somehow I'm a traditionalist. I want to inspire the audience. I think that, if you want to transpose an opera to a different time period, you have to have a reason for doing so.

Marta Domingo, who shares her husband's views on this, added:

> All these Greek tragedies could happen today—*Phaedra* or *Electra*, works like that. I saw *Electra* set against the background of pre–World War I tensions, and I found

it very, very convincing and depressing. If you can support it well and if the ideas are clearly worked out, you can alter the time frame [in which a work takes place]. By the same token, though, there are other eras that you can't change. *La traviata*, for example. You just can't change this time frame. The honor of a man, the honor of a woman have their meaning and their value in their time. Girls of ten or eleven would laugh at Violetta's tragic fate should it be set in our day. It would be ridiculous.

A better example for me would have been Mozart's *Figaro*. While one could still find fathers, especially in American society, willing and ready to break up a solid bond between their son and a former prostitute in order to ensure the reputation of the family and a good bourgeois match for their daughter, as in *La traviata*, it is difficult to transpose Beaumarchais–Da Ponte–Mozart's *Marriage of Figaro* into the New York of our day as Peter Sellars has recently done. Wherever in contemporary industrial New York, where Sellars's *Figaro* takes place, is there a count with the power of an absolute monarch (which is how he is addressed in the text); and where is there still the custom of the first night, which the count had abolished yet does not want to give up? In today's world, a woman either sleeps with her fiancé's boss or she does not. And even if there should be a boss who might entertain such ideas, he would harass much more brutally today than Almaviva did. No matter what, all the goings-on as depicted by Beaumarchais–Da Ponte–Mozart are simply unbelievable when one transposes the action to our time. The historical situation on the eve of the French Revolution, to which Da Ponte's text makes reference, is much more exciting and plausible.

{ 175 }

Although one can and should defend the Peter Sellars–
Da Ponte–Mozart production as important food for thought,
my objections, which both Plácido and Marta Domingo
share, cannot be dismissed out of hand. The problem is similar, but only similar, with Chéreau's staging of the *Ring* cycle,
which is readily available on video. Many things seem to be
antagonistic in this production. Take for example the setting
of *Die Götterdämmerung* in a kind of Krupp family, already
producing cannons, while Siegfried appears with sword in
hand and is killed with a spear by a member of the Krupp
clan. Despite such anachronisms and inconsistencies, however, Chéreau's staging was impressive, and it contributed
much to a new understanding of Wagner on my part. In this
case I do not agree with the criticism Domingo makes in his
autobiography to the effect that this vision has "negated the
direct, the human values of the theater" through its incom-
prehensibility.

For Domingo, the future of opera lies in the possibility
that people will simply be able to tune into an opera production on cable television. Even if this might be looking too far
into the future, it is already common practice to record a live
performance in a famous opera house and later broadcast it
or distribute the video. Domingo has done his part in further-
ing this development, which has made it more necessary than
ever that singers be actors as well, and that expressions and
eye movements onstage now have to be portrayed differently,
more realistically, than used to be the case. Domingo was
already writing about this in 1982:

> Learning how to act on camera should now be a normal
> part of a singer's training, because it is certain to be a
> major factor in the careers of most of today's and tomor-

row's singers. We must learn to make smaller and subtler gestures, for instance, and to bear in mind camera angles so as not to block our colleagues at key moments. Similarly, when a singer is working at, say, the Metropolitan, there is such distance between him and even the nearest member of the public that eye movement is of negligible importance. As a result, it is very difficult for us to learn to discipline our eyes as a cinema actor must do, when we are singing on television. An instant's loss of concentration can destroy the theatrical illusion for the viewer. (AB, 190)

Videotapes of operatic performances are one thing; the filming of an opera is another. Domingo has played his part in this development as well, and not only because of his magnificent voice but because of his extraordinary theatrical abilities. And even if he is not completely satisfied with the way opera films are made, he has produced some of his best vocal work in a few of them. The production procedure is cumbersome, at best: the entire part has to be sung before the filming begins, and only after it is recorded can the singer turn his attention to the acting, always keeping it in sync with the already recorded score. This is not as easy as it sounds, for should he sing the aria again during the filming itself just to appear more natural, he sometimes falls out of sync with the music because all he hears is his unaccompanied live voice. If he does not sing along, the visual impression loses its credibility because neither the mouth nor the throat muscles show the expected and appropriate signs of strain. "I do not normally have an angelic little smile on my face when singing a high B-flat," Domingo adds rather sarcastically (AB, 191).

Moreover, "for a fraction of a second you lose the theatrical aspect if you have to think about the way you should visually articulate something that was sung beforehand. One's concentration simply can't be complete, because the theatrical aspect is also dependent upon what's going on in the orchestra," he added during one of our conversations about the problems associated with filming operas.

On the other hand, in filming operas no one achieves as well as Domingo the visual harmony between his movements on screen and the lines and phrases he is singing. This includes breath control, throat movements, and facial expressions, for not even for a "fraction of a second" may the audience get the impression his thoughts are elsewhere (for instance, concentrating on what is happening in the orchestra).

Domingo sees other difficulties in the filming of an opera as well: "It is particularly hard to maintain the right frame of mind for a sad scene that has to be shot over and over again, because there are hundreds of people milling around all the time and, just before a take, loud warnings not to interrupt the proceedings are broadcast" (AB, 191).

Finally, a singer accustomed to stage performances misses the immediate and direct reaction from the audience. In spite of all these drawbacks, however, Domingo is well aware that the filmed version of an opera is a valuable tool, for it enables the singer to study himself in hindsight, something not possible with a stage production. One way or the other, though, he still prefers a stage production, not only because of the direct contact with the audience and the immediate tensions that are so great a part of every performance, but because, as singer or member of the audience, one remembers specific stage experiences much more vividly than one does a scene in a film. You can return to them again and again, both visually and emotionally.

DOMINGO AS
CONDUCTOR

Domingo's Career Crossover: Difficulties and Prejudices

Domingo is one of the few conductors who truly responds to each musician individually. This is particularly appreciated when members of the orchestra have to play in the pit, completely overshadowed by the singers onstage. . . . The way Domingo behaves toward the members of the orchestra on an individual basis is also the way he conducts them as a group: warmly and personably. But this, his greatest human asset, may yet prove to be a handicap in his career as conductor.

WHENEVER A FAMOUS SOLOIST—BE IT A SINGER, PIAnist, or cellist—turns conductor or just happens to conduct "on the side," there are always those who have difficulty in taking him seriously. Members of the audience and critics alike think in categories that, consciously or unconsciously, lead to critical prejudices. Musicians are not the only ones susceptible to this reaction. An actor, for example, who has made a name for himself in films and television as a romantic lead will find it difficult to be accepted one day as a character actor. Such a person is bound to have a harder time in the new field than the actor who started his career there in the first place. And this is true even apart from the fact that film and television producers are rarely amenable to such changeovers anyway.

There are musicians who, having attained world reputations as soloists, make a career switch to conducting or continue to work in both fields. One need think only of Yehudi Menuhin, Dietrich Fischer-Dieskau, Daniel Barenboim, Vladimir Ashkenasy, Iona Brown, Peter Schreier, and Mstislav Rostropovitsch, to name but a few. Of all these, though, perhaps the only one to have actually "made it" primarily as a career conductor is Daniel Barenboim. All the others are still surrounded by the aura of soloist, and the public as well as the critics remain skeptical when a famous soloist takes up the baton. Some go so far as to think it was only his or her fame as soloist that made the crossover to a conducting career possible in the first place.

Without now judging the various conducting skills of the artists named above, we can say with impunity that less qualified conductors have managed to make a career and a certain name for themselves in this field.

There is no doubt that Plácido Domingo has not or has not yet attained the acclaim and significance as a conductor that he enjoys, and will continue to enjoy, as one of the greatest tenors of the century. He would then have to be compared to Arturo Toscanini, Bruno Walter, Wilhelm Furtwängler, Herbert von Karajan, or Carlos Kleiber—and Domingo himself would not want that. Yet Domingo the conductor still stands very much in the shadow of Domingo the singer. In fact, many music lovers are surprised to learn of his second career. "Oh, Domingo's a conductor, too?" is the usual remark, tinged with a slightly skeptical undertone. When a musicologist from a prominent university recently told me, "Domingo is a great singer, and a good musician as well, but no conductor," I asked him whether he had ever heard Domingo lead an orchestra. The rather hesitant reply to this question was "No, but they let him conduct only because he is so famous."

In fact, Domingo is no newcomer to the conductor's podium. His early appearances on international stages date back at least two decades: in 1973 he conducted Verdi's *La traviata* at the New York City Opera and in 1975 Verdi's *Il trovatore* and *Aïda* in Hamburg. These performances were followed by appearances in such houses as the Vienna State Opera, Covent Garden, the Met, and the Los Angles Music Center Opera, where he has already conducted four operas since its opening in 1986. In fact, it was Lorin Maazel in Vienna who asked Domingo, who had already conducted the 1979 *Il trovatore* production, to lead the consummately Austrian work *Die Fledermaus*. In 1988, when the members of the Los Angeles Chamber Orchestra (which was founded by Sir Neville Marriner and which also in expanded form regularly accompanies the Los Angeles Music Center Opera) were polled as to which conductors from the previous season they preferred, Domingo came in second place. During the season in question, fourteen renowned conductors had led the orchestra.

Naturally, Domingo's popularity as conductor may have something to do with his personality as well as his ability. Domingo is one of the few conductors who truly responds to each musician individually. This is particularly appreciated when members of the orchestra have to play in the pit, completely overshadowed by the singers onstage. Domingo knows this and does not make light of the situation. He is aided by his great, one can almost say, phenomenal memory, musical as well as visual. He never forgets a face or a name.

Topper Smith, the music administrator of the Los Angeles Music Center Opera, once told me the following episode.

Domingo had just conducted his first Los Angeles production and was thus only slightly acquainted with the members of the Los Angeles Chamber Orchestra. One of those members bumped into him at the stage door in Vienna several months afterward. Domingo immediately remembered the man's first and last name, recalled his playing, and got him some tickets for one of the performances. Between their first acquaintance and this serendipitous meeting, Domingo had worked in dozens of roles in dozens of opera houses all over the world and had been steadily involved with film and sound recording engagements as well, so that during that time he had met and worked with hundreds of other musicians.

The way Domingo behaves toward the members of the orchestra on an individual basis is also the way he conducts them as a group: warmly and personably. But this, his greatest human asset, may yet prove to be a handicap in his career as conductor. If one watches him at work as conductor during rehearsals or performances, his warmth and amiability do not always serve the task at hand. Though he need not become a "tyrant" like Toscanini or humanly as well as artistically demanding and uncompromising like Carlos Kleiber, a little more distance and self-assertion would go a long way in increasing his ability to have his own desires prevail. Domingo is fully aware of this trait, for he says in his autobiography: "The conductor has two main tasks: to know exactly what he wants and to know how to get it [from the orchestra]" (AB, 112). As far as "knowing how to get it" goes, he is still too cautious, too considerate, perhaps even insecure, although the latter is not overtly obvious.

Ever since its beginnings in Mexico City, Domingo's conducting career has focused predominantly on operas in the Italian repertoire, although there have been excursions into other worlds. His *Fledermaus*, for instance, drew acclaim in Vienna, Munich, and Covent Garden, as did his work in orchestral concerts and on recordings of music by Beethoven and Tchaikovsky. The composer whose operas have so far constituted the bulk of his work as conductor is, of course, Giuseppe Verdi. Domingo considers the operas of Verdi's middle period the most difficult to lead. "*Aïda, Otello,* and *Falstaff* are written essentially in long segments, each within one basic tempo, while *Rigoletto, Trovatore,* and *Traviata* are made up of smaller units, each having its own tempo. The conductor must always be aware of making those tempi relate to each other and must concentrate on bringing off each change properly," he tells us (AB, 111). To my mind, *La bohème* is equally difficult to conduct, if not perhaps even more so. Still, *Rigoletto, Il trovatore, La traviata, La bohème,* and *Tosca* are the operas Domingo continues to conduct on a regular basis.

Ambitions and Reflections

*Domingo is a conductor who in any case has the right
feeling and the right "heart" for conducting, even
though he may still have much to learn. That which
"cannot be learned" Domingo already
knows intuitively.*

As we know, Domingo started to conduct early
in his career, beginning in Mexico City, where he worked as
singer and as assistant conductor in a production of *My Fair
Lady*. This initiation led to the opportunity to conduct two
zarzuelas in his parents' theater troupe. But his actual conducting career, as mentioned before, really began in 1973 in
New York and in 1975 in Hamburg. He has always considered conducting the continuation of his singing career, never
a mere safety net for the future. Conducting was his second
career right from the start. In 1986 he told Helena Matheopoulos: "Conducting is far more intriguing than singing because your feelings about the music must be expressed
through a hundred people" (*Divo*, 75). On the other hand,
he recently told the students at UCLA that singing is physically more difficult than conducting. As a singer, one has to
be very health conscious and watch one's lifestyle rather like
an athlete, whereas a conductor can lead a more normal life.
He repeated to them what he has told so many people over
the years: he still considers himself primarily a singer, and

singing still his actual career. Nevertheless, conducting seems to occupy him mentally at least as much as his singing does. Hence his autobiography pays almost equal attention to these two centers of interest, as does his frequently cited interview with Helena Matheopoulos.

> The least attractive quality is the need for an almost aggressive streak in one's character, and this is very hard for me to acquire. Because so far, as a singer, I've been involved on the right side, the nice side, of music-making where others tell *you* what to do. And, as I'm usually quite well-prepared, I've never had quarrels or problems with conductors, directors or colleagues. . . . But conducting is not about teamwork . . . it's about authority, the transmission of your ideas about the music to the orchestra. And if one is faced with an undisciplined orchestra . . . then one's character must change!
>   . . . I can sense intuitively when singers need more time to breathe and when it's better to keep going because the pulse of the tempo itself will help them. The disadvantage is that I cannot wholly disassociate myself from being a singer and helping too much even when I would actually prefer to impose my own view of the music and my own tempo. (*Divo*, 76)

About ten years after he said these things to Helena Matheopoulos, Domingo corrected and expanded upon his earlier remarks in his conversation with the UCLA students:

> The conductor has the whole performance in his hands, and that means it can also fall apart because of him. That's why it's best when the conductor knows each individual singer. He has to have a tremendous concentration and he has to see everything beforehand. . . .
>   When I'm conducting, the only time I think about

the fact that I'm a singer is when I want the best for the singers. I do and should understand them better than many other [conductors]. Except for this, I don't think like a singer while conducting, nor do I let the singer in me interfere with my conducting. I'm very disciplined. . . .

As conductor, I first start from the assumption that every instrument in the orchestra is a singer. The basis for all [music making] is proper breath control. For me, an orchestra consists of seventy, eighty, ninety singers, and I think that all these instruments have to sing, have to have the feeling of singing, even the percussionists have to sing—that's my attitude, my approach. My whole attitude as conductor stems from singing.

It's easier to conduct a symphony than an opera, because when conducting an opera, you also have to know what's happening onstage, and you occasionally have to deal with unmusical singers as well. Yes, there is such a thing as an unmusical singer! In an orchestra every player is a musician and musical. . . .

As conductor I still work a lot on my technique. Technique is something you practice and you improve—it can be learned. But there has to be a feeling there for the music and for conducting. That's something you can't learn—you have to be born with it.

Domingo added a few more things on the same subject during one of our subsequent conversations:

The fact that I'm a well-known singer makes it more difficult for me than for a normal conductor. There are some musicians who think, he cannot possibly be as good a conductor. I don't want to judge myself as a conductor. I don't even talk about my singing, and so I will never attempt to talk about my conducting. The only thing I know is that I have a definite idea of how things should be. I have the sound in my mind, and I think I can convey my ideas to the orchestra. Still, they have a hard time accepting me as one of them. Perhaps later, when my career is a bit more established, maybe then I will have more authority. That might be one thing. The other is, I am improving my technique, and most importantly, I am improving it from day to day. Even so, I still think a conductor's primary duty is to communicate [with the orchestra]; it goes without saying that he has to be musically very creative as well. I don't think it is enough to have a clean technique. Once in a while you see these technically clean conductors, but they have nothing to say. In any case my technique has improved, and I am very glad about that. And the important thing is precision, direction, and expressive force.

Domingo is a conductor who in any case has the right feeling and the right "heart" for conducting, even though he may still have much to learn. That which "cannot be learned" Domingo already knows intuitively.

Domingo intends to conduct for a long time to come, and his passion grows with each passing year. His aim is to continue his musical career as a conductor after he stops singing professionally or once his age dictates a certain easing of his heavy schedule. But to be a good conductor in the future means he must practice right now, and this involves "learning and improving."

When the Los Angeles Music Center Opera was established in 1986, Domingo thought he would be singing for another decade or so, but not much more than that. His original plan was to become that company's music director somewhere in the mid-1990s, but this idea has since given way to the thought of becoming a festival conductor someday. Being the music director of an opera that plays the whole year through, he is beginning to think, would involve too much administrative work. As a conductor of festival performances, on the other hand, he could devote full and uninterrupted concentration to the orchestra and the music for two full months. What he would most prefer is to work intensively with an orchestra on some work, Beethoven's symphonies, for example, or some operas, without being distracted by administrative duties, questions about repertoire, or casting responsibilities. With a festival performance everything is decided beforehand, and the musicians are especially chosen for the performance. All that remains is uninterrupted concentration on the music and the musicians during the two months it takes to rehearse and then perform the concert.

It is quite possible that someday Domingo will become the music director of the Los Angeles Music Center Opera in spite of himself, for when it comes down to it, this company is his "baby," and the general director and his staff can surely relieve him of a considerable amount of the administrative burden. Peter Hemmings remarks, however, "Domingo is just as busy today as he was ten years ago. That's why the possibility of becoming music director still lies in the distant future."

From Die Fledermaus *to* I Puritani

*When I asked those singers who had worked with him
in a number of productions how they felt about working under Domingo as conductor, the overwhelming
response was that they enjoyed singing under his direction and that he was easy to follow because he understood the singer's situation so well. . . . Members of
the orchestra were also unanimous and gave essentially
the same response, adding that, should things ever fall
apart . . . they were ready to do their best to patch
things up again. . . . Musical warmth is Domingo's
watchword in his role as conductor.*

WHEN HE DIRECTED JOHANN STRAUSS'S *DIE FLEDERMAUS*
at the Royal Opera, Covent Garden, for the worldwide 1983
New Year's Eve telecast of the performance, millions of
viewers discovered for the first time that Plácido Domingo
was a conductor as well as singer. Of course, this was not the
first time Domingo had publicly conducted an opera (or an
operetta, in this case), but a simultaneous telecast on New
Year's Eve featuring such stars as Hermann Prey, Kiri Te Kanawa, and Josef Meinrad as Frosch had to have a different
effect than an audio recording. The taped telecast is no longer
available, but there is a comprehensive chapter about the
preparation and performance of this *Fledermaus* production in
Daniel Snowman's book *The World of Plácido Domingo*.

Since I would like to begin my discussion of Domingo's

development as a conductor with Strauss's *Fledermaus*, I will use the 1986 CD recorded in Munich, which I have referred to before, and which features Domingo as conductor as well as in the role of Alfred.

On the whole, Domingo catches and conveys the Viennese buoyancy and dash very well. Yet right from the start, during the overture in fact, the listener is struck by a somewhat ponderous element. Domingo takes some things less lightly and briskly than Carlos Kleiber, for example, who is Domingo's model and who achieves his goals with much less effusive arm and body movements. Domingo's skill in leading the orchestra occasionally lacks a certain differentiation and nuance when it comes to the specific instruments. In this, too, Domingo has much to learn from Kleiber, whose exemplary performance with the Munich State Opera has been recorded on videotape. Under Domingo's baton, the transitional phrases leading up to the familiar central melodies occasionally suffer from too much emphasis. A bit more lightness or ease would have been appropriate here. Nevertheless, there is no lack of vitality, and the orchestra is guided by a rhythmic intuition.

If many things are not as light and subtle and brisk as one might wish, this is no reason to examine them too closely. After all, Domingo himself is well aware that, even today, he sometimes conducts with too many arm and hand movements. Back then, during the *Fledermaus* production in London, these problems were much more apparent and eventually produced the exhaustion and ponderousness mentioned above. "Earlier," he later told me, "I used to be completely exhausted from moving about so much; too much movement sometimes slows you down, tires you out. Especially if you're conducting something very fast and you want to communicate this through a great deal of movement: that's when you get tired. You beat the time too strongly just before you speed up, and in the end you become slower rather than faster. But these are the things you learn."

In 1989 I heard Domingo conduct *Tosca* and in 1993 *Rigoletto* and *La bohème*. Topper Smith reports on Domingo's debut as conductor of the Los Angeles Music Center Opera in a 1987 production of *Macbeth*, when the members of the orchestra anxiously watched to see if Domingo would come to the podium as a great world star who was unprepared and unable to do much in his new capacity, as one who would merely exploit the orchestra as other stars have been known to do.

> Naturally, they already knew him as a singer and knew how nice he is, that he often spoke with the individual members of the orchestra in his role as singer—during rehearsal breaks, for instance—and that he made a point of learning their names. But they didn't know him yet in his role as conductor. Since he was such a highly regarded musician, they were hoping he knew what he was supposed to do. . . . He approached the podium with an assurance born of moral and emotional readiness. The members of the orchestra quickly discovered that he was very well prepared and technically already very professional.

The poll putting Domingo in second place was taken at the end of this season. Topper Smith concludes his description: "Some of the musicians made comments to the effect that he treats the orchestra with affection, consideration, and respect; that he is very well prepared even if not always perfect in his technique. Ever since then they have liked working with him."

Smith further remarked:

Domingo dealt with the orchestra like a musician and
not like a soloist who wants to become a conductor at
their expense. There would have been great resistance
if he had turned up unprepared. But he knew the music.
Understandably, he still didn't know all the things a
conductor has to know, but one could and can follow
him as easily as many another of the so-called great conductors, some of whom the orchestra can hardly follow
at all. Back then we all expected him to be a conductor
of singers; we thought he would lose himself in the
beauty of the singing instead of concentrating on leading
the orchestra. But that is not the case now, nor was it
then. He knows how to establish the proper relation
between orchestra and singer. For him, the orchestra is
not merely an accompanying instrument.

This statement in no way contradicts Domingo's insistence
that the instruments should "sing," too. He always starts with
singing, and this holds true for his work as conductor as well.
As I witnessed during the preparation of the 1993 *La bohème*,
he sometimes actually sang along with the individual orchestral voices during the rehearsal. He makes sure, though, that
this approach never compromises the equality he fosters between the orchestra and the singers.

I was personally able to discern a great improvement in
Domingo's conducting skills between the *Tosca* production
in 1989 and his *La bohème* in 1993. In 1989 his conducting
was a bit too elementary for my taste, a bit too pedantic and
exact. He paid too much attention to the beat and the rhythm
and used too many memorized precise hand movements,
while still not keeping the singer and the orchestra in complete unison at every phrase. In the 1993 production, on the

other hand, he was considerably freer. Granted, there were still a few rather elementary aspects to his work, but he had made great progress in shaping the difficult phrases, in working out their transitions and extensions, and he was able to communicate the feelings he wanted to convey much more subtly in *La bohème* than previously in *Tosca*. In short, he was able to communicate much more through his direction, and the orchestra was better able to follow his intentions.

Yet what to me was even more interesting than this successful, professional rendition of *La bohème* was the way Domingo rehearsed Bellini's *I puritani* early in 1994 with a rather undistinguished student orchestra. He undertook this exercise as preparation for his forthcoming engagements in Vienna and showed that he could deal professionally with a nonprofessional orchestra.

Domingo had only four practice sessions at his disposal: one separate chorus rehearsal followed by individual sessions with the soloists and the combined chorus and orchestra for the first and then the second part of the opera; the fourth and final session was a full run-through. While working with the chorus, Domingo was very concerned about proper dynamics and the proper relation between legato and staccato. Rhythmic passages were less keenly observed than was a proper portamento. He was also concerned about carrying over the dramatics as well as the emotional context to the music of the chorus. In all of this, the singer in Domingo was quite clearly in charge.

During the orchestral sessions, on the other hand, his concentration focused on the orchestra itself, although here he was particularly interested in the relation between the various orchestral voices. The individual voices, especially those of the violins, were neglected in the beginning. Their playing was hopelessly lacking in bel canto, to put it mildly. Domingo's initial maxim was: "The orchestra should play in such a way that the instrumentalists can hear the singers, because if not, the audience can't hear them either." He was also preoccupied with the proper tempo, and to make it easier for the orchestra, he doubled the number of beats. He did now and again instruct the violins to play more softly and more melodically, but he neglected to use the appropriate signal with his left hand. Toward the end he devoted himself exclusively to the violins and rehearsed several passages with them alone, but it did not help very much. Once they were all playing together again, he was once again more concerned about rhythmic control.

During the second rehearsal with the orchestra he concentrated even more intensely on the individual voices, although here too his left hand failed to elicit the desired response (especially with respect to the strings).

Once the full run-through rehearsal had arrived, a small miracle happened. The warmth of Domingo's personality had so managed to win the students over that, despite all the musical and technical problems he encountered among individual instrumentalists, one could detect a certain cohesiveness and a certain overall control in the hands of the conductor. Although Domingo was still mainly (and rightly) concerned about rhythmic clarity—even though his directions could have been sharper at times and he could have been more authoritarian in exercising his will—he did manage to introduce certain musical impulses that moved beyond mere rhythmic cohesion. Unfortunately, his left hand was still not free enough of the right, and the right hand was still too elementary in its movements, which may actually have been justified in this case.

The progress he made with an inexperienced student orchestra within the span of two days showed what Domingo
could elicit from any orchestra. Following these rehearsals,
however, he rather humorously admitted to me: "If something goes awry during these sessions I can always blame it
on the students; but if something should go wrong with the
Vienna Philharmonic, the fault will be mine."

An orchestral concert with the London Philharmonia featuring Domingo as conductor is available on CD and cassette.
It contains works by Tchaikovsky: the *1812* Overture, *Cappricio italien,* and the *Romeo and Juliet* Overture-Fantasy. Although these are not the only orchestral pieces Domingo has
recorded so far, they are the ones I have chosen as the basis
of the following discussion.

In the *1812* Overture and especially at the beginning, Domingo seems a bit coarse in the rhythmic shaping and overall
dynamics of the piece. In addition, there are passages where
he could have placed greater emphasis on the weaker wind
instruments (the flutes, for example). On the other hand, in
other passages the strings are too heavy and his interpretation
lacks something by way of tenderness or, toward the end, of
differentiation. That may be more the fault of the players
than of Domingo's conducting. In any case, for my taste Domingo plays the end a little too energetically and noisily,
though the whole overture of course tends toward this anyway. But there are other places as well where greater distinction between crescendo and decrescendo would have been
desirable or the separation of phrases as well as their transitions could have been given a more distinct shape. Nevertheless, Domingo brings more musical spirit into this piece than
many of the conductors on the pop concert scene.

The beginning of *Cappricio italien* is also a bit too direct and elementary for me, so that I miss a contrasting swelling of the musical phases. Domingo soon moves into more convincing phrasing and dynamics, although he then takes the following descending tonal phrases a bit too coarsely. On the whole, his differentiation in the transition phases leading up to the famous folkloric melodies is less than it could be, even though the effectively orchestrated folk motifs are very well phrased. The vivacious, dancelike tempi are also well done, although they could have profited from a slightly lighter touch.

Again the transition phases are not completely successful: they are frequently too ponderous or else do not quite reach their proper relation to the main phrases. The final third does indeed have the proper vitality and the proper distinctions in dynamics and orchestral voices, except that the actual end, which is difficult to differentiate musically, is once again a bit blunt, noisy and direct.

The beginning of *Romeo and Juliet* also strikes me as being a bit coarse, too direct and undifferentiated in its upward phrasings and dynamics, and not sufficiently foreboding. Despite the lack of certain subtleties in the phrasing, however, Domingo does get very close to the dramatic nature of the work. Unfortunately, at times he fails to attain the tenderness and elegiac tension the strings are supposed to express, and the horns could be given freer reign in those passages where they supply the grieving background for the love theme. What the singer Domingo would have expressed in the love scenes—a great, tender, elegiac legato and portamento—the conductor Domingo does not quite succeed in eliciting from certain groups of instruments, again primarily the strings. Instead, he tries to lend an emotional emphasis to the very passionate as well as to the elegiac passages. The listener picks this up immediately, so that the tenderness and tension I occasionally missed may be less the fault of Domingo than of the string players themselves.

On the whole, Domingo succeeds in communicating the dramatic, even hostile altercations with his syncopes more graphically than he does the moods of presentiment and transfiguration. The transfiguration toward the end is not ethereal enough. The hostile and contrastive drums that accompany the fading away of the love motif could have been a bit more pronounced. In Domingo's rendition, the drums die out sooner than the love motif. Yet, like everything else I have suggested here, that too is a matter of individual interpretation. In any case, Domingo captures the essence of the work and succeeds in realizing it musically better than I have heard on other professional recordings; one immediately perceives how emotionally involved he is in the work and that he conducts it with heart. There is no doubt that Domingo has taken his place among the important conductors of the contemporary orchestral repertoire.

When I asked those singers who had worked with him in a number of productions how they felt about working under Domingo as conductor, the overwhelming response was that they enjoyed singing under his direction and that he was easy to follow because he understood the singer's situation so well. Even so, he still has difficulty pulling the piece back together quickly enough when the orchestra and singers fall out of sync, and this can lead to momentary chaos.

Members of the orchestra were also unanimous and gave essentially the same response, adding that, should things ever fall apart—which sometimes happens—they were ready to do their best to patch things up again. Since everyone knew how much he values each individual musician, they were all willing to do whatever it would take to help him out.

Because professional musicians appreciate Domingo's talents as conductor as well as his basic humanity and musicianship, he can count on their support. This is a bit of good fortune not every conductor has managed to earn.

David Shostac, a renowned American flutist and member of the Los Angeles Chamber Orchestra, has worked in a number of opera productions under Domingo's direction. During a recent conversation with me, he reflected on Domingo as conductor:

> The music [when Domingo conducts] sounds as if he's singing it. He makes the orchestra sing. Apart from his technique, the music flows, and he knows how to get that across. You can understand him very well. As far as the individual groups of instruments are concerned, he is not the type to dissect a score; he conveys it as a whole, makes it live, and we know what we have to do. Moreover, he has improved a great deal. Years ago everything was still a bit hesitant, clumsy, and experimental. Back then he could also conduct better with his bare hands; he was still a bit awkward with the baton. But today he knows how to use it, too. He uses a lot of arm and hand movements, but that's his style, and that's the way he elicits a warm sound from the orchestra. He doesn't conduct, say, the way Fritz Reiner does, who communicates everything with a minimum of movement and only gives slight indications. Domingo, on the other hand, demonstrates everything. The music sounds very warm under his baton, and his very expressive gestures are surely partly responsible for this. In addition to indicating the beat, they actually express the nuances he wants. His arm and hand movements are very expressive. In the beginning his left and right were still work-

ing together, but he has since learned how to let them work more independently. He always has a vision in mind and knows exactly what he wants—the only problem is that he is sometimes too indulgent toward the singers and their ideas at the expense of the orchestra. That's just another aspect of his technique that still needs honing. . . .

He could be a bit stricter with the singers at times, but he wants them to feel comfortable. I think he constantly puts himself in their position. In any case, he knows how the music is supposed to sound and tries to make the best of it even if he sometimes does not know exactly how he should convey his intentions technically to the individual orchestral groups. But he does know how to elicit the emotions and the flow of the music, and we understand that. He has to leave a lot up to the orchestra itself for the technical performance, since he isn't perfect in this, but the music is there. And besides, he gets better from one year to the next—I wouldn't be surprised if he has been studying conducting somewhere—and we love working with him. The orchestra likes him, and that's why we do everything we can to help him. He conveys his ideas about the music to us and lets us know what he finds important; we gladly help him out with the technical details, because he still has a bit to learn. There's a friendly relation between him and the orchestra, and we always learn something from him because he knows how the music is supposed to sound. That's what is most important to us.

There is certainly room for improvement in the technical direction of specific sections of the orchestra. Yet in the end, that is a matter of Domingo's technique and not his musical conception. When he was conducting Tchaikovsky's Serenade for Strings a few years ago during a concert with the Los Angeles Chamber Orchestra, the strings "sang" with a beauty that remains unforgettable. It did not matter how much these musicians had to add themselves by way of technique—the concept was Domingo's, and they have never again played as "vocally" as they did then.

Musical warmth is Domingo's watchword in his role as conductor. There are times when you can actually see it, as on the video of the 1991 concert he conducted in the amphitheater in Merida, Spain. The passage in question was his accompaniment of Mstislav Rostropovich in the adagio from Haydn's Cello Concerto in C. Here, as previously in Verdi's overture to *La forza del destino*, even the visual effect of his conducting is one of warmth and harmony. He conducts subtly, uses fewer elementary tempo beats than he used to, and has learned how to use his left and right arms in a more sophisticated way. The only criticism I have is that his friendliness toward and need for a harmonious adaptation to the soloist sometimes makes him hold the orchestra back a bit too much during the Haydn movement. Once again Domingo's amiability dominates over his authority as conductor.

A TRAVELING
SALESMAN IN THE
SERVICE OF MUSIC

Plácido Domingo in Concert

For those who know nothing about it, one result of these concerts is that opera is no longer some dusty old relic salvaged from Grandpa's attic; and they have surely won over several thousand first-time visitors to the opera house.

OUR TIMES ARE NOT THE FIRST TO SEE GREAT OPERA singers give concerts before mass audiences and combine serious music with popular tunes. Remember Richard Tauber, who sang popular tunes and melodies from operettas before large audiences and in recording studios long before Domingo was even born. He was as much of a singing personality in Europe back then as are Pavarotti and Domingo in the whole world today. The novelty today is that electronic amplification and computer-controlled transmission can fill even Olympic stadiums with the voices of tenors, and in such a way that the sound emerging from the loudspeakers is in perfect sync with the original sound two or three hundred yards away. In certain gala concerts today Domingo or Pavarotti no longer sings before several thousand people, as Richard Tauber did in Berlin, London, or New York. Hundreds of thousands can now hear them "live"—and this does not include the television audience.

Naturally, what draws such a crowd are their innate charisma and enormous vocal projection. The singer must also

be ready to make whatever adjustments the dynamically enhanced sound system requires. With his uncompromising and
somewhat cerebral subtlety, Nicolai Gedda would never have
made it as a star of New York's Madison Square Garden or
Los Angeles' Dodger Stadium. Pavarotti and Domingo, on
the other hand, are quite at home in such spaces: Pavarotti
because of his high trumpetlike tones (others compare his
voice to a flute or an oboe) and Domingo because of the
bronze, velvety, and textured sensuality of his voice. José
Carreras is, too, although his greatness lies more in an exquisite, subtle, and lean *piano*.

There is no question about it: if you hear Domingo's arias
in an arena in front of so many thousands of listeners, they
sound less nuanced than when he sings them on stage or on
a regular concert recording. The vastness of the space and the
echo of the loudspeakers affect the quality of the voice. He
may sing with more energy, a bit "happier" and more movingly in such situations simply because the mood of the
masses can help inspire him. But his singing is not any better
from an artistic point of view. Take Vasco da Gama's famous
aria "O Paradis" from the 1990 production of *L'africaine* that
he sang in the ruins of the Roman Baths of Caracalla (the
"Three Tenors" concert) and compare it with a 1988 recording taped live at the Royal Opera, Covent Garden. In Rome
everything sounded rather uniform because it was sung with
a dynamically full voice; in London he could add considerably more variations to his vocal colors and alternate between
piano, *mezzo forte*, and *forte*. Or another example: take the
Lensky aria from the 1991 production of *Eugen Onegin* that
Domingo sang in the Roman amphitheater in Merida, Spain,
and compare it with the studio recording of the same from
1993. In Merida his phrasing was much more uniform than

on the studio recording, while the latter, in turn, is more lyrical and more subtle in its modulation of vocal colors and rhythms.

When all three matadors—Carreras, Domingo, and Pavarotti—sing together in Rome and Los Angeles, each performing a preassigned verse of a popular song, the whole affair takes on a circus atmosphere. The most famous of all these gala performances are the ones that took place in the Baths of Caracalla and in Dodger Stadium in Los Angeles. They attracted an enormous live audience, millions of television viewers could follow their every movement, and millions more can still see them on video—not a bad return if you want to do something for opera. For those who know nothing about it, one result of these concerts is that opera is no longer some dusty old relic salvaged from Grandpa's attic; and they have surely won over several thousand first-time visitors to the opera house.

Yet only singers who possess the vocal quality and the charismatic personality of a Pavarotti or a Domingo can lure such huge numbers of people into such concerts. Domingo can look back with pride on the fact that he sang to three hundred thousand people in Madrid, and that at a time when the Rolling Stones drew only a few thousand. For Domingo, these concerts also fulfill a charitable purpose. The proceeds from the ticket sales of an opera have to be used to cover the enormous expense of each production, with all its singers, costumes, and sets. The proceeds of star concerts, on the other hand, can easily be apportioned to charitable purposes. After the earthquake in Mexico City, Domingo donated the proceeds of several concerts to the victims of that particular disaster.

In most of the great star concerts available on video today,

Domingo shares the stage with other artists. In the Merida concert mentioned above, it was Mstislav Rostropovitch. Domingo also conducted the orchestra and played the piano at this event. That same year witnessed a star concert in the Gran Teatro de la Maestranza in Seville featuring Alfredo Kraus, José Carreras, Teresa Berganza, and Pilar Lorengar. During this concert Domingo sang the arias from *Macbeth* that he rarely performs any more (I know of only one recording), and the sixty-four-year-old Alfredo Kraus still managed to produce one clear and strong (if perhaps not always elegant) high C after the other, just the way he used to. I should also mention the 1992 concert in the great stadium in Seville, where Domingo sang the final scene of *Carmen* with Julia Migenes, but the rendition was not nearly as moving there as it was onstage or in the film version with Migenes singing the title role. He also sang the aria "E lucevan le stele" from *Tosca* with deep feeling and great refinement. Still, as is always the case with such mass productions, Domingo did not quite attain the subtlety of his studio recordings or his stage performances. But this is a small price to pay compared to the enormous service such concerts provide for the world of opera as a whole.

Popular Music:
From the Hit Parade to Schmaltz

Domingo sees himself as a traveling salesman in the service of music, particularly opera. That he also happens to earn a lot of money doing this is only one of its many rewards. But this money is often reinvested in support of either music or other humanitarian projects, as was the case with the benefit concerts for the victims of the Mexico City earthquake.

DOMINGO GOT INVOLVED WITH POPULAR MUSIC VERY early in his career. While still a teenager in Mexico City he accompanied his then singer-girlfriend Cristina in her night-club gigs or wrote arrangements of American hit tunes for the Mexican recording industry. But that was just the beginning. The years between have seen a whole series of recordings featuring Domingo singing hit parade tunes, movie songs, or musical numbers. He recorded the CD *Domingo Sings Tangos* in the evenings following his last three *Otello* performances in Buenos Aires. "I chose that method," he writes in his autobiography, "because my voice is less fatigued by continuing to sing immediately after a performance than by 'opening up' again two days later—and two days before the next performance" (AB, 172).

Plácido Domingo Sings Tangos was released in 1981 on the Deutsche Grammophon label. While listening to these tangos one is struck by how perfect a match this is, perhaps because Domingo's own Spanish-Mexican origins are so closely related to this musical genre. Tangos are also a kind of night music meant for relaxation and dancing, so that the recording schedule and the "decompression" following a difficult opera like *Otello* could only enhance the whole project. Domingo's sensuously bronze and burnished tones are especially conducive for dreaming deep into the wee hours of the morning.

One of the greatest successes of the record industry was the 1981 collection of songs *Perhaps Love*, featuring the hit singer and songwriter John Denver. On it, Domingo and Denver sing solos or duets of popular tunes, many of which are Denver's own. Melding both voices, however, proved to be a rather difficult task. In one corner was the highly trained opera singer, who tried to adapt the quality of his voice to the sound of lighter tunes, and in the other the not so accomplished but vocally characteristic pop tune singer, who had no reason to try to be anything other than what he was.

Following the Denver album came the 1983 concert with the comedian Carol Burnett, and there are other CDs with Domingo singing light music with other artists whose names are not so internationally known.

Save Your Nights for Me (1985), *Be My Love* (1989/90), *The Domingo Songbook* (1992), *Entre dos mundos* (1992)—these are the titles of other recordings featuring Domingo singing popular tunes. He tries to adjust his vocal coloration from one song to another or within the songs themselves to match the mood of the text and the music while simultaneously trying not to come across as too "operatic." Other opera singers, whether male or female, occasionally fall into the trap of singing a popular song or a number from a musical with the high dramatics of an Ortrud from *Lohengrin* or a Siegfried from *Die Götterdämmerung*. One of Domingo's endearing qualities is that he knows how to differentiate between popular music and Otello. Of course, his voice will always sound too trained and musically too perfect for many of the tunes and tearjerkers he sings. After a while his pop songs seem too sophisticated despite the acoustical variations he introduces, and this leads to a certain uniform perfectionism. Just think of the hit tunes we have heard so often from the tobacco-drenched voice of a Dean Martin or the gravelly voice of a Jimmy Durante, songs we identify with these voices. The vocal brilliance of a Plácido Domingo can not improve upon their renditions—intentional or not, his singing tends to unmask or expose these selections for what they are. Since these tunes have little to offer musically, their existence and popularity depend on the characteristic style of specific singers who have nothing more than their vocal personality to fall back upon. That is why I prefer to hear a Beatles song sung by the Beatles, a John Denver song sung by John Denver, and a Charles Aznavour song performed by Charles Aznavour. When Domingo sings Aznavour's "The boats have sailed" ("Les bateaux sont partis") and introduces too much expression and brilliance by means of his unique *messa di voce*, I miss the simpler, thinner, chansonlike voice of the Frenchman, which is the intrinsic characteristic of his own work.

It is a different matter with hit tunes with a folk flavor or songs that embrace a traditional operatic or operetta style and are not identified with one specific voice such as that of Perry Como or Edith Piaf. With these songs Domingo occasionally produces small masterpieces. On the other hand, both *Save Your Nights for Me* and *The Domingo Songbook* contain a number of selections so inconsequential and forgettable that, when Domingo sings them, they sound almost like an insult to his voice, and I long to return to Dean Martin holding his cocktail glass in one hand and a cigarette in the other. When Domingo sang the musically rather undistinguished "Beautiful Maria of My Soul" from the film *The Mambo Kings* during the 1993 Academy Awards presentation ceremony, it came across as top-heavy from a vocal as well as musical perspective. There are limits—including lower ones—that a great artist simply has to respect. In the end, the great Domingo is still Domingo; he is an inappropriate choice for such popular pap.

However, when Domingo sings "Somewhere, My Love" (Lara's theme from the film *Doctor Zhivago*) on the CD *Be My Love*, for example, and then "La Golondrina" or "Valencia," these songs can take on a totally new dimension through his interpretation and can even get under one's skin. On this recording, Domingo actually sings "O Sole Mio" more impressively, more delicately, and more movingly than Luciano Pavarotti, who continues to rank as the foremost interpreter of Neapolitan songs. It might have to do with the way Domingo moves between a purple tone to a golden texture and back again. Although these songs are and remain Pavarotti's domain, I find Domingo's rendition of "O Sole Mio" much more enjoyable.

If I am particularly fond of any one of Domingo's light entertainment CD's, it would have to be *Be My Love*, although I still prefer the zinc-like voice of a Mario Lanza, with its metallic, somewhat sandpapery quality, for the title song, as well as the German version of the Richard Tauber song "Love Be My Guiding Star" ("Du bist die Welt für mich") sung more subtly, warmly, and in the upper regions more leanly by Nicolai Gedda, who has the added advantage of exquisite German diction. With these exceptions, Domingo's interpretations of the other selections on this disc are very convincing. In part, this is because many of these songs and tunes have a Spanish or Mexican folk quality. If, while listening to Edith Piaf's "La vie en rose"—regardless of how well Domingo sings it—we still yearn for the French chanteuse's more expressive interpretation, there is no doubt that Domingo's rendition of the Spanish and Mexican songs remains unbeatable.

Domingo's autobiography reveals why he devotes so much time to popular music: "The success of my recordings of Latin American and North American popular music," he says, "has been gratifying to me for two reasons, the first selfish and the second much broader: on the one hand, I can sing for and be appreciated by people who do not enjoy opera; and on the other, through these nonoperatic recordings I am helping to stimulate interest in opera" (AB, 203). Domingo sees himself as a traveling salesman in the service of music, particularly opera. That he also happens to earn a lot of money doing this is only one of its many rewards. But this money is often reinvested in support of either music or other humanitarian projects, as was the case with the benefit concerts for the victims of the Mexico City earthquake. One of the most recent contributions in support of music was the establishment in 1994 of the international Plácido Domingo Competition for Singers, the "Operalia 94." It began with preliminary elimination rounds in many countries and continued in Vienna with the semifinals in May. The final rounds were held in Mexico City in September. This Operalia is meant to be an annual event, and Domingo intends to continue financing it.

Zarzuelas, Viennese Operettas, and American Musicals

The way Domingo uses his dynamics, his color modulations, and his radiantly open (or somewhat darkened when appropriate) tonal phrasings to convey the music of . . . well-known zarzuela composers . . . all adds up to a vocal feast.

What Domingo does so masterfully in opera—use his theatrical talent to enhance his vocal phrasings—is turned around here: in the end, his singing disengages from what is going on in the music simply because his voice is too big and too perfected.

I BEGAN THIS STUDY WITH A DETAILED EXAMINATION OF Domingo's relation to zarzuela, the specifically Spanish form of opera and operetta. One could say that Domingo quite literally absorbed zarzuela with his mother's milk; later he grew up among his parents' zarzuela troupe. It is thus not surprising that Domingo is the greatest interpreter of this art form today. There may be a few Spaniards who might wish to contradict this assertion, but for me, at any rate, there is no comparison, even though I have heard other singers, international opera stars as well as local folk singers, on recordings featuring zarzuela excerpts. Domingo is the best interpreter of this type of music.

Consider the prize-winning recording (taped live during a 1983 concert in Salzburg) as an example. Here Domingo teams up with his compatriot Pilar Lorengar and gives a thrilling rendition of zarzuela selections. The way Domingo uses his dynamics, his color modulations, and his radiantly open (or somewhat darkened when appropriate) tonal phrasings to convey the music of such well-known zarzuela composers as Moreno Torroba or Pablo Sorozabal all adds up to a vocal feast. Several other CDs featuring Domingo singing solo selections have been released in the meantime.

A live videotape of a 1991 gala concert in Madrid features several other singers and a ballet troupe in addition to Domingo singing excerpts from several zarzuelas. Domingo's rendition of Torroba's "Los vareadores" (from *Luisa Fernanda*), for instance, is particularly distinguished by his dance-like vocal leaps, his soft staccato, and his transitions between *piano, mezzo forte,* and *forte.* Particularly striking in Soutullo and Vert's "Bella enamorada" (from *El ultimo romantico*) are the rather dramatic, radiant, artistically shaped phrases at the beginning of the stanzas and the following subtlety in the dynamic between *piano* and *forte.* And in Sorozabal's "No puede ser" (from *La tabernera del puerto*) Domingo occasionally employs melancholic and sentimental, rather broadly based tonal phrases that rise to the level of the dramatic and elegaic, especially toward the end of the aria.

The unmistakably Spanish sound defies description—it has to be experienced to be enjoyed. Or is the Spanish sound the artistic creation of Plácido Domingo himself?

If we listen to Chueca's prelude to *El bateo* or his "La gran via" from *Schottisch del Eliseo* on this video, we soon discover an undeniable similarity between certain aspects of this music and the Viennese light entertainment of the Johann Strauss era. Some zarzuelas are musically not far removed from the Viennese operetta or from other works of the Lanner-Suppé-Strauss period. It is no wonder, then, that Domingo owns four apartments in the Vienna he loves so much; not only does he sing and conduct for the Vienna State Opera, but he has also recorded songs from famous operettas. His familiarity with Viennese operetta dates back to his days in Mexico City, when he performed in Lehár's *Merry Widow* and *Der Graf von Luxemburg*. What follows refers to the 1991 CD recording of *Wien, du Stadt meiner Träume*, which features selections going back to 1985.

Domingo's main problem with the Viennese operetta has to do with the language. His failure to pronounce *ch* properly is only one problem among others, albeit a very disturbing one. His difficulties with the language and its pronunciation are less conspicuous when he sings works from the golden age of operetta (Strauss, Zeller, and Millöcker), where the phrasing is closer to that of opera itself, than when he sings works from the silver age (Lehár, Kálmán, Fall, and Oscar Straus). Here, as later in the Broadway musical, language determines the vocal phrasing to a considerably greater extent, which is to say, the rhythmic diction and articulation of spoken language dominates the work to a far greater degree.

This can be seen most clearly in Leo Fall's song "Ihr stillen, süßen Frau'n" (from *Die Rose von Stambul*). On this cut, Domingo reduces the rapid syllables into a mishmash of consonants and vowels, a vocal salad that strongly detracts from his otherwise good musical phrasing. The situation is similar, if perhaps not quite as marked, in his rendition of Fall's "O frag mich nicht" (from *Der fidele Bauer*). The tempi of the stanzas are too quick, Domingo has pronunciation problems, and the phrasing is compromised. Only during the refrain, with its slower phrases, is Domingo able to recover and sing with full voice. He is best in Lehár's "Dein ist mein ganzes Herz" (from *Das Land des Lächelns*), because this piece contains longer tonal phrases as it is, which are already a better match for Domingo's peculiar swell tones.

In sum, then, one can say that when Fritz Wunderlich and Nicolai Gedda sing these arias their articulation is clearer, and they neither slide over nor overly emphasize the consonants. That allows them (especially Wunderlich) to center the notes more firmly on the vowels. On the other hand, Domingo very rarely sings an inappropriate portamento and rarely extends the phrases longer than we have come to expect from professional operetta singers. The only times I have noticed the latter is in the second stanza of Oscar Straus's "Leise, ganz leise" (from *Ein Walzertraum*), for example, and then again in Emmerich Kálmán's "Komm Zigany" (from *Gräfin Mariza*) or in the second stanza of his "Grüß mir mein Wien" (also from *Gräfin Mariza*), where this artistic trick was expressly intended to form a contrast to the first stanza and does not appear to be simply mannered or affected, as in the other examples. When Wunderlich sings Viennese operettas, he strokes the listener's soul, and when Gedda sings Lehár's "Da geh' ich zu Maxim" from *The Merry Widow* (to whose style Domingo comes very close here), his rendition is brilliant and erotically thrilling.

When Domingo sings Viennese operetta, on the other hand, one can wax enthusiastic only about his voice. His expression lacks a great deal, although it is possible to enjoy several arias, such as Strauss's "Komm in die Gondel" (from *Eine Nacht in Venedig*), Lehár's "Dein ist mein ganzes Herz" and "Gern hab' ich die Frau'n geküßt" (the latter from *Paganini*), Kálmán's "Komm Zigany" and "Grüß mir mein

Wien," or Straus's "Leise, ganz leise," despite the deficiencies—mostly linguistic—mentioned above. The brilliance of Domingo's voice can still be heard here, and very frequently his artistic phrasing, which never fails to fascinate me, is right on the mark as well.

Surprisingly enough, it is easier to accept Domingo's pronunciation when he sings the musically difficult Florestan aria from Beethoven's *Fidelio* on the video *Hommage à Sevilla* than it is when he sings the simpler arias of an operetta. I have already mentioned this in the section on text and music. Here, too, one cannot understand everything in Florestan's aria, especially when it comes to the quicker tempi toward the end; Domingo has his characteristic problems with the *ch* sound (especially in the word *nichts*), and he slurs the consonants a bit too much. Despite all this, though, his pronunciation here does not get in the way of his musical phrasing. Domingo's German is actually quite easy to understand in the slower passages, and in those parts where he is not so easy to understand, the articulation is not quite so important anyway. Unclear diction or a foreign accent take a more serious toll in operettas.

Having recorded zarzuelas, songs from Viennese operettas, and American hit tunes, it goes without saying that Domingo could not very easily avoid that other form of light entertainment, the Broadway musical. We know that he had already sung the role of a drunkard in a production of Lerner and Loewe's *My Fair Lady* back in his Mexico City days. Since his New York apartment is not far from Broadway, one of his successful musical recordings is a 1991 CD called *The Broadway I Love*. It contains predominantly poorly arranged selections from musicals by George Gershwin, Cole Porter,

Rodgers and Hammerstein, Andrew Lloyd Webber, and Stephen Sondheim, among others.

Americans who have grown up with musicals have told me that Domingo frequently fails to produce the proper phrasing in these numbers, and they blame it on his language problems again, this time on his accent. After all, pronunciation is even more important in a musical than in an operetta. It certainly *sounds* beautiful when he sings selections from musicals, and he tries his best to give it the proper spirit, but his voice simply lacks the characteristic features. What seems to be missing is that special simplicity of timbre as well as those specific linguistic skills demanded by the genre which we have come to expect from singers in this field, singers who frequently come from the theater or film world. Domingo's voice is simply too big and too trained. He certainly understands better than other "heavy" opera singers how to adjust his singing to the genre even though he still cannot "come down" from his radiant, seamless singing and his particular vocal techniques to the sound characteristic of a musical. But Kiri Te Kanawa and José Carreras, who have sung in Leonard Bernstein's *West Side Story*, cannot make the transition from opera to musical fully, either.

On the whole, one could probably say that Domingo's voice is a better match for a musical score that is closer to operetta or even opera and that contains longer phrases rather like those in the refrain-like sections of "Oh, What a Beautiful Morning" (from *Oklahoma!*) or the extended phrases in "So in Love" (from *Kiss Me Kate*) and "Tonight" (from *West Side Story*). On the other hand, one has to admit that Domingo does not quite catch the character of the musical as well when he has to switch over into spoken dialogue or has to lend a dancelike rhythmic element to the language and the music (with the exception of his rendition of "Over There" from *George M!*, which is spectacular, even in terms of his vocal coloring). He doesn't feel his way into the language or the spoken phrases very well, and the listener is left with the impression that he conveys the sound of his voice more than the content of the text.

In his attempts to reproduce the characteristic Broadway sound moreover, he repeatedly holds back the sonority as well as the strength of his voice, so that his expression also suffers. In contrast, less perfect singers with less vocal resonance, poorer projection, and less broadly radiant tones (who usually sing these numbers) are compelled to deploy all their strength, including a fuller range of expression. As in his singing of Hollywood melodies, Domingo too often draws his voice like a golden, highly textured ribbon across the language and its musical phrases; it thus acquires its own identity in regard to the diction, the music, and the atmosphere of the scene in question. What Domingo does so masterfully in opera—use his theatrical talent to enhance his vocal phrasings—is turned around here: in the end, his singing disengages from what is going on in the music simply because his voice is too big and too perfected.

Folk Music

In his timbre, dynamics, and other aspects of phrasing,
Domingo never loses the folkloric essence, even in
those songs he routinely sings. On the one hand, he
produces tones more openly than he would normally
and consistently do in an opera. . . . On the other
hand, and appropriately so, he employs less dramatic
and lyrically refined phrasings and modulations . . .
than he does when portraying Canio or Otello.

Ever since the beginning of his career, Domingo
has strongly supported Spanish and Mexican folk music, and
this interest has only increased over the past few years. What
I fail to understand in this connection—and it goes back to
the theoreticians of the romantic school—is why only those
works are considered folk music that have been handed down
anonymously and that allegedly emerged straight from the
heart of the people. For me, every folk song of unknown
origin had its individual author at some time or other, regardless of how many generations sang it and passed it on down
the line. This is why I include under the rubric folk music
many works whose composers are known, as is the case with
most of the Neapolitan songs Pavarotti sings. I even consider
folk music those Spanish and Mexican songs, including several selections on Domingo's CD *Entre dos mundos*, that were
arranged with America's Hollywood taste in mind, as little

pleasure as I get out of such arrangements. As long as the melody and the rhythm of these songs maintain their folk character and can be recognized as such, I count them part of Domingo's repertoire of recorded folk music.

Domingo devotes a significant portion of his autobiography to explaining why he sings Spanish and Latin American folk songs. One of the main incentives is the presence of millions of Spanish-speaking people in the United States. He wants to help them remember and keep their cultural heritage alive. Fifteen years ago this was a more serious concern, but today the situation has changed. Today, culture bearers of the Hispanic tradition and heritage have carved out their own successful niche in the United States and have established themselves in it. Some of the credit for this success story is due to the efforts of Plácido Domingo.

As mentioned above, Domingo has recorded arrangements of Mexican folk songs on such CDs as *Be My Love* and *Entre dos mundos*. Also available on disc are recordings—*Adoro*, for instance—that feature popular Spanish folk songs, and some that combine folk songs and folk melodies with opera arias. There is even a cassette featuring Domingo with the Vienna Boys Choir. The CD *Canta para Mexico* pairs opera arias by Verdi, Bizet, Meyerbeer, and Donizetti with a selection of Mexican songs, and the double CD *Arias, Songs, and Tangos* on the Deutsche Grammophon label offers a combination of opera arias with selections from operettas, Hollywood hits, and Spanish and Latin American folk songs and tangos. Another disc on the Deutsche Grammophon label is called *Favorite Arias, Songs, and Tangos*. Less deserving of mention in my opinion is the 1993 CD *Christmas in Vienna*, with Domingo singing arrangements of well-known Christmas carols and songs along with José Carreras, Diana Ross, and the

Gumpoldskirchner Children's Choir. Apart from the fact that the vocal trio of Ross, Domingo, and Carreras just does not work, these recordings leave much to be desired in the area of technical reproduction as well. Domingo's voice is overwhelming, unfortunately even vis-á-vis Carreras, who sounds rather lackluster and brittle in the duet with Domingo.

On this, as on his other recordings of popular music, Domingo makes a point of singing one song by a young and talented composer by the name of Plácido Domingo Jr.

Folk music is also a component in his videos. Available, for example, are two volumes of the videotaped *Songs of Mexico*, replete with costumes and the usual colorful backdrop of Mexican life. In what follows I allude to volume 2 of this set because it is the most recent and thus the easiest to find, having been taped in 1990. Some songs sound a bit routine while others are more subtle; Domingo also occasionally stresses the undeniably inherent melodramatic element in several of these songs a bit too much. But in his timbre, dynamics, and other aspects of phrasing, Domingo never loses the folkloric essence, even in those songs he routinely sings. On the one hand, he produces tones more openly here than he would normally and consistently do in an opera. (And if some of the openness of these notes is the result of electronic manipulation, it was done in the proper spirit and does not detract from the whole.) On the other hand, and appropriately so, he employs less dramatic and lyrically refined phrasings and modulations of timbre or crescendo and diminuendo than he does when portraying Canio or Otello. Instead, the listener gets the impression that he finally feels comfortable enough to abandon himself to the long tones and phrases so typical of the relatively uncomplicated nature of folk music. Also impressive is the way he includes his personal support for the work of the Mexican composer Roberto Cantoral. This emerges from a conversation, also part of the video, that was taped in San Francisco to introduce this relatively unknown composer to the rest of the world.

It is not unusual for Domingo to lend his support to lesser known composers or their works. This was one of the motivating factors, for instance, behind his 1984 recording of *Always in My Heart: The Songs of Ernesto Lacuona* or again in 1989 with his recording of *The Unknown Puccini*, featuring unfamiliar songs and arias by this master.

Plácido Domingo on Video

Another videotape, Plácido Domingo: Hommage
à Sevilla, has been mentioned a number of times now,
and it really is a gem. It contains some of the most
beautiful shots of this exquisite city, which the viewer
enjoys in the company of a very charming tour guide.
Plácido Domingo leads us from one place to another
and sometimes to a few pretty girls, as well. . . . This
video shows both Ponelle and Domingo in their
personal warmth and charm and documents their
artistic versatility.

THERE ARE VIDEOTAPES MADE FOR AND WITH PLÁCIDO
Domingo that focus on operatic performances, gala concerts,
or folk music. For example, Domingo appears in the role of
narrator for the 1983 video portrait *Mario Lanza: The American Caruso.* While watching it, the viewer gets the impression
that Domingo here is putting his name more than his knowledge at the disposal of the moviemakers. On the other hand,
in a 1993 interview at the Met he—as well as Pavarotti—
named Mario Lanza as one of his role models. One reason
for his admiration is that Mario Lanza—like Domingo and
Pavarotti—did his share to attract millions of nonoperagoers
to this type of music through films and concerts.

On one very interesting video, called *Plácido: A Year in the
Life of Plácido Domingo* (1984), we see short takes of Domingo

recording *Lohengrin*, preparing himself to conduct *Fledermaus*, visiting his beloved Madrid, singing a duet with Charles Aznavour, rehearsing a television show with Carol Burnett that included a lot of dancing and fooling around, and attending a gala reception for film stars in Los Angeles. He also travels from one opera house to another, making us privy to his thoughts about Otello or the erotic fantasies of men and women. We also see him in excerpts from operas; his rendition of Otello's lament from the third act impressed me more here than in the Zeffirelli film discussed earlier. The aria is vocally more refined and more affecting on this video than in the film. The video also documents Domingo's radiant performance in a concert in spite of the nagging cold he was suffering at the time, and it eavesdrops on the advice he gave to young students in a master class. After warning them "not to jump into the phrases," he goes on to show them how to construct a legato by linking the vowels (portamento) without neglecting the consonants (this was part of an Italian clip) as well as how to alter the intonation of normal speech while singing successive repetitions of textual phrases. We also hear his description of how one's voice is affected by what goes on in one's head. As the reader has probably discerned by now, this video is episodic, but it conveys interesting insights into aspects of Domingo's life in 1983 and 1984.

Another videotape, *Plácido Domingo: Hommage à Sevilla*, has been mentioned a number of times now, and it really is a gem. It contains some of the most beautiful shots of this exquisite city, which the viewer enjoys in the company of a very charming tour guide. Plácido Domingo leads us from one place to another and sometimes to a few pretty girls as well. The high points, though, are some of the scenes designed by Jean-Pierre Ponelle for several operas that take place in Seville: *Don Giovanni* with Domingo in the title role and as Leporello (the latter only mimed), *The Barber of Seville* with Domingo as Figaro and Almaviva in a duet with himself, *Carmen* with Domingo as Don José, *La forza del destino* with Domingo as Alvaro, *Fidelio* with Domingo as Florestan against the background of Goya's famous etchings "Désastres de la guerre," and *El gato montés* with Domingo as Rafael Ruiz. Unfortunately, there is no clip from *The Marriage of Figaro*, an opera that also takes place in the vicinity of Seville.

This video shows both Ponelle and Domingo in their personal warmth and charm and documents their artistic versatility.

General Popularity

The number of people who know and admire Plácido Domingo can no longer be measured in the millions—it is no exaggeration to say that it goes into the billions today.

And should he decide to ease up on his schedule a bit—he has already started taking the odd day off now and again and allowing himself a holiday here and there—he can stay in his exquisitely appointed New York apartment and be inspired to practice new works of music not yet studied.

DOMINGO IS AT THE HEIGHT OF HIS POPULARITY RIGHT now. This is not something he likes to hear, of course, for he believes that an artist on top has nowhere left to go but down. The number of people who know and admire him can no longer be measured in the millions—it is no exaggeration to say that it goes into the billions today. He knows this, but it has not affected his amiable and respectful attitude toward every person he meets. One might wonder, though, what is really on his mind. Does he fear the day he will no longer walk out on the world's great opera stages and renowned concert halls as the celebrated tenor? He will never be as idolized as a conductor as he is today as *tenorissimo*, even if he were to become the greatest conductor of all time. Even the greatest baritone or bass is not as celebrated as a great tenor. The higher and more radiant the tones a man can produce, the more erotic the relation between the singer and his public. It is a phenomenon that has yet to be explained. Add to it the corresponding charisma that Domingo, Pavarotti, and Carreras obviously possess, and concerts like theirs can lead to something close to mass hysteria.

Of these three, Pavarotti is the one usually showered with the greatest ovations in such concerts. But that is probably because he can blare out his high C's more directly than Domingo, who has to build up to them. Apart from this, though, Domingo is no less popular than Pavarotti: perhaps even more so because of his greater versatility. After all, at the writing of this book Domingo had already released close to one hundred LPs, cassettes, and CD recordings offering selections or full performances of fifty-seven different operas. If we tally up all the individual recordings of arias, songs, popular music, and so on, that Domingo has made, the total comes to more than eight hundred titles.

But what is behind this enormous versatility and output? Is Domingo driven and pursued by some invisible inner demon? Has this demon enslaved him to his desire to do and achieve as much as possible? No one knows. What we do know, though, is that ten years ago he was already toying with the idea of at least cutting down his busy schedule, if not ending his singing career altogether, by the time today had finally rolled around. The possibility of an imminent end to his career has always been on his mind, and it continues to occupy his thoughts today. He spoke about this to the UCLA students, and he also spoke to me about it. "I have a fanatic love for my career," he told me. "That's why I'm constantly searching and watching myself, and believe me, I will be the first to say good-bye at the right time. . . . I think there is a big respect, first of all to yourself and then to the public. It is always better if they say, "Why is he gone, he could still sing," rather than, 'Oh my God, he is still singing. When is he retiring?' "

Things have not come that far, not by any means. If anything, his voice has become broader, more radiant, and even more flexible in the years after the dire predictions of his critics following his performances of Otello and Lohengrin and even after his Siegmund. He may have lost a certain leanness of sound since that time, but nothing else, and thus he will probably continue to sing even after his planned performance of Tristan.

However, should his voice lose a little of its strength and vitality to the point that he can no longer expect to fill the great opera houses and concert halls with the music of Verdi and Puccini, he can always fall back on an old dream of his, which is to concentrate, finally, on the subtle lied. A previous chapter has already quoted him as saying that this genre demands a lot as far as expression is concerned, but does not require that much vocal energy. Another attractive option is that he will finally be able to sing the Evangelist in Bach's *Saint Matthew Passion* while simultaneously conducting this monumental work.

Thus, as always when reflecting on his past in his autobiography, Domingo recognizes the positive side of calculations that went wrong or other setbacks he may have experienced, and there is no reason to believe he will not continue to seek out the positive side of things in the future. In the last analysis, Plácido Domingo is much more than merely a great singer and a great musician: he is also a highly intelligent man who knows himself very well. This self-knowledge helps him recognize where certain weaknesses lie and when they might emerge. The question is only, does he let himself be driven and hounded onward against his better judgment? In 1986 he told Helena Matheopoulos:

> All of us have both God and devil, both good and bad, in us. But you have to negotiate with this devil, find out which way he is trying to lead you and decide on which occasions you may agree to go along with him, to some extent. For in many cases you make a sort of pact with this devil within you, because you see some things in him which you may like or feel you can use creatively, while certain other traits may be too much and lead to chaos. . . . The secret is to find the very delicate dividing line between the creative and the destructive side of the devil's influence. (*Divo*, 70–71).

I for one do not believe the "destructive side" of the "devil's influence" will ever gain the upper hand with Plácido Domingo. And since the constructive side will win out in the end, he is not likely to overextend himself, either. In the years to come, we can expect to hear quite a bit from and about Plácido Domingo. And as always, he will still be the one to determine the quality of his work; from what we know of him, it will continue to be very high.

And should he decide to ease up on his schedule a bit—he has already started taking the odd day off now and again and allowing himself a holiday here and there—he can stay in his exquisitely appointed New York apartment and be inspired to practice new works of music not yet studied. His apartment, with its adjoining office, is papered in warm, reddish tones (the living quarters in a reddish orange, the office in burgundy), and the furniture, accoutrements, and paintings work together to produce an aesthetic—in the most positive sense of the word, plush—combination that cannot fail to delight the eye. One gets the impression that the color, warmth, and richness of Domingo's voice are nourished and strengthened in this environment, which was designed for the most part by his wife, Marta.

Between 1994, when the book *PLÁCIDO DOMINGO* first appeared in Germany, and today, Domingo has not curtailed but rather expanded his unusually diversified career. In addition to all his other worldwide obligations, he has since become the artistic director of the Washington Opera and has extended his function as artistic consultant for the Los Angeles Music Center Opera to include the duties of artistic advisor and principal guest conductor. He has reduced his vocal obligations in Los Angeles, however, to the singing of only one role per season, and his appearances as principal guest conductor have turned out to be fewer than might have been expected. During the 1996–97 season he directed only four performances of *Norma* and is scheduled to conduct no operas whatsoever in the upcoming 1997–98 season. On the other hand, his loyalty to the Los Angeles Opera remains unchanged. He still sings the featured role in each season's opening production: in August 1995 it was Stiffelio in the opera of the same name, in 1996 Canio in *I pagliacci*, and in August 1997 it will be the role of Loris in Giordano's *Fedora*. He is also scheduled to inaugurate the 1996–97 season of the Washington Opera by singing the starring role in Antonio Carlos Gomes's *Il guarany*.

A new trend is becoming increasingly characteristic of Domingo's operatic career: he now turns more often toward singing either shorter operas (*I pagliacci*) or those more conventional and less strenuous roles (such as Loris in *Fedora*, for instance), as a way to "recuperate." These excursions into shorter or less demanding roles are then balanced out by his singing of longer and more difficult parts by Wagner and

Verdi in other productions. At the same time his interest in Wagnerian roles has grown considerably. He sang the role of Lohengrin onstage a number of years ago to great critical acclaim, and although his renditions of Tannhäuser and Walter von Stolzing are as yet only available on his complete recordings of *Tannhäuser* and *Die Meistersinger,* he continues to sing Siegmund in *Die Walküre* as well as the role of Parsifal. Moreover, he not only intends to make a CD recording of *Tristan*, a role he had wanted to sing in the Vienna State Opera in 1996, but also still plans to perform it someday onstage as well. The dangerous weight and length of the music were not the only aspects that deterred Domingo from performing these roles in the past. The text itself presented and remained a problem, even when it could be projected onto the stage floor as was done in the Vienna production of *Lohengrin*. As far as Verdi's music is concerned, Domingo continues to sing Otello, the role of his life, and since 1993 has also taken on the demanding role of Stiffelio.

But what can be said about the vocal quality of Domingo's singing today? Does it betray Domingo's age and his multifaceted obligations? The answer is yes and no. There is no doubt that Domingo's voice has lost the leanness of the early days. Yet this development was already noticeable fifteen years ago. By way of compensation, Domingo's voice has been growing in fullness, breadth, and color ever since. I have discussed this positive phenomenon in great detail in the book. Furthermore, Domingo today tends to avoid the more lyrical roles of Alfredo (*La traviata*) or the youthfully heroic parts of Rudolfo (*La bohème*). He continues to do so today, not only because, at fifty-five, he appears somewhat too old for a young lover, but also because he knows his voice has acquired a greater dramatic fullness and has expanded the breadth of its sound spectrum. Both characteristics would fall out of the expected frame for such roles. On the other hand, Domingo is still expanding his repertoire, even today, by including new roles that extend all the way to Benjamin Britten.

It's truly remarkable that Domingo, who had already feared the approaching end of his singing career twelve years ago, is still convincingly singing the roles, for instance, of Otello, Canio, and Alvaro (*La forza del destino*). Of course, occasionally he does have to take some time off. When he sang Otello in Los Angeles in the spring of 1995, there were certain unmistakable signs of fatigue and a slight break in his voice, not to mention a brief resort to the routine in the love duet. When his private jet then flew him to Spain immediately after the last performance to sing Stiffelio in that country, it was evident that both body and voice had been overtaxed. He was forced to cancel the last performances of the engagement. After several weeks of rest and recuperation he sang a very impressive Parsifal in Bayreuth, an accomplished Stiffelio in Los Angeles, and one of his best Otellos ever in New York. Neither breaks nor signs of fatigue were evident in his voice, and the tonal spectrum was full of radiance and beauty, especially in the difficult Stiffelio role, even if in two performances it no longer displayed the glorious evenness in certain tones within his otherwise so artistically subtle vibrato. I have described this *messa di voce* so specifically characteristic of Plácido Domingo in the chapter "World Fame."

Domingo's voice has retained its full radiance and beauty to this day, a fact amply demonstrated by his renditions of Siegmund and Canio, for example. Yet with regard to the latter, during the performance I attended in Los Angeles, his unique vibrato was not able to vary its sound quite so flexibly and expressively as before; and in several transitional phrases one could hear slight dynamic weaknesses. The latter was also evident in his most recent portrayal of Alvaro at the Met, especially during Alvaro's great aria. And while Domingo's Siegmund (which I followed closely in Vienna) radiated with all the qualities of bel canto in the higher positions, his voice had lost something of the evenness of its acoustical columns in the transitions to the deeper passages.

Even today, and in most of the roles Domingo sings, these columns still display their former harmonic transition from one color spectrum to another, and they still range, without any interruption in register, from the deep notes to the high ones. He uses these columns, now as before, to construct the artistic bridges and capitals he needs to produce his higher notes. In his rendition of Siegmund, however, Domingo's columns were not as consummately uniform in the transitions to the deep tones as his previous performances have accustomed us to expect. Particularly unexpected is the fact that Domingo, who originally began as a baritone, continues to shine in the higher notes of his fascinating bel canto interpretation of Siegmund, even though he no longer possesses quite the radiance and his usual poise in the deeper positions.

The reason for this may, in fact, lie in the role itself, for Domingo's rendition of Otello at the Met last fall did not betray any of these problems at all. On the contrary! Moreover, he enhanced his dramatic portrayal of Otello with new theatrical nuances: this is an older Otello; hence within this man of maturity and statesmanlike stature the feelings of mistrust, jealousy, degradation, and aggression grow out of the depths of his personality. His maturity makes these emotions all the more tragic and fatalistic. Domingo knows how to employ the expressive qualities of his voice to convey this maturity, this stature, this grief, pain, and aggression with an intensity that continues to mark him as the greatest Otello of our times.

Close-ups of Domingo like those in this year's gala concerts featuring the "Three Tenors" give the impression he is straining. This appearance is deceptive. In spite of the physical problems Domingo might conceivably have to deal with at his age, his voice continues to peal out effortlessly. Were this not the case, clear and distinct breaks would be increasingly noticeable. However, it is fair to say that, in a concert held in an enormous arena before an audience of one hundred thousand people, even the musically consummate artist Plácido Domingo is tempted to pay more attention to the strength than to the subtlety of his singing, despite the presence of a microphone.

Musicality, however, remains one of Domingo's most highly perfected and dominant traits. This musical perfection goes so far that in one production of the past year, during which the singing of his female partner repeatedly tended to be flat, Domingo deliberately (or unconsciously) slightly, but only very slightly, transposed his voice into a higher pitch and brighter overtones in order to raise his partner's pitch and timbre.

Musicality is also the primary characteristic of Domingo's conducting. When he conducted a Verdi concert in Los Angeles last year with Carol Vaness and Vladimir Chernov, one was still aware of his occasional dependency on an elementary emphasis on the beat, though his performance was considerably more fluid than ten years ago. Nevertheless, he conveyed a warmth and an empathy with the orchestra and the singers that are sadly missing in the work of many other,

purely professional conductors. Under Domingo's direction
the orchestra played both overtures in such a way that, from
the sound, if perhaps not always the technical precision, it
could not have been better.

And when Domingo conducted *Norma* this year in Los
Angeles, many technical aspects still appeared less sovereign
than under the baton of a professional routine conductor, and
yet he led the orchestra into a bel canto sound that one would
not have expected from musicians who were unfamiliar with
the works of Bellini. Although Domingo did not always succeed when trying to unite the bel canto sound with a dramatic impulse, in precisely shaping the transitions between
musical phrases or clearly distinguishing the phrases one from
another, the warmth and the dramatic orchestral performance
he did achieve, as well as his empathetic support of the singers, outweighed all these deficiencies. Even in the few orchestral rehearsals that were allotted to Domingo, he
managed within a very few minutes each time to bring the
orchestra into harmony with both the bel canto sound and
the spatial acoustics of the Dorothy Chandler Pavilion. He
frequently also sang along with the individual orchestral
voices during these rehearsals.

The man Domingo has remained full of humor, even-tempered, and friendly toward other people, despite his new and
additional obligations. Very rarely is he ever even somewhat
impatient, even during rehearsals, and he still enjoys a good
joke among friends and acquaintances.

A source of great joy in Domingo's life is the fact that his
son Plácido Jr., a talented composer who lives in Los Angeles,
has presented him with another grandchild. For Domingo
and his wife, Marta, family life remains a deep and central
focus.

Domingo also continues to follow his wife's career as stage director with great interest. Her accomplishments include the 1991 production of *Samson et Dalila* in Puerto Rico, the 1992 production of *Tosca* in Seville, the 1993 production of *Rigoletto* in Los Angeles, the 1994 production of *Il barbiere di Siviglia* in Puerto Rico, and the 1995 production of *La rondine* in Bonn. 1997 will witness her *La traviata* in Washington. Domingo himself occasionally works with her as singer or conductor in one of these or another production during the same time period to demonstrate his commitment to family ties. He has never forgotten that, decades ago, it was his wife who gave up her own singing career to support him both professionally and domestically and that she remains to this day his most critical while at the same time his most understanding advisor.

Los Angeles, September 1996

The FOLLOWING DEFINITIONS OF CERTAIN MUSICAL AND technical terms having to do with singing are based on the specific way in which they are used in the text. The sources consulted include the standard works on the different schools of singing technique. Since even the standard references contradict each other in certain respects, however, it seemed advisable to append my own brief glossary here.

Bel canto: A type of singing historically associated with Italian opera from the seventeenth century to Bellini, Donizetti, and Rossini. The term originally referred to the art of the castrati. Guidelines for bel canto singing still exist today and should be studied primarily by those singers with a particular inclination toward declamatory singing. This type of singing is dominated by the musical line built on vowels. Particular techniques are the art of swelling and then diminishing the tones (*messa di voce*), producing a clear and cleanly executed portamento, and making an uninterrupted transition in the passaggio region from one register to another.

Falsetto: In this book, the word *falsetto* denotes the controlled, well-supported vibration of the edges of the vocal cords in the head register accompanied by a slight opening of the glottis. This tone sounds soft, tender, and high because it is produced without any admixture of the chest voice. Musically, falsetto belongs to the realm of *mezza voce*. In this definition, falsetto is a technical term referring to how a tone is produced and not to the acoustical frequency of the tone so produced. I also make a distinction between falsetto and the falsetto-like sound of a whistling voice, which is not discussed in this book at all. I also avoid using the term in the sense of something "false," which the linguistic root of the term implies. Nor do I use the term to refer to a type of middle register or *voix mixte*, as Manuel Garcia tended to do.

Legato: A series of tones bound together, which sound like a musical line carried on one stream of breath and are usually sung without interruption. Tones or syllables are not separated by staccato, exaggerated articulation of consonants, or excessively marked glottal stops, even though distinct consonants, the clear separation of syllables, and a good pronunciation of vowels are still mandatory.

Messa di voce: Originating in the bel canto school of singing, this term refers to the dynamic swelling and diminishing (crescendo and diminuendo) of a tone without producing a wobbling sound. In general terms it also refers to the proper placing or positioning of a tone. Part of the secret of Domingo's voice is that he enhances, or "feeds," his tones with artistic, subtle, and shaping vibrations. This results in his unique style of *messa di voce.* And since his tones are usually concentrated on the subtle crescendo (except in those passages where the music demands something else), one can also speak of a "semi" *messa di voce* in Domingo's case.

Mezza voce: Literally, to sing with half a voice, which is to say, lightly and tenderly while still maintaining good support. Also associated with falsetto in this book; thus it is not only a light tone, a full-voiced *piano,* but also the sound of a "half" voice that is produced by not completely vibrating the vocal chords.

Overtones and formants: These terms are defined in detail in the first chapter.

Passaggio: The transition between the chest voice to the head voice or between the chest register to the head register (see definitions of vocal register below). For tenors, the passaggio lies somewhere in the region of d^1 and g^1, usually at e^1 and f^1, depending on the makeup of the individual singer. One of the most important challenges posed by the art of singing is to navigate this transition between the registers as smoothly and as inaudibly as possible. In the bel canto schools, the *messa di voce* is strongly concentrated in the passaggio region.

Portamento: The formation of a legato whereby in one single phrase the tones are so melded together from one vowel to another or from one syllable to another as to give the impression that each successive pitch simply glides out of the level of the previous vowel.

Portato: Tonal steps or musical phrases sung between legato and staccato. It is sometimes called the "half staccato." The consonants in a syllable and the glottal stops before an initial vowel in German are more audible than in a portamento-legato, but they still have to be relatively soft and articulated as one flowing unit. The same holds true for the separation and non-separation or the legato and non-legato of individual steps and syllables. Portato is the art of being clearly in the middle.

Support: Explained in detail in the first chapter.

Swell tones: The dynamic swelling or diminishing of tones, as explained in the definition of *messa di voce* (q.v.). Domingo's artistic enhancement of swell tones through a subtle and expressive vibrato is discussed in detail in the first chapter.

Vocal register: In general, there are two registers: the chest and the head. Sometimes professionals also speak of a third, a middle register, meaning either the passaggio region or the mixing of the two other registers in the *voix mixte*. They also occasionally speak of a middle voice and relate it either to the chest register or, as Martienssen-Lohmann does, to the head register. There is great confusion among voice teachers concerning the concept of register, rather similar to that concerning falsetto. Even when they mean the same thing, they usually disagree about the terminology. Some, for instance, differentiate between a chest voice and a chest register or between a head voice and a head register, while others use these terms synonymously insofar as they associate the chest voice with the region of the chest register and the head voice with the region of the head register and relate it all to regions of pitch. In this case, the chest voice is not only a full *forte* singing, regardless of whatever region it is in, and the head voice is not only *piano* singing, especially in *mezza voce*, as Martienssen-Lohmann would have it. Instead, the head voice begins above the passaggio, or to put it another way, in the region of the head register, and the chest voice lies in the region below. According to this definition, then, with men the chest voice encompasses the lower two-thirds and the head voice the upper one-third of the vocally trained range of a voice, and with women the proportions are the opposite.

I subscribe to this latter definition. For me, the chest register is associated with the chest voice just as the head register is associated with the head voice, and both refer to regions of pitch. Above a certain height, the vocal cords vibrate differently because they now have a different muscular tension and thus sound softer. In male voices, these tones sound less resonant. What is missing is the so-called chest resonance (that is, the chest cavity no longer vibrates along with these notes), and therefore one speaks of a head voice. The extreme manifestation of the head voice, then, is naturally the falsetto (q.v.).

Part of the art of today's tenor singing is to try to combine as much as possible of the sound of the chest voice in the region of the head register, which Nicolai Gedda achieved with notes as high as d^2. A pure head voice sound in the region of the head register is thus more a matter of artistic shaping and no longer a mere vocal necessity for the most accomplished singers. Domingo actually tries to raise his chest voice to higher and higher pitches. He is frequently effective in this, but it occasionally costs him some of his lyrical tenderness. This tenderness is more easily attainable by means of a clear head voice or, if you will, a falsetto.

DISCOGRAPHY

Compiled by Dieter Fuoß

THE FOLLOWING DISCOGRAPHY LISTS PLÁCIDO DOMIN-go's studio recordings and "legal" live recordings. Bootleg recordings are not included here.

Also not included are the by now almost unsurveyable compilations and reissues: regroupings of arias and scenes, anthologies, cross-sections, and excerpts from complete recordings. The reason for this omission is simply the enormous, almost daily explosion of such offerings.

In principle this list indicates only the order numbers of the CD versions, since these have since been standardized just about all over the world. The original LP number is given only in those instances where the recording still has not been issued on compact disc.

Since Domingo recorded several works a number of times over the course of several years, these recordings are listed chronologically. Recordings whose original date of production is not available are usually designated as ⓟ, which means that this work was released in the indicated year. An asterisk means that the recording is no longer available.

Complete Operas

BELLINI

Norma (Pollione) – 1972
Caballé, Cossotto, Raimondi;
Cillario, London Philharmonic
Orchestra
BMG-RCA GD 86502
(3 CD)

BERLIOZ

Béatrice et Bénédict (Bénédict) –
1979
Cotrubas, Minton, Fischer-
Dieskau, Soyer; Barenboim,
Orchestre de Paris
DG 2707 130 (2 LP)★

La damnation de Faust (Faust) –
1978
Fischer-Dieskau, Minton,
Bostin; Barenboim, Orchestre de
Paris
DG 2740 199 (3 LP)★

BIZET

Carmen (Don José) – 1975
Troyanos, Te Kanawa, van Dam;
Solti, London Philharmonic
Orchestra
DECCA 414 489-2 (3 CD)

1978
Berganza, Cotrubas, Milnes;
Abbado, London Symphony
Orchestra
DG 419 636-2 (3 CD)

1982
Migenes, Esham, Raimondi;
Maazel, Orchestre National de
France
ERATO 2292 45 207-2 ZB
(3 CD)

BOITO

Mefistofele (Faust) – 1973
Treigle, Caballé; Rudel, London
Symphony Orchestra
EMI 7 49522 2 (2 CD)

1988
Ramey, Marton; Patané,
Hungarian State Orchestra
SONY S2K 44 983 (2 CD)

CHARPENTIER, GUSTAVE

Louise (Julien) – 1976
Cotrubas, Bacquier, Berbié;
Prêtre, New Philharmonia
Orchestra
SONY S3K 46 429 (3 CD)

CILEA

Adriana Lecouvreur (Maurizio) –
1977
Scotto, Milnes; Levine, New
Philharmonia Orchestra
SONY M2K 79 310 (2 CD)

DONIZETTI

L'elisir d'amore (Nemorino) –
1977
Cotrubas, Evans, Wixell;
Pritchard, Royal Opera House,
Covent Garden
SONY M2K 79 210 (2 CD)

Lucia di Lammermoor (Edgardo) –
1990
Studer, Pons, Ramey; Marin,
London Symphony Orchestra
DG 435 309-2 (2 CD)

GIORDANO

Andrea Chenier (title role) – 1976
Scotto, Milnes; Levine, National
Philharmonic Orchestra
BMG-RCA GD 82 046 (2 CD)

GOMEZ

Il guarany (title role) – 1995
"live"
Villarroel, Alvarez, Bogart,
Martinovic; Neschling, Oper
Bonn
SONY 66 273 (2 CD)

GOUNOD

Faust (title role) – 1978
Freni, Ghiaurov, Allen; Prêtre,
Théâtre National de l'Opéra de
Paris
EMI 7 47493 8 (3 CD)

Roméo et Juliette (Roméo) – 1995
Swenson, Graham, Miles;
Slatkin, Münchner
Rundfunkorchester
BMG RCA 09026-68440-2
(2 CD)

LEONCAVALLO

I pagliacci (Canio) – 1971
Caballé, Milnes, McDaniel;
Santi, London Symphony
Orchestra
plus arias from operas by
Leoncavallo (*La bohème, Zazà,
Chatterton*)
RCA LSC 7090 (2 LP)★
plus *Il tabarro* (Puccini)
BMG-RCA CD 60 865

1983
Stratas, Pons, Rinaldi; Prêtre,
Teatro alla Scala, Milano
(original soundtrack of Zeffirelli
film)
PHILIPS 411 484-2 (1 CD)

MASCAGNI

Cavalleria rusticana (Turiddu) –
1978
Scotto, Elvira; Levine, National
Philharmonic Orchestra
BMG-RCA RD 83 091 (1 CD)

1983
Obraszowa, Bruson; Prêtre,
Teatro alla Scala, Milano
(original soundtrack of Zeffirelli
film)
PHILIPS 416 137-2 (1 CD)

1989
Baltsa, Pons; Sinopoli,
Philharmonia Orchestra
DG 429 568-2 (1 CD)

Iris (Osaka) – 1988
Tokody, Pons, Giaiotti; Patané,
Münchner Rundfunkorchester
SONY M2K 45 526 (2 CD)

MASSENET

Le Cid (Rodrigue) – 1976
"live"
Bumbry, Plishka; Queler, Opera
Orchestra of New York
SONY M2K 79 300 (2 CD)

Hérodiade (Jean) – 1994
"live"
Fleming, Zajick, Pons; Gergiev,
San Francisco Opera
SONY 66 847 (2 CD)

La Navarraise (Araquil) – 1975
Horne, Milnes, Zaccaria,
Bacquier; Lewis, London
Symphony Orchestra
RCA ARL 1-1114 (1 LP)★

Werther (title role) – 1979
Obraszowa, Grundheber, Moll,
Augér; Chailly, Kölner
Rundfunk-Sinfonie-Orchester
DG 413 304-2 (2 CD)

MONTEMEZZI

L'amore dei tre re (Avito) – 1976
Moffo, Elvira, Siepi; Santi,
London Symphony Orchestra
RCA RL 01945 (2 LP)★

MOZART

Idomeneo (title role) – 1994
Bartoli, Murphy, Vaness,
Hampson, Lopardo, Terfel;
Levine, Metropolitan Opera,
New York
DG 447 737-2 (3 CD)

OFFENBACH

Les contes d'Hoffmann (Hoffmann)
– 1971
Sutherland, Tourangeau,
Bacquier; Bonynge, Orchestre
de la Suisse Romande
DECCA 417 363-2 (2 CD)

1988
Gruberova, Eder, Schmidt,
Bacquier, Morris, Diaz; Ozawa,
Orchestre National de France
DG 427 682-2 (2 CD)

PENELLA

El gato montés (Rafael Ruiz) –
1991
Villarroel, Berganza, Pons; Ros,
Orquesta Sinfónica de Madrid
DG 435 776-2 (2 CD)

PUCCINI

La bohème (Rodolfo) – 1973
Caballé, Blegen, Milnes,
Raimondi, Sardinero; Solti,
London Philharmonic Orchestra
BMG-RCA RD 80 371 (2 CD)

La fanciulla del West (Dick
Johnson) – 1977
Neblett, Milnes; Mehta, Royal
Opera House, Covent Garden
DG 419 640-2 (2 CD)

1991
"live"
Zampieri, Pons, Roni; Maazel,
Teatro alla Scala, Milano
SONY S2K 47 189 (2 CD)

Gianni Schicchi (Rinuccio) – 1977
Gobbi, Cotrubas; Maazel, New
Philharmonia Orchestra
SONY M3K 79 312 (3 CD) (plus
Il tabarro and *Suor Angelica*)

Madama Butterfly (Pinkerton) –
1978
Scotto, Knight, Wixell; Maazel,
New Philharmonia Orchestra
SONY M2K 35 181 (2 CD)

Manon Lescaut (Chevalier Des
Grieux) – 1971/72
Caballé, Sardinero; Bartoletti,
New Philharmonia Orchestra
EMI 7 47736 8 (2 CD)

1983
Freni, Bruson; Sinopoli,
Philharmonia Orchestra
DG 413 893-2 (2 CD)

La rondine (Ruggero) – 1982
Te Kanawa, Nicolesco, Rendall,
Nucci; Maazel, London
Symphony Orchestra
SONY M2K 37 852 (1 CD)

Tosca (Cavaradossi) – 1972
L. Price, Milnes; Mehta, New
Philharmonia Orchestra
BMG-RCA RD 80 105 (2 CD)

1980
Scotto, Bruson; Levine,
Philharmonia Orchestra
EMI 7 49364 2 (2 CD)

1990
Freni, Ramey; Sinopoli,
Philharmonia Orchestra
DG 431 775-2 (2 CD)

Il trittico: Il tabarro (Luigi) – 1971
L. Price, Milnes; Leinsdorf, New
Philharmonia Orchestra
BMG-RCA GD 60 865 (2 CD)
(plus *La bohème*)

1977
Scotto, Wixell; Maazel, New
Philharmonia Orchestra
SONY M3K 79 312 (3 CD) (plus
Suor Angelica and *Gianni Schicchi*)

Turandot (Calaf) – 1981
Ricciarelli, Hendricks,
Raimondi; Karajan, Wiener
Philharmoniker
DG 423 855-2 (2 CD)

Le villi (Roberto) – 1979
Scotto, Nucci; Maazel, National
Philharmonic Orchestra
SONY MK 76 890 (1 CD)

ROSSINI

Il barbiere di Siviglia (Figaro) – 1992
Battle, Lopardo, Gallo,
Raimondi; Abbado, Chamber
Orchestra of Europe
DG 435 763-2 (2 CD)

SAINT-SAËNS

Samson et Dalila (Samson) – 1978
Obraszowa, Bruson, Lloyd;
Barenboim, Orchestre de Paris
DG 413 297-2 (2 CD)

1991
W. Meier, Fondary, Ramey;
Chung, L'Opéra-Bastille
EMI 7 54470 2 (2 CD)

STRAUSS

Die Frau ohne Schatten (Kaiser) –
1991
Varady, Behrens, Runkel, van
Dam; Solti, Wiener
Philharmoniker
DECCA 436 243-2 (3 CD)

Der Rosenkavalier (Italian singer)
– 1971
Ludwig, Jones, Popp, Berry,
Gutstein; Bernstein, Wiener
Philharmoniker
SONY M3K 42 564 (3 CD)

VERDI

Aïda (Radames) – 1970
L. Price, Bumbry, Milnes,
Raimondi, Sotin; Leinsdorf,
London Symphony Orchestra
BMG-RCA RD 86 198 (3 CD)

1974
Caballé, Cossotto, Cappuccilli,
Ghiaurov, Roni; Muti, New
Philharmonia Orchestra
EMI 7 47271 8 (3 CD)

1981
Ricciarelli, Obraszova, Nucci,
Raimondi, Ghiaurov; Abbado,
Teatro alla Scala, Milano
DG 410 092-2 (3 CD)

1990
Millo, Zajick, Morris, Ramey,
Cook; Levine, Metropolitan
Opera, New York
SONY S3K 45 973 (3 CD)

Un ballo in maschera (Riccardo/
Gustav III) – 1975
Arroyo, Cossoto, Grist,
Cappuccilli; Muti, New
Philharmonia Orchestra
EMI 7 69576 2 (2 CD)

1980
Ricciarelli, Obraszowa,
Gruberova, Bruson; Abbado,
Teatro alla Scala, Milano
DG 415 685-2 (2 CD)

1989
Barstow, Quivar, Jo, Nicci;
Karajan, Wiener Philharmoniker
DG 427 635-2 (2 CD)

Don Carlos (title role) – 1970
Caballé, Verrett, Raimondi,
Milnes; Giulini, Royal Opera
House, Covent Garden
EMI 7 47701 8 (3 CD)
*Recording of the five-act Italian
version*

1983/84
Ricciarelli, Valentini-Terrani,
Raimondi, Nucci; Abbado,
Teatro alla Scala, Milano
DG 415 316-2 (4 CD)
*Recording of the five-act final version
in French, plus six scenes from the
original French version*

Ernani (title role) – 1982
"live"
Freni, Bruson, Ghiaurov; Muti,
Teatro alla Scala, Milano
EMI 7 47082 2 (3 CD)

La forza del destino (Don Alvaro)
– 1976
L. Price, Cossotto, Milnes,
Giaiotti, Bacquier; Levine,
London Symphony Orchestra
BMG-RCA RD 81 864 (3 CD)

1986
Freni, Zajick, Zancanaro,
Plishka, Bruscantini; Muti,
Teatro alla Scala, Milano
EMI 7 47485 8 (3 CD)

Giovanna d'Arco (Carlos VII) –
1972
Caballé, Milnes; Levine, London
Symphony Orchestra
EMI 7 63226 2 (2 CD)

I Lombardi (Oronte) – 1971
Deutekom, Raimondi, Dean;
Gardelli, Royal Philharmonic
Orchestra
PHILIPS 422 420 2 (2 CD)

Luisa Miller (Rodolfo) – 1979
Ricciarelli, Obraszowa, Bruson,
Howell, Ganzarolli; Maazel,
Royal Opera House, Covent
Garden
DG 423 144-2 (2 CD)

1991
Millo, Quivar, Chernov,
Rootering, Plishka; Levine,
Metropolitan Opera, New York
SONY S2K 48 073 (2 CD)

Macbeth (Macduff) – 1976
Verrett, Cappuccilli, Ghiaurov;
Abbado, Teatro alla Scala,
Milano
DG 415 688-2 (3 CD)

Nabucco (Ismalele) – 1982
Dimitrova, Cappuccilli,
Nesterenko; Sinopoli, Deutsche
Oper Berlin
DG 410 512-2 (2 CD)

Otello (title role) – 1978
Scotto, Milnes; Levine, National
Philharmonic Orchestra
BMG-RCA GD 82 951 (2 CD)

1985
Ricciarelli, Diaz; Maazel, Teatro
alla Scala, Milano
EMI 7 47450 8 (2 CD)

1992
Studer, Leiferkus; Chung,
L'Opéra Bastille
DG 439 805-2 (2 CD)

Rigoletto (The Duke) – 1979
Cappuccilli, Cotrubas,
Obraszowa, Ghiaurov; Giulini,
Wiener Philharmoniker
DG 415 288-2 (2 CD)

Simon Boccanegra (Gabriele
Adorno) – 1973
Cappuccilli, Raimondi,
Ricciarelli; Gavazzeni, RCA
Orchestra
BMG-RCA RD 70 729 (2 CD)

La traviata (Alfredo Germont) –
1976/77
Cotrubas, Milnes; C. Kleiber,
Bayerisches Staatsorchester
DG 415 132-2 (2 CD)

Ⓟ 1983
Stratas, MacNeil; Levine,
Metropolitan Opera, New York
(original soundtrack of Zeffirelli
film)
WEA 25-0072-1 (2 LP)★

Il trovatore (Manrico) – 1969
L. Price, Cossotto, Milnes,
Giaiotti; Mehta, New
Philharmonia Orchestra
BMG-RCA RD 86 194 (2 CD)

1983
Plowright, Fassbaender,
Zancanaro, Nesterenko; Giulini,
Accademia Nazionale di Santa
Cecilia
DG 423 858-2

1993
Millo, Zajick, Chernov, Morris;
Levine, Metropolitan Opera,
New York
SONY S2K 48 070 (2 CD)

I vespri siciliani (Arrigo) – 1973
Arroyo, Milnes, Raimondi;
Levine, New Philharmonia
Orchestra
BMG-RCA RD 80 370 (3 CD)

WAGNER

Lohengrin (title role) – 1985/86
Norman, Randová, Nimsgern,
Sotin, Fischer-Dieskau; Solti,
Wiener Philharmoniker
DECCA 421 053-2 (4 CD)

Die Meistersinger von Nürnberg
(Walther von Stolzing) – 1976
Ligendza, Ludwig, Fischer-
Dieskau, Hermann, Laubenthal,
Lagger; Jochum, Deutsche Oper
Berlin
DG 415 278-2 (4 CD)

Parsifal (title role) – 1991/92
Meier, Moll, Morris, Wlaschiha,
Rootering; Levine, Metropolitan
Opera, New York
DG 437 501-2 (4 CD)

Tannhäuser (title role) – 1988
(Paris version)
Studer, Baltsa, Salminen,
Schmidt; Sinopoli, Philharmonia
Orchestra
DG 427 625-2 (3 CD)

WEBER

Oberon (Hüon) – 1970
Nilsson, Auger, Hamari, Grobe,
Prey; Kubelik, Orchester des
Bayerischen Rundfunks
DG 419 038-2 (2 CD)

Operettas & Musicals

LEIGH

Man of La Mancha (Don
Quixote) – 1990
Migenes, Domingo Jr., Elias,
Hadley, White, Ramey;
Gemignani, American Theatre
Orchestra
SONY 46 436 (CD)

JOHANN STRAUSS JR.

Die Fledermaus (Alfred and the
Conductor) – 1986
Popp, Lind, Baltsa, Seiffert,
Brendel, Rydl; Münchner
Rundfunkorchester
EMI 7 47480 8 (2 CD)

VARIOUS COMPOSERS

Wien, Du Stadt Meiner Träume –
1985
Songs by Lehár, Zeller, Kálmán,
others; Rudel, English Chamber
Orchestra
EMI 7 47398 2 (CD)

Operatic Recitals

Plácido Domingo
Arias by Handel, Mozart,
Halévy, Wagner, Tchaikovsky,
others; Downes, Royal
Philharmonic Orchestra
RCA SAR 22067 (LP)★; DECCA
SXL 6451 (LP)★

Domingo Sings Caruso
Arias by Leoncavallo, Donizetti,
Massenet, Puccini, others;
various orchestras and
conductors
BMG RCA 09026-61356-2
(CD)

The Plácido Domingo Album
Arias by Bizet, Donizetti,
Flotow, Gounod, Verdi, Wagner,
others; various orchestras and
conductors
BMG RCA GD 60 866 (2 CD)

*Gala Opera Concert: Domingo,
Giulini*
℗ 1981
Arias by Donizetti, Verdi,
Halévy, Meyerbeer, others; Los
Angeles Philharmonic Orchestra
DG 400 030-2 (CD)

Mozart Arias
1991
Arias from *La finta giardiniera*,
Idomeneo, *Don Giovanni*,
Entführung, *Tito*, *Le nozze di
Figaro*, *Così fan tutte*, *Die
Zauberflöte*; Kohn, Münchner
Rundfunkorchester
EMI 7 54329 2 (CD)

Roman Heroes
1989
Arias from *Nerone, Julius Caesar,
Norma, Benvenuto Cellini, La
vestale, Ezio, Rienzi*, others;
Kohn, National Philharmonic
Orchestra
EMI 7 54053 2 (CD)

Duets with Katia Ricciarelli
1972
Excerpts from *Otello, Madama
Butterfly, Un ballo in maschera,
Francesca da Rimini*
RCA SAR 22.128 (LP)
The duets from *Otello* and *Un
ballo in maschera* have been
rerecorded on the solo CD *Katia
Ricciarelli*
(BMG-RCA GD 86 534)

Duets with Renata Scotto
1978
Excerpts from *Manon, Roméo et Juliette, Fedora;* Adler, National Philharmonic Orchestra
SONY 39030 (CD)

Plácido Domingo: "Nessun Dorma"
Arias by Donizetti, Verdi, Ponchielli, Giordano, Leoncavallo, Mascagni, Puccini, Cilea; Santi, Orchester der Deutschen Oper Berlin
TELDEC 9031 73 741-2 ZS (CD)

Plácido Domingo & Leontyne Price
– 1970–74
Duets from Verdi and Puccini operas; Santi, Leinsdorf, Mehta; various orchestras
BMG-RCA GD 9026 61 634-2 (CD)

Opera Gala – 1995
Arias by Bellini, Rossini, Donizetti, Verdi, Bizet, Thomas Swenson, Hampson; Kohn, Philharmonia Orchestra
EMI 5 555 54 2 (CD)

Live Operatic Concerts

Metropolitan Opera Gala in Honor of Sir Rudolf Bing
1972
Arroyo, Caballé, Corelli, Nilsson, Price, others; various conductors
DG 2530 260 (LP)★

Domingo at the Philharmonic
New York, 1988
Giordano, Lehár, Mascagni, Verdi, others; Mehta
SONY MK 44 942 (CD)

Live in Tokyo
1988
Mozart, Donizetti, Rossini, Verdi, Gounod, Lehár; Battle; Levine, Metropolitan Opera Orchestra
DG 427 686-2 (CD)

Covent Garden Gala Concert
1988
Meyerbeer, Verdi, Puccini, J. Strauss; Studer, Randová, Allen; Barker
EMI 7 49811 2 (CD)

Concert for Planet Earth
Rio de Janeiro, 1992
Marsalis, Chang; DeMain, Municipal Theater of Rio de Janeiro
SONY SK 52 570 (CD)

Gala Lirica
Seville, 1991
Berganza, Kraus, Pons, Aragall, Caballé, Lorengar, Carreras; various conductors
BMG-RCA RD 61 191 (CD)

From the Official Barcelona Games Ceremony
1992
Carreras, Caballé, Aragall, Berganza, Pons; Navarro, City of Barcelona Symphony Orchestra
BMG-RCA 09026-61381-2 (CD)

Sacred and Secular Works for Soloists, Chorus, and Orchestra

BEETHOVEN

Symphony No. 9 in D Minor, op. 125 (tenor solo) – 1969
Marsh, Veasey, Milnes;
Leinsdorf, Boston Symphony Orchestra
RCA LSC 7055 (2 LP)★

Ⓟ 1981
Norman, Fassbaender, Berry;
Böhm, Wiener Philharmoniker
DG 427 802-2 (1 CD)
DG 413 721-2 (2 CD) plus
Symphony No. 6

Missa solemnis (tenor solo) – 1991
"live" from Salzburg
Studer, Norman, Moll; Levine,
Wiener Philharmoniker,
Leipziger Rundfunkchor, and others
DG 435 770-2 (2 CD)

BERLIOZ

Requiem (tenor solo) – 1979
Barenboim, Orchestre de Paris
DG 437 638-2 (2 CD)★

LLOYD WEBBER

Requiem (tenor solo) – 1984
Brightman and others; Maazel,
English Chamber Orchestra
EMI 7 47146 2 (CD)

VERDI

Requiem (tenor solo) – 1970
Arroyo, Veasey, Raimondi;
Bernstein, London Symphony Orchestra
SONY SM2K 47 639 (2 CD)

1979
Ricciarelli, Verrett, Ghiaurov;
Abbado, Teatro alla Scala,
Milano
DG 415 976-2 (2 CD)

1980
Caballé, Berini, Plishka; Mehta,
New York Philharmonic Orchestra
CBS D2 36927 (2 LP)★

1992
Marc, Meier, Furlanetto;
Barenboim, Chicago
Symphony Orchestra & Chorus
ERATO 4509 96357-2 (2 CD)

VARIOUS COMPOSERS

Domingo and the Vienna Choir Boys – 1985
Fauré, Franck, Handel, Bizet,
Kienzl, others; Froschauer,
Wiener Symphoniker
BMG-RCA 07863-53835-2 (CD)

Light Entertainment

Be My Love: Evergreens
"Granada," "Mattinata,"
"Siboney," others; Peeters,
London Symphony Orchestra
DG 413 451-2 (CD)

Domingo Sings Tangos
1981
R. Pansera
DG 415 120-2 (CD)

Perhaps Love
Ⓟ 1981
"He Couldn't Love," "Time after Time," "Perhaps Love," "Yesterday," others; Denver/Holdridge
SONY MK 73 592 (CD)

My Life for a Song
Ⓟ 1983
"Besame Mucho," "Follow Me," "Blue Moon," others; Holdrige
SONY MK 45 5448 (CD)

"Save Your Nights for Me" and Other Love Songs
Ⓟ 1985
SONY MK 39866 (CD)

Great Love Songs
Ⓟ 1988
"Maria," "Siboney," "Besame Mucho," others; Denver/McGovern
SONY MK 44 701 (CD)

Placido Domingo and Itzhak Perlman: Together
1990
Toselli, Massente, Kreisler, Richard Strauss, Godard, Handel, others
EMI 7 54266 2 (CD)

The Broadway I Love
1991
Kohn, London Symphony Orchestra
east west 9031-75590-2 (CD)

De Mi Alma Latina: Popular Latin Songs
Ana Gabriel, Pandora Daniela Roma, Patricia Soso; VVC Symphonic Orchestra
EMI 7 54878 2 (CD)

Spanish Music

For Our Friends, from Spain
Zarzuela melodies with Caballé, Carreras, Berganza, Lorengar, Sardinero, others; various conductors
DP VL 30445 (2 LP)★

Music of My Country
1974
Zarzuela arias; Navarro, Orquesta Sinfónica de Barcelona
DECCA SXL 6988 (LP)★

Duo de Dolores y Rafael
with T. Berganza
RCA VL 30445 (2 LP)★

Romanzas de Zarzuelas
1987
Moreno-Buendia, Orquesta Sinfónica de Madrid
EMI 7 49148 2 (CD)

Zarzuela Arias and Duets
Ⓟ 1985
P. Lorengar; Navarro
SONY MK 39 210 (CD)

The Songs of Ernesto Lecuona
"Siboney," "Noche azul,"
"Andalucia," others; Holdridge,
Royal Philharmonic Orchestra
SONY MK 38828 (CD)

Entre dos mundos
"Sevilla," "El grito de America,"
"Te quiero merena," others
SONY SK 48479 (CD)

Por fin juntos!
Kohn and Chova, Ensemble
Paloma San Basilio
EMI 7 99611 2 (CD)

Suite Espanola
Ⓟ 1996
WC Symphony Orchestra
SONY 99 706 (CD)

BRETON

La Verbena de la Paloma (Julian) –
Ⓟ 1994
Bayo, Pierotti; Ros-Marbá
Valois/Auvidis V 4725 (CD)

SOROZABAL

La Tabernera del puerto (Leandro)
– Ⓟ 1996
Bayo, Pons; Pirez
Valois/Auvidis V 4766 (CD)

TORROBA

Luisa Fernanda (Javier) – Ⓟ 1995
Villarroel; Ros-Marbá
Valois/Auvidis V 4759 (CD)

VIVES

Dona Francisquita (Fernando) –
1993
Arteta, Perelstein, Alvarez,
Mirabal, Chausson; Roe
SONY 66 563 (2 CD)

Noces de Zarzuela
1991
Moreno, Torroba, Vives,
and others
RTVE 650005 (CD)

Miscellaneous

*Domingo Sings and Directs
Tchaikovsky*
1993
the Philharmonia Orchestra
EMI 5 55018 2 (CD)

The Unknown Puccini
1989
J. Rudel, piano and organ
SONY MK 44 981 (CD)

*Premier Concours International de
Foix d'Opéra*
1993
Arteta, Stemme, Mula-Tchako,
Youn; Kohn, Orchestre de
l'Opéra Bastille
SONY 46 691 (CD)

Specials

Carreras, Domingo, Pavarotti: The Rome Concert
1990
Mehta; Maggio musicale fiorentino and Teatro dell'Opera di Roma
DECCA 430 433-2 (CD)

Carreras, Domingo, Pavarotti: The Los Angeles Concert
1994
Mehta; Los Angeles Philharmonic
TELDEC 4509 96 200-2 ZK (CD)

Christmas with Plácido Domingo
Ⓟ 1985
Holdridge, Wiener Symphoniker
SONY SK 37 245 (CD)

A Carnegie Hall Christmas Concert
"live," 1991
Battle, von Stade; Previn, Orchestra of Saint Luke's
SONY SK 48 235 (CD)

Christmas in Vienna
"live," 1992
Carreras, Ross; Sutej, Wiener Symphoniker
SONY SK 53 358 (CD)

Christmas in Vienna II
1993, "live"
Warwick, Mozart Boys' Chorus; Sutej, Wiener Symphoniker
SONY 64 304 (CD)

Christmas in Vienna III
1994, "live"
Krykjebö, Aznavour; Sutej, Wiener Symphoniker
SONY 66 846 (CD)

Christmas with Carreras, Domingo, and Pavarotti
(compilation)
SONY 47 186 (CD)

Domingo, Plácido. *My First Forty Years.* New York: Knopf, 1983.

Fischer, Jens Malte. *Große Stimmen: Von Enrico Caruso bis Jessye Norman.* Stuttgart: J. B. Metzler, 1993.

Kesting, Jürgen. *Die großen Sänger unseres Jahrhunderts.* Düsseldorf: Econ, 1993.

Matheopoulos, Helena. *Divo: Great Tenors, Baritones and Basses Discuss Their Roles.* New York: Harper & Row, 1986. Published in Great Britain as *Bravo.*

Snowman, Daniel. *The World of Plácido Domingo.* New York: McGraw-Hill, 1985.

Wagner, Cosima. *Cosima Wagner's Diaries.* Edited and annotated by Martin Gregor-Dellin and Dietrich Mack. Translated and with an introduction by Geoffrey Skelton. 2 vols. New York: Harcourt Brace Jovanovich, 1977.

Wagner, Richard. *Richard Wagner's Prose Works.* Translated by William Ashton Ellis. 8 vols. Reprint. New York: Broude Brothers, 1966.

INDEX

8c com.
8-23-01

subject   8 /05